Turn into the Wind

Volume II

US Navy, Royal Navy, Royal Australian Navy, and Royal Canadian Navy Light Fleet Aircraft Carriers in the Korean War and through End of Service, 1950–1982

American and British light fleet aircraft carriers, an expedient of war at a time of dire need in World War II, answered their nations' call a second time during the Korean War. While larger US Navy fleet carriers plied their trade in the deeper Sea of Japan off Korea's east coast, their svelte sisters — USS *Bataan*, HMS *Glory*, HMS *Ocean*, HMS *Theseus*, HMS *Triumph*, and HMAS *Sydney* — were consigned to the Yellow Sea. Operating off the west coast, ragged and heavily indented with numerous small islands, aircraft aboard the carriers repeatedly struck the enemy. Winters were cold, with occasional gales and blinding snow squalls; summers were hot and humid, with heavy rains and fog. While the piston-engine aircraft attacked enemy supply lines, fortifications, and troop positions, enemy MiG jet aircraft were a constant threat, some flown by Russians. Carrier air also provided protection to friendly islands, from which guerillas mounted operations behind enemy lines. Following the Korean War, Australia acquired two additional former Royal Navy light fleet carriers, and Canada three in succession, as centerpieces for naval fixed air programs. Former CVLs served in new roles during the Cold War/Vietnam War: USS *Wright* as a "doomsday" afloat White House, HMAS *Sydney* as a troop transport, and USS *Arlington* as a communications link between the Pentagon and commanders in the field. One hundred fifty-five photographs, maps, and diagrams; appendices; and an index to full-names, places, and subjects add value to this work.

Turn into the Wind

Volume II
US Navy, Royal Navy, Royal Australian Navy, and Royal Canadian Navy Light Fleet Aircraft Carriers in the Korean War and through End of Service, 1950–1982

Cdr. David D. Bruhn, USN (Retired)

HERITAGE BOOKS
2021

HERITAGE BOOKS
AN IMPRINT OF HERITAGE BOOKS, INC.

Books, CDs, and more—Worldwide

For our listing of thousands of titles see our website
at
www.HeritageBooks.com

Published 2021 by
HERITAGE BOOKS, INC.
Publishing Division
5810 Ruatan Street
Berwyn Heights, Md. 20740

Copyright © 2021 Cdr. David D. Bruhn, USN (Retired)

All rights reserved. No part of this book may be reproduced or transmitted in any form or by any means, electronic or mechanical, including photocopying, recording or by any information storage and retrieval system without written permission from the author, except for the inclusion of brief quotations in a review.

International Standard Book Number
Paperbound: 978-0-7884-0869-4

To the Light Fleet Carrier officers and men who plied dangerous waters, and their embarked pilots and aircrewmen who flew in harm's way in the Korean War and Vietnam War, and steadfastly helped maintain the peace during the Cold War

Contents

Foreword by Rear Adm. Allan du Toit, AM RAN (Retired)	xv
Foreword by Commodore Hector Donohue, AM RAN (Retired)	xix
Foreword by Commander Larry Wahl, USN (Retired)	xxiii
Acknowledgements	xxv
Preface	xxxi
1. Downed Pilot Saved in Daring Rescue	1
2. Korean War, June 1950 - January 1952	9
3. Korean War, February 1952 - July 1953	53
4. Royal Canadian Naval Air Service Historical Overview	87
5. Acquisition/Service of RCN Aircraft Carriers	109
6. Post-WWII Service of the *Independence*-class CVLs	133
7. National Emergency Command Post USS *Wright*	141
8. *Saipan* (CVL-48) / Later *Arlington* (AGMR-2)	147
9. The Australian Aircraft Carrier Program	167
10. Some Australian Fleet Air Arm Personalities	195
Postscript	217
Bibliography/Chapter Notes	231
Index	253
About the Author	271

Photos and Illustrations

Foreword-1: Group portrait of twelve former RAAF pilots	xxi
Acknowledgements-1: Richard DeRosset	xxv
Acknowledgements-2: Rear Adm. Allan du Toit AM RAN (Ret.)	xxvi
Acknowledgements-3: Cdre Hector Donohue AM RAN (Ret.)	xxvii
Acknowledgements-4: Lt Cdr. Rob Hoole, RN (Ret.)	xxviii
Acknowledgements-5: Cdr. Larry Wahl, USN (Ret.)	xxviii
Acknowledgements-6: Dwight Messimer	xxix
Acknowledgements-7: George Duddy	xxx
Preface-1: Light Fleet Carrier USS *Langley* (CVL-27)	xxxi
Preface-2: Fleet carrier USS *Essex* (CV-9) under way	xxxiii
Preface-3: Command Post Afloat USS *Wright* (CC-2)	xxxv
Preface-4: British light fleet carrier HMS *Triumph*	xxxvi
Preface-5: Painting *Recovered Apollo 11 Module, USS Hornet*	xlii
Preface-6: Australian light fleet carrier HMAS *Sydney*	xlvi
Preface-7: Australian corvette HMAS *Junee*	li
Preface-8: Painting of recue of downed pilot by Richard DeRosset	lii

Contents

1-1: Light fleet carrier USS *Bataan* — 1
1-2: F4U Corsairs of VMA-312 readied for flight operations — 2
1-3: F4U Corsair launching from USS *Bataan* — 4
1-4: Drawing by Herbert C. Hahn of a F4U Corsair firing rockets — 5
1-5: Sikorsky H-19A Chickasaw rescue helicopter — 7
2-1: British light fleet carrier HMS *Triumph* at Kure, Japan — 9
2-2: U.S. 24th Infantry Division members at the Battle of Osan — 11
2-3: Vice Adm. Arthur D. Struble, USN — 13
2-4: Vice Adm. William G. Andrewes, RN — 14
2-5: North Korean railroad train just south of Pyongyang — 15
2-6: Canadian destroyer HMCS *Crusader* under way off Korea — 17
2-7: Drawing by Herbert C. Hahn of U.S. fleet attacking Inchon — 20
2-8: Rear Admiral Doyle congratulates Silver Star Medal winners — 23
2-9: Light fleet carrier HMS *Theseus* at sea, circa 1952 — 24
2-10: Admirals rowing Lord Louis Mountbatten across a harbor — 24
2-11: A Grumman F9F-2 Panther aboard the USS *Philippine Sea* — 27
2-12: USS *Bataan* with F4U-4B Corsair fighter-bombers on board — 30
2-13: F4U-4 Corsair from the aircraft carrier USS *Boxer* — 32
2-14: USS *St. Paul* bombarding enemy installations at Wonsan — 33
2-15: The Han River, Korea, in 1871 — 34
2-16: HMAS *Bataan* in company with USS *Bataan* — 37
2-17: Hawker Sea Fury F.B.11 fighter launched from HMS *Glory* — 40
2-18: A Sikorski S-51 helicopter lands aboard HMAS *Sydney* — 40
2-19: Launching of HMS *Terrible* at Devonport, England — 41
2-20: USS *New Jersey* conducting shore bombardment — 42
2-21: A Fairey Firefly of the RAN — 43
2-22: *New Jersey* bombarding targets near Hungnam — 47
2-23: Airmen ('birdies') sweep snow and ice from HMAS *Sydney* — 49
2-24: Rear Adm. Alan Kenneth Scott-Moncrieff, DSO RN — 50
3-1: British cruiser HMS *Belfast* coming alongside USS *Bataan* — 53
3-2: Hill 355 (Kowang San), but referred to as "Little Gibraltar" — 56
3-3: Lt. Col. Frank G. Hassett with Majors Shelton and Finlayson — 58
3-4: British aircraft maintenance carrier HMS *Unicorn* at anchor — 60
3-5: Escort carrier USS *Bairoko* off San Diego, California — 61
3-6: Marine Corps F4U Corsair dropping napalm — 62
3-7: Members of the "Checkerboards" on board USS *Bataan* — 63
3-8: British light fleet aircraft carrier HMS *Ocean* at anchor — 65
3-9: *Bataan*'s flight deck, island structure, and flight deck personnel — 68
3-10: Comdr. William Landymore and Lt. George MacFarlane — 71
3-11: Republic of Korea submarine chaser *Kum Kang San* — 73
3-12: MiG-15B fighter of North Korean Senior Lt. No Kum-Sok — 75
3-13: USS *Bataan* sailors manning a gun mount — 78

3-14: USN Captains Harry Ray Horny and Shirley Snow Miller	82
3-15: Members of 2RAR celebrate the signing of the cease fire	85
4-1: German battleship *Tirpitz* in a Norwegian fjord	92
4-2: Escort carrier HMS *Nabob* after being torpedoed by *U-354*	94
4-3: Escort carrier HMS *Puncher* off Chesapeake Bay, Virginia	96
4-4: US Navy F4F Wildcats flying in formation	97
4-5: Fairey Barracuda taking off from an aircraft carrier deck	99
4-6: HMS *Formidable* with a Wildcat fighter about to land	101
4-7: Japanese escort ship *Etorofu*	104
5-1: HMCS *Warrior* passing under the Lions' Gate Bridge	109
5-2: Harland and Wolff's Musgrave shipyard, Belfast	110
5-3: HMCS *Magnificent* under way	114
5-4: Cocooned RCAF Sabres aboard HMCS *Magnificent*	115
5-5: An Avenger torpedo bomber flying past *Magnificent*	117
5-6: Hawker Sea Fury with *Magnificent* in the background	117
5-7: Royal Marine detachment and band aboard HMS *Vanguard*	120
5-8: 1953 Naval Review at Spithead, England	122
5-9: AD-4 Skyraider taking off from the USS *Philippine Sea*	123
5-10: HMCS *Bonaventure* at sea	127
5-11: CS-2F Tracker in flight over *Bonaventure*	128
5-12: McDonnell F2H-3 Banshee	128
6-1: USS *Monterey* under way in the Gulf of Mexico	133
6-2: Painting *Coming into Golden Gate Bridge* by Franklin Boggs	135
6-3: Bikini Atoll A-Bomb Tests involving USS *Independence*	136
6-4: Battleship USS *Iowa* passes the hulk of USS *Independence*	137
6-5: Grumman AF-2W Guardian aircraft of VS-24	138
6-6: Oran, Algeria, street scene	139
6-7: The Casbah in Tangiers	139
7-1: USS *Wright* in June 1963	141
7-2: USS *Northampton* at sea in 1962	143
7-3: Waving the Texas flag from aboard USS *Wright*	144
7-4: USS *Wright* arriving at San Diego, California	145
8-1: USS *Saipan* with FH-1 Phantom jet fighters aboard	147
8-2: The Navy's First Jet Pilots	148
8-3: USS *Saipan* at Sasebo, Japan	149
8-4: Hong Kong, British Crown Colony	150
8-5: USS *Saipan* transiting the Suez Canal	151
8-6: French Riviera	152
8-7: USS *Arlington* under way	153
8-8: USS *Arlington*'s crew aboard ship for her commissioning	154
8-9: *Arlington* sailors on liberty in Lisbon, Portugal	155
8-10: Bremerhaven, Germany	156

xii   Contents

8-11: Oslo, the largest city and capital of Norway   156
8-12: *Arlington* sailor makes a close friend in Oslo   157
8-13: USS *Arlington* as viewed by the Apollo 8 astronauts   159
8-14: Descent of the Apollo 10 space capsule   160
8-15: U.S. Naval Air Station, Midway   162
8-16: President Richard M. Nixon and entourage   162
8-17: President Nixon and President Thieu shaking hands   163
8-18: Navy helicopter recovering the Apollo 11 astronauts   164
8-19: Armstrong, Aldrin, and Collins enter Quarantine Facility   165
8-20: Banner depicting USS *Arlington*'s nickname and motto   166
9-1: Lt. Victor Smith, RAN, wearing the ribbon of the DSC   168
9-2: Maintenance work on the engine of a Sea Fury fighter   172
9-3: Hawker Sea Fury fighter aircraft aboard HMAS *Sydney*   173
9-4: HMAS *Sydney* in Korean waters   174
9-5: Captain Harries, RAN, and Commander Kiggell, DSC RN   175
9-6: Monte Bello Islands, Australia   177
9-7: His Royal Highness, The Duke of Gloucester   177
9-8: HMAS *Vengeance* and HMAS *Sydney* off Queensland coast   179
9-9: Royal Yacht *Gothic* being escorted by HMAS *Vengeance*   181
9-10: 1RAR formed up on the flight deck of HMAS *Sydney*   182
9-11: *Melbourne* undergoing trials off Barrow-in-Furness, England   184
9-12: USS *Ponchatoula* replenishing HMAS *Melbourne* at sea   186
9-13: View from the cockpit of a Tracker landing on *Melbourne*   188
9-14: Tracker landing on HMAS *Melbourne*'s flight deck   188
9-15: Officers in Flight Control watch a Skyhawk land   189
9-16: Skyhawks, Trackers, and helicopters aboard *Melbourne*   190
10-1: Captain Jeffrey Gledhill, DSC RAN   195
10-2: Royal Australian Navy Auster J/4 Archer aircraft   198
10-3: Lieutenants Bob Bluett, RN, and Peter McNay, RN   201
10-4: Commodore Norman Lee standing in front of a Firefly   202
10-5: An aerial view of a bridge between Haeju and Yonan   203
10-6: Firefly landing on HMAS *Sydney* during Korean War   206
10-7: HMAS *Tobruk* in Korean waters   207
10-8: RAN Firefly from HMAS *Sydney* in Korean waters   207
10-9: Aircraft handlers about to remove chocks from a Sea Fury   209
10-10: Sea Venom onboard HMAS *Melbourne*   213
10-11: Burnt out Sea Venom after crash   216
Postscript-1: Lt. Comdr. Guy Beange, RAN, receiving the DSC   217
Postscript-2: Beange while a soldier in the New Zealand Army   218
Postscript-3: Corsair of 1831 Squadron landing aboard HMS *Glory*   220
Postscript-4: Surrender ceremony onboard HMS *Glory*   221
Postscript-5: *Sydney* with Fireflies and Sea Fury aircraft overhead   222

Postscript-6: *Sydney*'s flight deck during Typhoon Ruth 224
Postscript-7: A Hawker Sea Fury landing aboard HMAS *Sydney* 225
Postscript-8: Lieutenant Commander Beange aboard HMAS *Junee* 226
Postscript-9: Sea Venoms flying in formation 227
Postscript-10: Medals of Commander Guy Alexander Beange 229

Maps and Diagrams
1-1: Northwest Coast of Korea 3
1-2: Area around Haeju in North Korea 4
2-1: Korean Peninsula 10
2-2: Northeast coast of Korea 18
2-3: Korea and relatively nearby ports of Sasebo and Kure, Japan 29
4-1: Portion of Scandinavia, including the west coast of Norway 98
7-1: The National Military Command System 142
10-1: Cartoon from the cover of *Slipstream* 212

Foreword

Few changes in naval warfare have been as all-embracing as the role played by the aircraft carrier. It is undoubtedly the most impressive and, at the same time, the most controversial manifestation of sea power. From experiments conducted by Britain before 1914, the aircraft carrier rose to pre-eminence during and after the Second World War following its eclipse of the battleship as the principal capital ship in the world's navies.

The Royal Australian Navy's dalliance with aircraft at sea dates as far back as 1917 when the light cruiser HMAS *Brisbane* embarked a Sopwith seaplane for use in the hunt for a German armed merchant cruiser in the Indian Ocean. Although the Australian Naval Board decided to construct a purpose-built seaplane carrier in 1925, the locally built HMAS *Albatross* was only destined to spend four years in RAN service. As a consequence of the Great Depression, *Albatross* was transferred to the Royal Navy, in part payment for the new cruiser HMAS *Hobart* in 1933. While its cruisers continued to operate seaplanes, this ended the RAN's first active participation in the arcane and stimulating art of operating aircraft from purpose-built ships.

Although Churchill made the offer of a light fleet carrier during the war in the Pacific in 1944, and the British Admiralty offered the RAN two light fleet carriers for the price of one in 1946, it was not until mid-1947 that a decision was finally taken to introduce carriers into the Australian Fleet. The acquisition of two light fleet carriers and the establishment of a Fleet Air Arm, as part of Australia's post-war Defence Plan, added a whole new dimension to the RAN's sea control capability. It was undoubtedly one of the most significant developments in the RAN's history.

From the arrival of HMAS *Sydney* in 1948, until 1983 when the Australian government finally decided not to replace HMAS *Melbourne*, the aircraft carrier formed the core component of the Australian Fleet. Its place in defence strategy and the force structure seemed relatively secure. But, as Commodore Donohue has argued, the significant decision to introduce naval air power was made without any real consideration of other force structure implications. This would ultimately distort the RAN force structure for more than three decades.

After the arrival of *Sydney*, the development of the RAN's naval aviation capabilities became the RAN's highest priority until the Korean

War intervened. The war waged by *Sydney* in Korean waters demonstrated the versatility of an aircraft carrier beyond the sea control role for which carriers had been acquired and involved the RAN in naval power projection operations. And significantly, the commitment of a carrier to the Korean War gave Australia the distinction of being the third nation, after the U.S. and Britain, to gain operational experience with aircraft carriers in the post-war period.

But, while the Korean War was being fought, naval aviation was undergoing fundamental changes, the operation of jet aircraft at sea being the most significant development. This was quickly followed by the introduction of three crucial devices by the Royal Navy – the steam catapult, the angled flight deck, and the mirror landing aid. This made it possible for light fleet carriers to operate modern high-performance jet aircraft. As a result, delivery of Australia's second carrier, HMAS *Melbourne*, was significantly delayed while these improvements in aircraft carrier design were incorporated.

It was not long, however, before this new centrepiece of the Australian Fleet was found to be unsustainable. As a result, the two-carrier plan was dropped to save money. By 1959, even the future of Australia's only remaining operational carrier, HMAS *Melbourne*, was looking bleak. Largely based on cost considerations, the Australian Government was actively considering phasing-out fixed wing naval aviation altogether. This thinking was, however, reversed not long afterwards. There was a growing concern that Australia needed a capability for independent operations in defence of Australian interests, at least until help from powerful friends arrived. The 1960s was consequently characterized by steady growth in Australia's independent maritime capability. This included the acquisition of new naval aircraft for *Melbourne* for sea control and power projection missions.

By the 1970s, the United States, like Britain before it, made it clear that Australia had to look after itself. The RAN argued that strategic guidance demanded credibility in the maintenance of a naval presence, the conduct of sustained naval operations, and a shift of force balance towards naval offensive capability. It saw the core of the required naval force based around two carriers. This was, however, at odds with the new Whitlam Labor Government's policy of minimizing defence expenditure and concentrating on defending continental Australia.

With a change of government in 1975, the new Fraser government reverted to a more outward looking defence policy. It was favourably disposed towards acquiring a new carrier to replace *Melbourne* which was rapidly nearing the end of her useful life. As a result, the decision was finally made to acquire a new purpose-designed helicopter carrier with the potential to operate STOVL aircraft in a sea control role. (A Short Take-off and Vertical Landing aircraft is a fixed-wing plane that is able to take off from a short runway and land vertically.) This decision was, however, greeted by much resistance, and it stimulated detailed public enquiry, intense and prolonged parliamentary debate, and caustic inter-service rivalry.

This decision was reconsidered in mid-1981 following an offer from Britain to sell the new but surplus British STOVL carrier HMS *Invincible* to Australia at a substantially reduced price following British defence cuts. This offer was accepted by the Australian Government. The major refit planned for *Melbourne* was immediately cancelled. And she was paid-off into contingency reserve to free up personnel for *Invincible* which was planned to commission in 1983 and be renamed HMAS *Australia*.

Arrangements to take over *Invincible* had scarcely begun when the Falklands conflict occurred in the South Atlantic. By this time, the Australian government was facing significant budgetary woes. With some relief it offered to forego the purchase of *Invincible* if the Royal Navy wished to retain the ship. This offer was quickly accepted, and the sale was cancelled.

Following this unexpected setback, the search for a replacement for *Melbourne*, which languished in reserve, resumed. But politics finally intervened. One of the first moves of the new Hawke Labor Government in 1983, which firmly believed that the capability represented by an aircraft carrier was not needed, was to announce that *Melbourne* would not be replaced. This brought to an end an important era in the RAN's history and ended one of the most bitter and long-running debates on the structure of the Australian Defence Force.

In retrospect, the long battle to maintain a carrier force was always the victim of attempting to do too much with inadequate resources. But cost and resources alone can obscure the fundamental reordering of Australia's defence posture and strategic thinking which significantly contributed to the decision not to replace *Melbourne*. Following the painful loss of *Melbourne*, the RAN was forced to come to grips with effectively operating and developing a fleet without a carrier. This required shifting its emphasis from fixed wing aviation to helicopters operating predominantly from frigates and, more recently, versatile flat top amphibious assault ships, which are now substantially larger than the light fleet carriers covered in the pages of this highly commended book.

Allan du Toit, Rear Admiral, RAN, retired

Foreword

David Bruhn's *Turn in to the Wind Volume II* provides a valuable insight into the U.S.- and British-built light fleet carriers, that served in the US Navy, Royal Navy, Royal Canadian Navy, and Royal Australian Navy (RAN) in the Korean War, Cold War and Vietnam War. The book concludes with the decommissioning of HMAS *Melbourne* in 1982 and the cessation of fixed-wing carrier flying in the RAN.

The Korean War has been referred to as the 'Forgotten War' in terms of both public interest and historical research. But for those who served there, Korea was a deadly conflict against a well-armed and disciplined enemy. The detailed descriptions in the book of the impact that light fleet carriers made, provides a valuable insight into that war. From the British Commonwealth forces perspective, the most conspicuous role in the war was undertaken by the British and Australian light fleet carriers. Their performance was assessed as outstanding but rendered possible only by the virtual absence of enemy air activity. However, despite this, the results achieved demanded extremely hard work, much improvisation, machinery driven to the limit and the acceptance of calculated risks.

HMAS *Sydney*'s Carrier Air Group performance must have been of particular satisfaction to her Executive Officer, Commander VAT Smith, (later Admiral Sir Victor Smith) who only a few years earlier had been instrumental in the planning and execution of forming the new Air Arm – an exercise fraught by the politics of the day. In the post-World War II force structure planning process in Australia, it had been accepted within the defence establishment that a balanced naval task force should include aircraft carriers and that these should be included in the RAN's force structure. The issue remained whether the RAN should manage naval air or whether the Royal Australian Air Force (RAAF) should perform the task.

Convinced that effective air power required unity of effort and maximum flexibility of employment, the RAAF firmly believed that it should maintain overall command of both land-based and ship-borne aircraft. The RAN in contrast, feared the withdrawal of operational control in national emergency and stressed the uniqueness of naval service and the need to weld a ship's company – including its embarked aircrew - into a cohesive unit. With air force recording its strong dissent, the Council of Defence accepted the naval arguments and on 15 August

1947, Cabinet endorsed the decision to create a separate Naval (later Fleet) Air Arm.

The Fleet Air Arm (FAA) came into being with the commissioning in 1948 of the Naval Air Station at Nowra, HMAS Albatross, with two Naval Air Squadrons, 805 equipped with the Hawker Sea Fury FB11, a single seat fighter-bomber and 816 with the Fairey Firefly Mk 5 two-seat armed reconnaissance/strike and anti-submarine aircraft. Prior to this, an extensive recruitment drive was undertaken to seek personnel for the new branch. The obvious lack of trained Australian personnel necessitated significant reliance on experienced Royal Navy (RN) officers in both operational and training capacities.

For these first FAA trainee pilots and the many who followed, the RAAF conducted the initial flight training until trainees reached a level of competence where they were awarded their 'wings'. Following this milestone, FAA aircrew completed their training in a wholly maritime environment. In the 1940s Australia did not possess either the trained instructors, facilities, ships or the aircraft to ensure their naval aviators reached the required competence so, once again, the RN and her Fleet Air Arm filled the breach while training was conducted in UK.

When the British Pacific Fleet came to Australia in the latter part of the war, about 24 RAAF pilots volunteered to transfer to the Royal Australian Navy Volunteer Reserve (RANVR) and they subsequently served aboard RN aircraft carriers and at RN Air Stations established in Australia. Post-war many joined the RAN's new FAA. During *Sydney*'s deployment to Korea six aircrew had been awarded the Distinguished Flying Cross and one a Distinguished Flying Medal, from their time in the RAAF.

Photo Foreword-1

Group portrait of 12 former Royal Australian Air Force, (RAAF), pilots, who were the first group selected for training as naval aviators with the British Pacific Fleet (Fleet Air Arm), HMS Nabthorpe, at Schofields, NSW. Back row from left: Acting Sub-Lieutenant (A/Sub Lt) Leslie John Norton, of Sydney, NSW, killed in a flying accident at Schofields on 29 November 1945; A/Sub Lt Robert Lindsay Davies (later Lieutenant Commander, (Lt Cmdr)), of Adelaide, SA; A/Sub Lt John Bradley (Jack) O'Connor, of Yarrawonga, Vic, formerly of 80 Squadron (Sqn), RAAF; A/Sub Lt Charlie Bowley, who later crash landed, going over the side of HMS *Indomitable* but was rescued by a following destroyer; Acting Lieutenant (A/Lt) Kenneth Brian Innes Smith, of Adelaide, SA, formerly of 80 Squadron, RAAF, A/Lt George Edward Pagan, of Damar, Qld; A/Lt Arthur John 'Nat' Gould, of Queensland, 2 Operational Training Unit and formerly of 75 and 457 Sqns, RAAF; A/Lt Clifford Herald Gray of Dungog, NSW. Front row: A/Sub Lt George Firth Spencer 'Spanky' Brown, DFC, (later Lt Cmdr) of Echuca, Vic, formerly of 8 Operational Training Unit, who was killed in a flying accident on 5 January 1956; A/Lt Roy Clayson 'Shorty' Carroll, of Blackall, Qld, formerly of 1 Aircraft Depot; A/Sub Lt Philip Crothers, of Northhampton, WA, formerly of 2 Operational Training Unit; A/Lt Ian Sandford Loudon, of Port Moresby, PNG, formerly of 76 Sqn, RAAF. (AWM)

Sydney's initial Carrier Air Group comprised experienced RN personnel and RN trained RAN recruits who were joined by HMAS Albatross trained Safety Equipment, Aircraft Handler, Ordnance and Photography recruits. Almost all the key air related positions in *Sydney* during that deployment were RN loan officers including: Commander Air, Operations Officer, Deck Landing Officer, Carrier Air Group Commander and two of the three Squadron Commanding Officers.

Turn in to the Wind Volume II describes the evolution, deployment and the ultimate demise of the aircraft carrier within the RAN's force structure. Aviation within the maritime environment was and remains a versatile weapon in any modern navy and after finally coming into existence in 1948, the Australian Fleet Air Arm operated from the three Australian aircraft carriers: HMA Ships *Sydney*, *Vengeance* and *Melbourne* as well as the shore establishment at Nowra, HMAS Albatross. These carriers embarked, operated and fully maintained various fixed-wing aircraft and the naval personnel needed for operational deployments until 1982. These deployments included contributions to national and multinational combat, peacekeeping and humanitarian operations.

The FAA deployed a helicopter Flight to Vietnam with aircrew and maintenance personnel from 723 Squadron serving in-country with the United States Army's 135th Assault Helicopter Company from October 1967 until June 1971. This is outlined in David Bruhn's *Gators Offshore and Upriver* pages 85 – 87.

The FAA met every operational challenge during its years of service but faced its most significant challenge in 1982, when the newly elected Labor Government made the decision not to replace *Melbourne*, the last of the aging aircraft carriers. Several factors influenced this decision, including the end of the Cold War and the prohibitive cost of replacing and operating both an aircraft carrier and its associated aircraft.

Although it was a testing time, this major transition from fixed wing to rotary wing aircraft was ultimately very successful and the role of the FAA was expanded rather than curtailed by the transformation. This was a major turning point for Australian Naval Aviation; with the FAA concentrating on helicopters and adapting to flight operations from frigates and destroyers. Today, the Fleet Air Arm continues its role in providing sea-borne air power with the focus on the embarked helicopters.

The Fleet Air Arm has seen active service in Korea, the Malaya Emergency, Indonesian Confrontation, Vietnam, the Gulf War, East Timor and more recently, the War Against Terrorism. Since 1948, the FAA has operated 22 different types of aircraft - a real challenge to the aircrew and the maintenance personnel. It has forged a proud tradition over the years. a tradition of professional service and outstanding achievements.

Turn in to the Wind Volume II puts into perspective the impact of light fleet carriers in four navies' force structure. The book provides a valuable insight into the role of carriers in the post-World War II era and the professionalism of those personnel involved in flying and maintaining this unique capability.

Hector Donohue AM
Commodore RAN (Rtd)

Foreword

On a cool fall afternoon in 1976, while assisting the Spanish Navy in training carrier pilots aboard the light fleet carrier SNS *Dedalo*, I met retired Rear Admiral Joseph "Joe" Coleman on the pier and escorted him aboard the ship. *Dedalo*, formerly the USS *Cabot* (CVL-28) had just arrived at Mayport, Florida, from Spain, to pick up AV-8A Harriers, pilots, maintainers, and equipment for transport home.

Passing through the quarterdeck and into the hangar bay, Admiral Coleman stopped, looked around, and commented that this was the cleanest ship he had ever seen. That the ship was so clean was, perhaps, one reason the USS *Cabot* served both the American and Spanish navies for so many years as a CVL. It was kept in great shape by its crews. Admiral Coleman had been the commanding officer of the attack carrier USS *Ranger* (CV-61) during Vietnam some years earlier. He was a stickler for detail!

The CVL was somewhat of an unsung hero of WWII, Korea, and beyond. Several took heavy damage in combat but usually in the shadow of the large carriers. The fact that several nations possessed light carriers was a testament to their effectiveness and efficiency. During my time with the *Dedalo*, I was assigned a stateroom that had in it a plaque commemorating those who had died from a Kamikaze attack on 25 November 1944. That stateroom always inspired a feeling of reverence and quiet.

Operations from the deck of the *Dedalo* were not unlike those of a wartime CVL. Harriers used a deck run to get airborne as did the aircraft of earlier days. However, landings were always vertical because of the aircraft design and there were no arresting wires on the deck. Flying off the short-deck, *Dedalo* gave pilots an appreciation for what Corsair and Hellcat pilots faced in earlier times. The missions were the same: fighter, attack, and reconnaissance. Helicopters were also aboard the *Dedalo* for Search and Rescue (SAR), ASW (Anti-Submarine Warfare), and transport.

As one of the last pilots to fly from a CVL, I understood why the *Dedalo*, as a light carrier, was tailored for the Spanish Navy mission of coastal protection. The ship was maneuverable, relatively quick, and carried a solid mix of mission-capable aircraft for rapid launch, deployment, and recovery.

During this same time frame of the 1970s, the US Navy was evaluating less-expensive, small-deck carriers, known at the time as the Sea Control ship. The USS *Guam* (LPH-9) was the platform used in the trials. The idea being that, with VSTOL (Vertical Take-Off and Landing) aircraft on a small deck, an expensive attack carrier could be better deployed elsewhere. This vision never came to complete fruition but, due to VSTOL aircraft such as the AV-8A Harrier and F-35 Lightning II, several classes of aviation ships provide that capability today.

Unknown in the 1940s and 1950s, the CVL would become the genesis of smaller deck, multi-mission aviation ships we see today from several countries. With missions of jets and helicopters ranging from fighter, attack, reconnaissance, ASW, transport, and SAR, these descendants of the light carrier have become front line warships of today.

CDR Bruhn has provided an extremely well researched and written account of multi-nation CVL operations during the Korean War. His accounts of aviators in Dog Fights and Bombing attacks are even more fascinating because David is not an aviator, yet he captures the exhilaration of such flying. This book belongs in both your aircraft and ship collections.

Larry Wahl, CDR, USN (Retired)
Naval Aviator

Acknowledgements

Brilliant maritime and aviation artist Richard DeRosset has completed over a thousand paintings to date in his illustrious art career, which followed much time spent at sea as a sailor in the US Navy, deckhand on a commercial fishing vessel, and finally as master of the small tanker *Pacific Trojan*. To date, fifteen of those paintings have been created as the cover art for an equal number of my books. I provide Richard details about a particularly compelling action or event, often little known to the public. Following his own research, he brings the resultant painting to life in a way that draws in viewers of his masterful work, and makes them feel like they were there. I eagerly await unveilings, and am always stunned when his genius is revealed on canvas.

Photo Acknowledgements-1

Richard DeRosset at work in his art studio in Lemon Grove, California.
Courtesy of Victoria Maidhof

Several very distinguished individuals have assisted with this book, including Rear Adm. Allan du Toit AM RAN, who retired from naval service four years ago after forty years combined service in two Commonwealth navies (South Africa and Australia). Born and raised in South Africa, he entered the South African Navy in 1975 and joined the Royal Australian Navy in early 1987. As a Warfare Officer at sea, du Toit served in mine counter measures vessels, submarines, frigates, destroyers and amphibious ships, commanding at each rank from Lieutenant to Rear Admiral. Flag officer assignments included two Middle East coalition command appointments. His final appointment was as Australia's Military Representative to NATO in Brussels.

Admiral du Toit authored two books, *Ships of the South African Navy* and *South Africa's Fighting Ships - Past and Present*, during his operationally-focused career, and over the years contributed to various other books, journals and naval history conferences. Keenly interested in academics, he is currently a visiting fellow and adjunct lecturer at the University of New South Wales (UNSW) Canberra, and has just completed all requirements for his doctorate degree, the defence of the Cape Sea Route during the Cold War being the focus of his research.

Photo Acknowledgements-2

Rear Adm. Allan du Toit AM RAN (Retired)
Courtesy of Admiral Allan du Toit

I am particularly grateful for the considerable assistance provided by Commodore Hector Donohue AM RAN (Retired). Donohue has generously provided, for several of my previous books, much material from his own books and articles, and has penned forewords reflecting the perspective of a Royal Australian Navy flag officer. He has done so again; this time, crafting two compelling chapters and the postscript, in addition to his foreword to the book.

Donohue began his career in the RAN in 1955 as a seaman officer and subsequently sub-specialized as a clearance diver and torpedo and anti-submarine officer. His service in the RAN included command of the destroyer escort HMAS *Yarra* and the guided missile frigate HMAS *Darwin*. Ashore, he held a number of senior positions in Defence policy and force development prior to retirement in mid-1991.

Photo Acknowledgements-3

Hector Donohue while in command of HMAS *Darwin*.
Courtesy of Commodore Donohue, AM RAN (Rtd.)

Rob Hoole co-authored with me the *Home Waters/Nightraiders/Enemy Waters* trilogy of mine warfare books and, for this book, reviewed the Royal Navy-related material. Rob is a former Royal Navy mine clearance diving officer and commanding officer of the mine countermeasures vessel HMS *Berkeley*. An acknowledged expert on mine warfare, he is a long-standing member of the Ton Class Association and a regular contributor to its publications. Hoole is also founding Vice Chairman and Webmaster of the Royal Naval Minewarfare & Clearance Diving Officers' Association, and holds key positions in related organisations.

Rob spearheaded successful efforts to establish a memorial at Gunwharf Quays in Portsmouth, UK, in remembrance of the tens of thousands of service personnel who passed through the gates of the training establishment HMS Vernon. These personnel included the mine warfare and diving specialists, mine designers, minefield planners, bomb & mine disposal personnel and the crews of the minelayers, minesweepers, and minehunters who were trained or based there.

Photo Acknowledgements-4

Rob Hoole standing in front of the Vernon Mine Warfare
& Division Monument at the Gunwharf Quays in Portsmouth, UK.
Courtesy of Rob Hoole

I am also grateful to retired US Navy commander Larry Wahl, a former naval aviator and fighter pilot, for his critical review of the dogfighting action and other pilot-related material in the book. Larry was also kind enough to provide a foreword offering an assessment of the light fleet carriers from the perspective of a pilot who had spent time aboard the Spanish SNS *Dedalo*, formerly the USS *Cabot* (CVL-28).

Photo Acknowledgements-5

Larry Wahl entering cockpit of an AV-8A Harrier ground-attack aircraft.
Courtesy of CDR Larry Wahl, USN (Retired)

Wahl served two combat tours in Vietnam flying 178 combat missions from aircraft carriers. Other duty included serving as an exchange pilot with the US Marine Corps for three years testing, evaluating, and training new pilots in early Harrier Vertical/Short Take Off and Landing (V/STOL) jets. During the Reagan presidency, he was the Liaison Officer to the White House Military Office in support of "Western White House" aircraft operations.

Dwight Messimer, a former university lecturer, and acclaimed military historian and author, lent his considerable expertise on aviation to the project and provided material for the book. A specialist on the German Navy and U-boats, he has written nearly a dozen books on this subject and on naval aviation covering the period 1925-1942. Messimer's work has also appeared in many periodicals, including *The American Neptune*; *The Quarterly Journal of Military History*; *War, Revolution and Peace;* and *Naval History*.

Photo Acknowledgements-6

Dwight Messimer, 2020.

This book would not have been possible without the considerable involvement of Canadian George Duddy, a retired Professional Engineer with a keen interest in maritime subjects, particularly those relating to the maritime history of western Canada and the Arctic. Duddy has deep family roots in the British Isles. His father, as a schoolboy, took photographs of surrendered German Battleships in the Firth of Forth near the end of World War I; his great grandfather was a pioneering Leith steamship owner and his great great grandfather, as Master in both sail and steam, ended his career as marine superintendent for the Leith, Hull & Hamburg Steam Packet Co. One of his other relatives, Midshipman Percival George, fell to his death from the mast of a Royal Navy ship during the age of sail. His dirk is on display in a museum in South Africa.

Duddy offered many suggestions for improvement during his technical review and editing of this book, as he has done for others. Additionally, he was extensively involved in the research and the crafting of the chapters devoted to early Royal Canadian Navy aviation and its former aircraft carrier program.

Photo Acknowledgements-7

George Duddy in Glacier Bay aboard the MS *Volendam* during an Alaskan cruise in 2019. A contributor and U.S. Military & Naval Vessel Correspondent for Nauticapedia.ca Project, he is sporting an organization ballcap.
Courtesy of George Duddy

Canadian John M. MacFarlane allowed use of material from his article "Some Notes on HMCS *Iroquois* in the Korean War," as well as a photograph of *Iroquois* conducting shore bombardment of enemy targets in North Korea. Formerly the Director and Curator of the Maritime Museum of British Columbia in Victoria, MacFarlane is now the Curator of the website, The Nauticapedia.ca, which shares a vast resource related to British Columbia's nautical history, and has two extensive searchable databases of ships and people. He has written many articles and books on this theme. His latest book, *Around the World in a Dugout Canoe: The Untold Story of Captain John Voss and the Tilikum*, co-authored with Lynn J. Salmon, was recently published.

Finally, much thanks to my editor, Lynn Marie Tosello. Lynn has now edited a half dozen or more of my books. Her scouring and polishing of hundreds of pages of text, while gently, in most cases, identifying to the author overlooked omissions, or the need to better explain nautical-related subject matter, adds much to these works.

Preface

Turning into wind now,
Ship goes full ahead.
All eyes on the island,
Light's remaining red.
Up pops the Flag, your leader's gone!
Pour on the coal, the thrust so strong!
Off brakes, you navy pilot,
Get up where you belong.

—From the poem *Flight of Angels* by Bill Babbitt.[1]

Photo Preface-1

Light fleet carrier USS *Langley* (CVL-27) berthed in port, location and date unknown. This starboard bow aspect clearly shows that she, and her eight *Independence*-class sister ships were laid down as cruisers in builders' yards, then had flight decks affixed atop their hulls during construction.
Naval History and Heritage Command photograph #NH 67579

Turn in to the Wind Volume II is devoted to the American- and British-built light fleet carriers that served as units of the United States Navy, Royal Navy, Royal Canadian Navy, and Royal Australian Navy in the Korean War, Cold War, UN Peace Keeping Missions, Vietnam War, and up until 1982 when HMAS *Melbourne* was decommissioned. The WWII service of USN and RN light fleet carriers is the subject of

Volume I of *Turn in to the Wind*, but it's worthwhile to describe here the desperate conditions in that war that spurred America and England to acquire small carriers with modest capabilities, whose contributions, nevertheless, would be considerable.

When America was thrust into World War II by the Japanese attack on Pearl Harbor on 7 December 1941, the US Navy had only five fleet carriers in the Pacific. As a result, for the first four months of 1942, the carrier admirals were ordered to avoid engaging the Japanese fleet and were relegated to raiding actions against island bases. The dearth of fleet aviation capabilities became even more acute following the loss in 1942 of four carriers to combat action:

- USS *Lexington* (CV-2): Torpedoed and bombed by Japanese carrier-based aircraft on 8 May 1942, in the Battle of the Coral Sea
- USS *Yorktown* (CV-5): Torpedoed by a Japanese submarine on 7 June 1942, after being disabled by Japanese carrier aircraft bombs and torpedoes, 4 June 1942, in the Battle of Midway
- USS *Wasp* (CV-7): Torpedoed by a Japanese submarine on 15 September 1942, while operating in the Southwestern Pacific in support of forces on Guadalcanal
- USS *Hornet* (CV-8): Hit by Japanese carrier aircraft bombs and torpedoes on 26 October 1942, in the Battle of the Santa Cruz Islands[2]

The Navy's solution was the *Essex*-class fleet aircraft carrier. Twenty-four of the 30,000-ton ships were built in American shipyards between 1943 and 1950. As shown in the following table, twelve of the carriers were completed in time to collectively earn 84 battle stars in the Pacific Theater in World War II.[3]

Essex-class Aircraft Carriers
(that saw combat in WWII)

Aircraft Carrier	Commissioned	Battle Stars
USS *Essex* (CV-9)	31 Dec 42	13 WWII
USS *Yorktown* (CV-10)	15 Apr 43	11 WWII
USS *Intrepid* (CV-11)	16 Aug 43	5 WWII
USS *Hornet* (CV-12)	29 Nov 43	7 WWII
USS *Franklin* (CV-13)	31 Jan 44	4 WWII
USS *Ticonderoga* (CV-14)	8 May 44	5 WWII
USS *Randolph* (CV-15)	9 Oct 44	3 WWII
USS *Lexington* (CV-16)	17 Mar 43	11 WWII
USS *Bunker Hill* (CV-17)	24 May 43	11 WWII
USS *Wasp* (CV-18)	24 Nov 43	8 WWII
USS *Hancock* (CV-19)	15 Apr 44	3 WWII
USS *Bennington* (CV-20)	6 Aug 44	3 WWII[4]

Photo Preface-2

USS *Essex* (CV-9) under way in May 1943. The aircraft on her flight deck include 24 SBD scout bombers (located aft), about 11 F6F fighters (after midships area) and some 18 TBF/TBM torpedo planes (amidships).
National Archives photograph #80-G-68097

INTERVENTION OF PRESIDENT ROOSEVELT

President Franklin D. Roosevelt, not content with the ship completion schedule for the *Essex*es, directed the conversion of *Cleveland*-class light cruiser hulls already laid down in yards, to produce light carriers. A former Assistant Secretary of the Navy (17 March 1913 to 26 August 1920), Roosevelt had a keen interest in, and periodically personally directed, naval matters during World War II.[5]

In this case, Roosevelt ignored the warnings of naval architects that the fine lines of the cruiser hulls would preclude a roomy hangar and large island, and make it difficult to position the elevators or support the forward flight deck. Modifications made to address these issues included: truncating the flight deck, designing a very small island resembling those of escort carriers, making do with a rather small hangar, and bulging the hull to maintain stability.[6]

Interestingly, these 619-foot petite carriers with 71-foot beam and 26-foot draft would earn more battle stars on average than the larger, more well-known *Essex*-class carriers. The *Essex*es stretched 872 feet in length, with twice the girth (147-foot beams), and slightly deeper drafts of twenty-eight feet. Both ship classes were fast; the *Essex* could make 33 knots, and the *Independence* one knot less.

Independence-class Light Fleet Aircraft Carriers

Aircraft Carrier	Commissioned	Battle Stars
Independence (CVL-22)	14 Jan 1943	8 WWII
Princeton (CVL-23)	25 Feb 1943	9 WWII
Belleau Wood (CVL-24)	31 Mar 1943	12 WWII
Cowpens (CVL-25)	28 May 1943	12 WWII
Monterey (CVL-26)	17 June 1943	11 WWII
Langley (CVL-27)	31 Aug 1943	9 WWII
Cabot (CVL-28)	24 July 1943	8 WWII
Bataan (CVL-29)	13 May 1943	5 WWII/7 Korean War
San Jacinto (CVL-30)	15 Dec 1943	6 WWII

POST-US NAVY SERVICE IN FOREIGN NAVIES

Three of the nine *Independence*-class light fleet carriers later served in the French or Spanish navies, whose service is not included in the book.

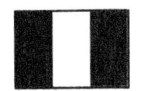

US Navy and Subsequent Service of *Independence*-class Ships

USS *Belleau Wood*	USS *Langley*	USS *Cabot*
France	France	Spain
Bois Belleau (R97)	*Lafayette* (R96)	*Dedalo* (R01)
Comm: 23 Dec 53	Comm: 1951	Loan: 30 Aug 67
Decom: 12 Dec 60	Decom: 1963	Struck: 1989

SAIPAN-CLASS LIGHT FLEET CARRIERS

In addition to the nine *Independence*s, the US Navy completed two other light fleet carriers, post-World War II. *Saipan* and *Wright* were follow-on ships to the earlier light fleet carriers. Their design remedied some of the problems the *Independence*-class had suffered. With a hull design based on the *Baltimore*-class heavy cruisers, the 683-foot, 19,086-ton *Saipan*s were a little larger. Instead of being fitted with above water-line bulges, their hulls were widened several feet at the design stage, allowing a much greater growth margin than their predecessors. The general configuration of *Saipan* and *Wright* was the same as the earlier CVLs.[7]

Neither ship saw any combat duty as light fleet aircraft carriers. Both were decommissioned following their service as carriers, then later brought out of "mothballs" and reconfigured for other duties. Following *Saipan*'s conversion to Major Communications Relay Ship, and renaming as *Arlington* (AGMR-2), she served off Vietnam in the late 1960s. Her duties included relaying communications between "top brass" in the Pentagon and combat commanders in theater. She was decommissioned on 14 January 1970.[8]

Wright (former CVL-49 and AVT-7) was converted to a National Emergency Command Post Afloat in March 1962. Fitted with extensive presidential command and control facilities, she was redesignated *Wright* (CC-2). Her service to the Navy ended a little after *Saipan*'s. She was decommissioned on 27 May 1970.

Photo Preface-3

USS *Wright* (CC-2) under way on 17 June 1963, following her conversion to National Emergency Command Post Afloat. An extensive array of large communications antennas was installed on her flight deck to provide presidential command facilities. Naval History and Heritage Command photograph #NH 97621

Saipan-class Light Fleet Aircraft Carriers

Ship	Comm	Decom
Light Fleet Aircraft Carrier *Saipan* (CVL-48)	14 Jul 1946	3 Oct 1957
Major Communications Relay Ship *Arlington* (AGMR-2)	27 Aug 1966	14 Jan 1970
Light Fleet Aircraft Carrier *Wright* (CVL-49)	9 Feb 1947	15 Mar 1956
National Emergency Command Post Afloat (CC-2)[9]	11 May 1963	27 May 1970

THE ROYAL NAVY'S LIGHT FLEET CARRIERS

Ten *Colossus*-class light fleet aircraft carriers were built in UK shipyards in the 1940s to Royal Navy design. They, like their American cousins, were intended to serve as an intermediate step between the expensive, full-size fleet aircraft carriers and less costly but limited-capability escort carriers. Sixteen of these ships were laid down in 1942 and 1943. However, only eight were completed to the specified design; of these only four entered service before the end of the war, and none saw front-line combat operations in WWII.[10]

Four of the *Colossus*es—HMS *Triumph*, HMS *Theseus*, HMS *Ocean*, and HMS *Glory*—served, along with the Australian and American light fleet carriers HMAS *Sydney* and USS *Bataan*, in the Korean War. HMS *Warrior* was deployed as a transport for troops and aircraft to support British forces during the conflict, but did not engage in combat and did not receive battle honours.

Photo Preface-4

Light fleet carrier HMS *Triumph* off Subic Bay, Philippines, during joint U.S. and UK naval exercises, 8 March 1950. Planes on her deck include Supermarine Seafire 47s of 800 Squadron, forward, and Fairey Fireflys aft.
Naval History and Heritage Command photograph #NH 97010

Colossus-class Light Fleet Aircraft Carriers
695 feet, 18,000 tons, 23.3-foot draft, 25 knots, 1,050 ship's complement
Four Admiralty 3-drum boilers, Parsons turbines (40,000hp), 2 shafts
Six 4-barrelled 2-pounder AA guns, sixteen twin 20mm Oerlikon AA guns
(all weapons later replaced by 40mm Bofors in varying configurations)
Full flight deck and hangar for up to 52 aircraft

Ship	Builder	Comm	Paid off
HMS *Colossus* (R61)	Vickers-Armstrong Shipbuilding, Barrow-in-Furness, Cumbria, UK	16 Dec 44	1946 UK
HMS *Glory* (R62)	Harland & Wolff Shipbuilding, Belfast, Northern Ireland, UK	2 Apr 45	1956 UK
HMS *Ocean* (R68)	Stephen & Sons Shipbuilding, Glasgow, Scotland, UK	8 Aug 45	1960 UK
HMS *Venerable* (R63)	Cammell-Laird Shipbuilding, Birkenhead, UK	17 Jan 45	April 1947 UK
HMS *Vengeance* (R71)	Swan Hunter Shipbuilding, Wallsend, Tyne and Wear, UK	15 Jan 45	April 1952 UK
HMS *Pioneer* (R76)	Vickers-Armstrong Shipbuilding, Barrow-in-Furness, Cumbria, UK (maintenance carrier)	8 Feb 45	1954 UK
HMS *Warrior* (R31)	Harland & Wolff Shipbuilding, Belfast, Northern Ireland, UK	2 Apr 45	April 1946 UK
HMS *Theseus* (R64)	Fairfield Shipbuilding and Engineering, Govan, Glasgow, Scotland, UK	9 Feb 46	1957 UK
HMS *Triumph* (R16)	R&W Hawthorn Leslie & Company, Tyneside, UK	9 May 46	1975 UK
HMS *Perseus* (R51)	Vickers-Armstrong Shipbuilding, Barrow-in-Furness, Cumbria, UK (maintenance carrier)[11]	19 Oct 45	1957 UK

As indicated in the table, two of these ten carriers—HMS *Pioneer* and HMS *Perseus*—were fitted with maintenance and repair facilities instead of aircraft catapults and arresting gear, and entered service as aircraft maintenance carriers.[12]

POST-ROYAL NAVY SERVICE IN FOREIGN NAVIES

Following their service to the Royal Navy, four *Colossus*-class light fleet carriers collectively sailed under the flags of Australia, Argentina, Brazil, Canada, France, and the Netherlands. *Vengeance* and *Warrior* first assisted the Commonwealth countries Australia and Canada in developing their fledgling aircraft carrier programs. Later acquired by Brazil and Argentina, respectively, the World War II-vintage ships continued their long service and, in the case of *Vengeance*, until October

2001. Only the Australian and Canadian service of these ships is covered in this book.

Royal Navy and Subsequent Service of *Colossus*-class Ships

HMS *Colossus*	HMS *Venerable*	HMS *Vengeance*	HMS *Warrior*
France	Netherlands	Australia	Canada
Arromanches (R95)	HNLMS *Karel Doorman* (R81)	HMAS *Vengeance* (R71)	HMCS *Warrior* (R31)
Acquired: 1946	Comm: 28 May 48	Comm: 13 Nov 52	Comm: 14 Mar 46
Decom: 1974	Decom: 29 Apr 68	Decom: 25 Oct 55	Decom: 23 Mar 48
	Argentina	Brazil	Argentina
	Veinticinco de Mayo	*Minas Gerais* (A11)	*Independencia* (V1)
	Comm: 12 Mar 69	Comm: 6 Dec 60	Comm: 8 Jul 59
	Decom: 1997	Decom: 16 Oct 01	Decom: 1970

After decommissioning, HNLMS *Karel Doorman* was transferred to Argentina and renamed ARA *Veinticinco de Mayo*, where she would later play a role in the 1982 Falkland Islands Conflict. She was commissioned into the Argentine Navy on 12 March 1969 and finally decommissioned in 1997. After being stripped of spares to support the Brazilian carrier *Minas Gerais*, *Veinticinco de Mayo* was scrapped in India in 2000.[13]

MAJESTIC (MODIFIED *COLOSSUS*) CLASS SHIPS

The final six, of the sixteen *Colossus*-class light fleet aircraft carriers laid down, were modified during construction to handle larger and faster aircraft. Redesignated the *Majestic*-class, their construction was suspended at the end of World War II. Five were eventually completed with the last one commissioning in 1961. These ships were transferred, loaned, or sold to Australia, Canada, and India, assisting these countries in the development of carrier air warfare capabilities.

Majestic-class Light Fleet Aircraft Carriers

695-feet, 19,500-tons, 24.9-foot draft, 25 knots, 1,050 ship's complement
Four Admiralty 3-drum boilers, Parsons turbines (40,000hp), 2 shafts
Thirty Bofors 40mm AA guns (6 twin/18 single)
Full flight deck and hangar for up to 52 aircraft

Ship	Builder	Comm	Decom
HMS *Majestic* (R77)/HMAS *Melbourne* (R21)	Vickers-Armstrong Shipbuilding, Barrow-in-Furness, Cumbria, UK (transferred to Australia)	28 Oct 55 RAN	30 May 82 RAN
HMS *Terrible* (R93)/HMAS *Sydney* (R17)	HM Dockyard, Devonport, UK (transferred to Australia; aircraft carrier service until 30 May 1958)	16 Dec 48 RAN	12 Nov 73 RAN
HMS *Magnificent* (R36)/HMCS *Magnificent* (CVL-21)	Harland & Wolff Shipbuilding, Belfast, Northern Ireland, UK (loaned to Canada)	21 Mar 48 RCN	14 Jun 57 RCN
HMS *Hercules* (R49)/INS *Vikrant* (R11)	Vickers-Armstrong Shipbuilding, Barrow-in-Furness, Cumbria, UK (sold to India, 1957)	4 Mar 61 INS	31 Jan 97 INS
HMS *Powerful* (R-95)/HMCS *Bonaventure* (CVL-22)	Harland & Wolff Shipbuilding, Belfast, Northern Ireland, UK (transferred to Canada)[14]	17 Jan 57 RCN	3 Jul 70 RCN

USN, RN, RAN, AND RCN LIGHT FLEET CARRIERS

A summary of the *Independence*- and *Saipan*-class light fleet aircraft carriers that served in the United States Navy, and those of the British *Colossus* and *Majestic* classes that sailed under the ensigns of the Royal Navy, Royal Australian Navy, and Royal Canadian Navy follows:

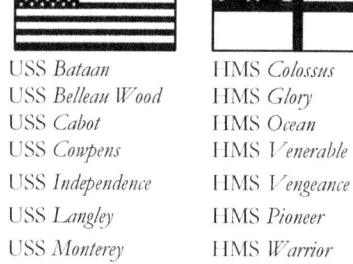

USS *Bataan*	HMS *Colossus*	HMAS *Sydney*	HMCS *Warrior*
USS *Belleau Wood*	HMS *Glory*	HMAS *Vengeance*	HMCS *Magnificent*
USS *Cabot*	HMS *Ocean*	HMAS *Melbourne*	HMCS *Bonaventure*
USS *Cowpens*	HMS *Venerable*		
USS *Independence*	HMS *Vengeance*		
USS *Langley*	HMS *Pioneer*		
USS *Monterey*	HMS *Warrior*		
USS *Princeton*	HMS *Theseus*		
USS *San Jacinto*	HMS *Triumph*		
USS *Arlington*	HMS *Perseus*		
USS *Wright*			

OVERVIEW OF THE BOOK

Turn in to the Wind opens with an account of the daring rescue, of a downed fighter pilot on a frozen reservoir in North Korea, by a US Air Force air commando helicopter. Marine Corps major David Cleeland, USMC, was not having a particularly good day on his 101st mission, lying aside his crashed F4U Corsair, under fire from enemy forces, and with no good options for his survival available. The H-19A Chickasaw then swooped in and picked him up. The normal activities of this "bird" and other three members of H-19 Helicopter Flight based at Seoul City Airbase were so highly classified, they were blended in with elements of the 2157th Air Rescue Squadron. Standard operations for the pilots and aircrews involved nighttime insertion of agents behind enemy lines.

Action-packed Chapters 2 and 3 are devoted to the six light fleet carriers identified previously that served in the Korean War—four Royal Navy, one Royal Australian Navy, and one US Navy.

The Royal Canadian Navy did not acquire its first carrier (HMCS *Warrior* on loan from Britain) until 1946. However, the RCN's entry into naval aviation extended back to a fledgling pilot training program undertaken in the closing months of WWI. Pilot training in England ceased at war's end, but eight Canadians were later awarded RCNAS wings. Chapter 4 takes readers from this point through World War II. Britain, short of personnel for newly built ships coming off the ways, requested that the Royal Canadian Navy operate two RN carriers, with the RN Fleet Air Arm providing the aircraft and aircrews. The RCN commanded and manned HMS *Nabob* and *Puncher*, which participated in combat operations off German-occupied Norway—gaining valuable experience in fleet operations before launching its own carrier program.

ROYAL CANADIAN NAVY AIRCRAFT CARRIERS

HMCS *Warrior*	HMCS *Magnificent*	HMCS *Bonaventure*
"Haul together"	"We stand on guard"	"Not for us alone"
Colossus-class	*Majestic*-class	*Majestic*-class

Chapter 5 describes the sequential service of three aircraft carriers in the Canadian Navy between 1946 and 1970, the first being HMCS *Warrior*. The Royal Navy's HMS *Warrior* was transferred to the RCN on 14 March 1946 and commissioned HMCS *Warrior* that same day. After her heating system proved insufficient to deal with the cold waters of the North Atlantic, she was transferred to Canada's west coast until returned to the RN in exchange for a more suitable light fleet carrier, the *Magnificent*.[15]

Warrior arrived at Belfast, Northern Ireland, in February 1948. Her crew transferred the stores on board to *Magnificent*, then took possession of their new ship. *Magnificent* operated both fixed and rotary-wing aircraft. The former included Fairey Fireflies and Hawker Sea Furies. In 1953 she participated in the Coronation Spithead Review off Portsmouth, England. (In addition to HMCS *Magnificent*, the light fleet carriers HMS *Perseus*, HMS *Theseus*, and HMAS *Sydney* were also present, as were the larger carriers HMS *Eagle*, *Indomitable*, *Implacable*, *Indefatigable*, and *Illustrious*.) Near the end of her Canadian service, *Magnificent* functioned as a transport during the Suez Crisis, carrying a large part of the Canadian peacekeeping force to Egypt, its vehicles parked on her deck. *Magnificent* was decommissioned at Plymouth, England, on 14 June 1957, and turned over to the Royal Navy.[16]

Magnificent's successor was HMCS *Bonaventure*, named after the bird sanctuary in the Gulf of St. Lawrence. Work on the former HMS *Powerful* had stopped three months after her launching in February 1945. However, the lengthy delay before construction resumed in 1952, allowed improvements to be incorporated. The most significant was an angled flight deck, which provided a longer landing run without sacrificing forward parking space. Other associated improvements included the removal of the unpopular crash barrier, and the addition of a steam catapult and a mirror landing sight. The latter went far in helping to eliminate human error in landing.[17]

"Bonnie" was commissioned at Belfast on 17 January 1957, and arrived at Halifax, Nova Scotia, six months later on 26 June. Unlike her predecessors, *Bonaventure* boasted F2H-3 Banshee jet fighters and CS2F-2 Tracker anti-submarine aircraft as her complement. Over the next thirteen years, she enjoyed a busy career of flight training and participation in anti-submarine exercises with ships of other North Atlantic Treaty Organization nations, and served as the flagship for the commander, Canadian Fleet Atlantic. In March 1964, *Bonaventure* transported Canadian UN forces and materiel to Cyprus. She was paid off on 3 July 1970.[18]

POST-WORLD WAR II, COLD WAR, AND VIETNAM WAR SERVICE OF THE US NAVY LIGHT CARRIERS

The service of USS *Bataan*, *Cabot*, and *Monterey*, less the combat duty of *Bataan* during the Korean War, is taken up in Chapter 6. USS *Princeton* was lost during World War II—scuttled following a Japanese dive-bomber attack on 24 October 1944, in which she suffered great damage and loss of life. Of the remaining eight CVLs, seven took part in Operation MAGIC CARPET, to transport home former POWs during the immediate aftermath of the war. *Independence* participated in nuclear tests at Bikini Atoll in 1946. Her ruined, radioactive hulk was towed to San Francisco and, following study, later sunk off the Californian coast. The remaining seven light carriers were laid up in 1947. Three—*Bataan*, *Cabot*, and *Monterey*—were returned to service, and ultimately, *Cabot*, *Langley*, and *Belleau Wood* were transferred to Allies.

Chapters 7 and 8 introduce readers to the very interesting duty of the two *Saipan*-class ships—*Saipan* and *Wright*—commissioned in 1946 and 1947, respectively. As noted earlier, following service with the fleet as aircraft carriers, *Saipan* was laid up in the Reserve Fleet in 1956, followed by *Wright*, a year later.

Both ships were later "brought out of mothballs" in the early 1960s and, following modification, were utilized for duties other than mobile bases for the operation and support of naval aircraft. *Saipan* was renamed *Arlington*, and served as a major communications relay ship during the Vietnam War. In addition to multiple tours in the combat zone, she also supported the recovery of the Apollo 8, 10, and 11 space capsules.

Photo Preface-5

Painting *Recovered Apollo 11 Module, USS Hornet* by Cliff Young, 1969, depicting the space capsule aboard the recovery ship, the aircraft carrier *Hornet*. *Arlington* was nearby, functioning as a communications relay link for Navy and NASA radio and voice circuits. Naval History and Heritage Command photograph 88-163-AM

During the Cold War, the U.S. government devised top-secret plans to ensure its survival if the Soviet Union launched a nuclear attack. USS *Wright* was specially configured as an Emergency Command Post Afloat, and either she or the USS *Northampton* (CC-1) was always at sea in the Atlantic Ocean, Chesapeake Bay, or shadowing the president around the world, serving as a "Floating White House/Pentagon." In readiness for a possible national military command role, the ships carried special Joint Chiefs personnel and featured elaborate staterooms with full communications capabilities.[19]

Plans also existed for the evacuation and safeguarding personnel for critical government functions, other than the president and his key advisors and senior military leaders. A secret bunker was built beneath Greenbrier, a luxury resort in White Sulphur Springs, West Virginia, 250 miles southwest of the capital city, to host the U.S. Congress. Members of the Supreme Court were to relocate to the Grove Park Inn in Asheville, North Carolina. To ensure continuity of government finances, the chairman, board of directors, and staff of the Federal Reserve System were to move into a bunker built into a hillside at Culpeper, Virginia, 75 miles south of Washington, D.C.[20]

COLD WAR CRISES AND HOT SPOTS

The Korean War marked the last combat duty of the USN *Independence*-class ships. Subsequent conflicts/hotspots involved only RN, RCN, and RAN light fleet carriers. These included the Suez Crisis of 1956, and associated peace keeping operations the next year; the Cyprus Crisis, 1963-1964; and the Indonesia–Malaysia confrontation, 1965-1966.

THE SUEZ CRISIS (OPERATION MUSKETEER) 1956

In the summer of 1956 President Nasser of Egypt seized the Suez Canal from the Anglo-French Company which administered it. Some eight weeks prior to this action, Britain had withdrawn its military presence in the Canal Zone, which it had maintained since 1953. In response, the British and French Governments subsequently decided to reoccupy the Canal Zone via a sea and airborne assault of Port Said, Egypt.[21]

On 6 November 1946, aboard HMS *Ocean* and HMS *Theseus*, the Royal Marines of No. 45 Commando unit prepared for the first helicopter-borne assault landing in history. In eighty-three minutes, 22 Sycamore and Whirlwind helicopters from the light fleet carriers landed alongside the statue of canal builder Ferdinand de Lesseps, and put ashore 415 marines and 23 tons of stores. The helicopters then brought in reinforcements and more supplies, and ferried out wounded, including 18 Marines who had been strafed in error by a Fleet Air Arm fighter-bomber.[22]

In a day of street fighting, the Royal Marines seized Port Said, but political pressure from the United States, the Soviet Union, and the United Nations, resulted in military operations being suspended after the objectives had been achieved. Following a cease-fire, the Royal Marines were withdrawn and a UN force took over.[23]

THE SUEZ CRISIS UNITED NATIONS EMERGENCY FORCE (UNEF) PEACE KEEPING OPERATION 1957

In an operation suggested by Canada, a force made up of troops from eleven separate countries was organized to supervise the reopening of the canal and the ceasefire between Egyptians and Israelis. Then Foreign Minister (and later Prime Minister) Lester B. Pearson received consideration for this when awarded the 1957 Nobel Peace Prize. In her penultimate duty in the RCN, HMCS *Magnificent*, known affectionately by her crew as the "Maggie," transported 406 troops, 233 vehicles, four Otter aircraft, one helicopter, and 400 tons of equipment to Port Said in Egypt.[24]

Her final mission, before being paid off in June 1957, was to transport home from Scotland to Halifax 59 RCAF Sabre jets, which Canada had been employing as part of their NATO commitment.[25]

CYPRUS CRISIS OF 1963-1964

Cyprus, a small island in the eastern Mediterranean located south of Turkey, has a very tumultuous history, including the period leading up to and after the island gained independence. In 1960, the former British crown colony became the Republic of Cyprus. However, long-standing conflict between the Greek Cypriot majority and the Turkish Cypriot minority continued and, because of this unrest, Cyprus asked the UN to establish a peacekeeping force for the island in 1964.[26]

In March 1964, HMCS *Bonaventure* transported Canadian Army peacekeeping elements to Cyprus. A large Canadian contingent served on the island from 1964 to 1993, and today, a small Canadian Armed Forces presence remains there as UN peace efforts continue. More than 25,000 Canadian Armed Forces members have served in Cyprus over the decades, and this effort is one of Canada's longest and best-known overseas military commitments.[27]

MALAYSIA 1964-1966

Between 1962 and 1966, Indonesia and Malaysia fought a small, undeclared war which came to involve military forces from Australia, New Zealand, and Britain. The conflict resulted from Indonesia's President Sukarno believing that the creation of the Federation of Malaysia represented a British attempt to maintain colonial rule behind the cloak of independence granted to its former possessions in southeast Asia. Malaysia was officially formed in September 1963, when what had been British Malaya (nine Malay states and the British Straits Settlements Penang and Malacca) united with the Singapore, North Borneo, and Sarawak Crown Colonies.[28]

Australia's commitment of military forces to operations against Indonesia in Borneo and West Malaysia fell within the context of its membership in the Far East Strategic Reserve. Australian Army units fighting ashore during the Confrontation, as part of a larger British and Commonwealth force under British command, were supported by ships of the Royal Australian Navy serving in surrounding waters.[29]

Two of the fleet units were light fleet carriers. HMAS *Melbourne* garnered Battle Honours MALAYSIA 1965-66 battling communist uprisings. HMAS *Sydney* (the RAN's most decorated carrier) had earlier earned Battle Honours MALAYSIA 1964, adding to battle honours for KOREA 1951-52, and preceding those for VIETNAM 1965-1972.

Among the officers and men who served aboard light fleet carriers in the American, British, Canadian, and Australian navies, former crewmembers of HMAS *Sydney* have bragging rights as being the last such engaged in war duty, before departing Vietnam for the last time in March 1972. (*Sydney* was then functioning as a troop transport). USS *Arlington*, serving as a major communications relay ship, earned her last Vietnam Service Medal for the period 26 June to 8 July 1969.

ROYAL AUSTRALIAN NAVY AIRCRAFT CARRIERS

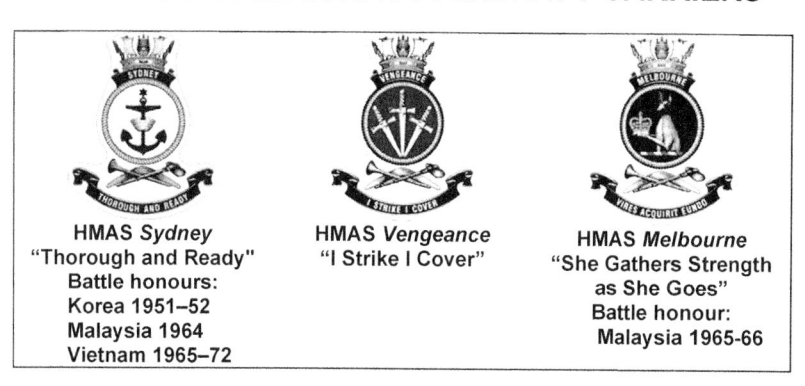

HMAS *Sydney* "Thorough and Ready" Battle honours: Korea 1951–52 Malaysia 1964 Vietnam 1965–72	HMAS *Vengeance* "I Strike I Cover"	HMAS *Melbourne* "She Gathers Strength as She Goes" Battle honour: Malaysia 1965-66

The final two chapters of the book and the Postscript, authored by Commodore Hector Donohue AM RAN (Retired), introduce readers to the rich history of the Royal Australian Navy's former aircraft carrier program. This warfare capability, like that of Canada, perished as a result of limited military funding, and fierce interservice fighting for those monies.

The next four pages of the Preface provide schema for Chapter 9, aptly titled "The Australian Aircraft Carrier Program."

In 1947 the Australian government decided to acquire two of the *Majestic*-class carriers for the Royal Australian Navy. Work therefore resumed on HMS *Terrible*, which was to be the first "flattop" operated by the RAN. She was handed over to Australia during a ceremony at Devonport, England, on 16 December 1948, at which she was renamed HMAS *Sydney*, and went into service on 5 February 1949 under the command of Capt. Roy Russell Dowling, DSO RAN.[30]

Photo Preface-6

HMAS *Sydney* at anchor in an unidentified harbor during the Korean War. The *Sydney* was mainly involved in patrolling off the western coast of Korea, while its Hawker Sea Fury aircraft of 805 and 808 Squadrons, and Fairey Firefly aircraft of 817 Squadron, carried out strikes against North Korean units and supply lines.
Australian War Memorial photograph P05890.033

Sydney and the planes of her embarked air groups engaged in extensive combat in the Korea War. In 1962, *Sydney* was converted to a fast troop transport. Two years later, owing to tensions associated with Indonesia's opposition to the creation of the Malaysian State, she engaged in her first operational tasking since the Korean War.[31]

After embarking Army personnel, vehicles, and operational cargo in Sydney at the Fitting Out Wharf at Garden Island, *Sydney* sailed shortly after midnight on 25 May 1964 with 1,245 personnel on board. Her tasking was to transport the soldiers and equipment to Malaysia as part of the Australian Army's commitment to the confrontation. *Sydney* and her escorts arrived at Jesselton, Borneo, on 4 June, and discharged all personnel, vehicles, stores and equipment for that location by noon the following day. Leaving Jesselton, she proceeded to Singapore, then Penang on the northwest coast of peninsular Malaysia, and discharged the remainder of her cargo. She then set a course for Fremantle, arriving on 26 June, via a stop at Sumatra, a large island located to the west of Java and south of the Malay Peninsula.[32]

On 29 April 1965, the Australian Government made the decision to commit an infantry battalion to serve in South Vietnam. *Sydney* subsequently received orders to make preparations to transport the 1st Battalion, Royal Australian Regiment (1RAR) to Vung Tau. This military commitment was increased on 8 March 1966, to a force of approximately 4,500 men. Establishment of the 1st Australian Task Force (1ATF), based in Nui Dat, Phuoc Tuy Province, required the deployment of 5RAR battalion and 6RAR battalion. With Australian ground forces well established in Vietnam, *Sydney* began a regular deployment pattern of ferrying troops to and from Australia, disembarking one battalion at Vung Tau and back loading another for the return passage to Australia.[33]

She regained some air capability when a detachment of four Wessex MK 31A helicopters from 725 Squadron was embarked in April 1967, to provide additional anti-submarine protection during transits. The Wessex Flight was later replaced by a similar flight, with the detachment (Flight) usually drawn from a component of the HMAS *Melbourne* Carrier Air Group.[34]

Australia's combat role in the Vietnam War ceased in March 1972 when HMAS *Sydney* transported home the last combat elements. She was decommissioned the following year on 12 November 1973.[35]

SHORT SERVICE OF HMAS *VENGEANCE*

Thirty-one years earlier, HMS *Vengeance* had been commissioned into the Royal Australian Navy as HMAS *Vengeance*, on loan from the Royal Navy, at Devonport, England, on 13 November 1952. She arrived at Sydney on 11 March 1953, having proceeded via Gibraltar, Malta, Port Said, the Suez Canal, Colombo, Fremantle, and Melbourne. Following a three-month refit, *Vengeance* began operations with the Australian fleet in June 1953, working up in preparation for a deployment to Korea. At the end of July, it was announced that HMAS *Sydney* would deploy to Korea in lieu of *Vengeance*.[36]

Her duties over the next three years included serving as escort ship for Queen Elizabeth II and Prince Phililp (the Duke of Edinburgh), during a trip by the Royal Party aboard the Royal yacht SS *Gothic* (a former passenger-cargo liner) to the Cocos Islands.[37]

Following her return to Australia, *Vengeance* later departed Sydney on 27 October 1954 for Japan to embark aircraft, men and equipment of No. 77 Squadron, Royal Australian Air Force, and return them to Australia. *Vengeance* sailed from Sydney for the final time, on 16 June 1955, to commence the long passage to England and her return to the Royal Navy. Aboard her were almost 1,000 officers and sailors who were to commission HMAS *Melbourne*.[38]

Vengeance arrived at Devonport, on 13 August 1955, at which time administrative control was assumed by the Senior Officer Reserve Fleet, Plymouth. She was decommissioned, on 25 October 1955, and turned over to the Royal Navy. HMAS *Melbourne* was commissioned three days later, on 28 October 1955.[39]

EXTENSIVE SERVICE OF HMAS *MELBOURNE*

The first aircraft to touch down on *Melbourne*'s flight deck, the former HMS *Majestic*, was a Westland Whirlwind helicopter of the Royal Navy, on 6 December 1955. Thereafter, the first fixed-wing aircraft, a Hawker de Havilland Sea Venom and a Fairey Gannet, arrived during trials in the English Channel. *Melbourne* left Glasgow, Scotland, for Australia, on 11 March 1956, with 808 Squadron (Sea Venom all-weather fighters) and 816 and 817 Squadrons (Gannet anti-submarine aircraft) embarked.[40]

Melbourne arrived at Sydney, on 9 May 1956, with thousands of people turned out to watch her enter the harbour. Three days later, she replaced HMAS *Sydney* as the flagship of the RAN when Rear Adm. Henry Mackay Burrell 'broke' (hoisted) his flag in her. In September, *Melbourne* sailed for what was to be the first of many deployments to South East Asia. The Australian Government had by this time committed naval forces to what became known as the Far East Strategic Reserve, which provided for the annual participation of an aircraft carrier in training exercises as part of the RAN's contribution. The deployment was also notable as it was the only occasion on which both RAN aircraft carriers, *Melbourne* and *Sydney*, deployed overseas together.[41]

Over the next several years, *Melbourne* maintained a regular program of fleet exercises, training and maintenance, and annual deployments to the Asia-Pacific region.[42]

Australian budgetary constraints from the late 1950s had placed some doubt over the future of naval aviation, given the large financial outlay required to operate aircraft carriers and their associated aircraft.

A two-carrier navy was no longer feasible, and HMAS *Sydney* was relegated to a training vessel before being placed into reserve in 1958. To save costs, a decision was made to eliminate fixed-wing naval aviation in 1963, when *Melbourne* became due for a major refit, and retain her in an anti-submarine capacity. Twenty-seven Westland Wessex anti-submarine helicopters were ordered, the first having come into service in November 1962. Nevertheless, the service life of the Sea Venoms and the Gannets was extended past 1963.[43]

While deployed on a South East Asia cruise in 1965, *Melbourne* joined HMAS *Sydney*'s escort force for four days during the troop carrier's voyage to Vietnam in early June. The Royal Australian Navy received a boost that year with the decision to re-equip its Fleet Air Arm with Douglas A4G Skyhawk fighter bombers and Grumman S2E Tracker anti-submarine warfare aircraft. The Douglas and McDonnell aircraft companies later merged, and the Skyhawk was known as the McDonnell-Douglas Skyhawk by the time it entered RAN service.[44]

The standard routine of South East Asia cruises and fleet exercises was broken in 1977, when *Melbourne* made a 5-month cruise to Europe for the Royal Silver Jubilee and Naval Review. (These events marked the 25th anniversary of Queen Elizabeth II's accession to the thrones of the United Kingdom and other Commonwealth realms.) On 28 June, with some 175 ships from 18 nations (and around 30,000 sailors embarked) assembled at the Spithead anchorage, Her Majesty's Yacht *Britannia* with the queen aboard anchored at the head of the review columns. After weighing anchor, she proceeded down the lines, conducting the review over the course of two hours.[45]

Melbourne arrived back in Sydney on 4 October 1977. In February 1982, the Australian government announced that arrangements had been made to purchase HMS *Invincible* from the Royal Navy to replace the ageing *Melbourne*. HMAS *Melbourne* was decommissioned on 30 June 1982. Subsequently, Britain decided it was necessary to retain the aircraft carrier following lessons learned during the 10-week Falklands War with Argentina (2 April-14 June 1982), and the RAN lost many of the advantages accorded by the carrier it had hitherto enjoyed in the Pacific region.[46]

AUSTRALIAN FLEET AIR ARM

Following the introduction in Chapter 9 of the ships that carried the aircraft and crews of the Royal Australian Navy's Fleet Air Arm, Chapter 10 takes readers inside the world of carrier pilots. The chapter's title, "Some Australian Fleet Air Arm Personalities," provides a hint of the material that follows. The twenty-two pages—offering gripping action, colorful escapades, and humorous misadventure—begin with a short first-hand account by Capt. Jeffrey Gledhill, DSC RAN, of his combat experience during World War II. We then join (vicariously) Robert Bluett and Peter McNay, two officers on loan from the Royal Navy, dispatched to shoot down a pilotless aircraft (this occurred only by accident back then) loose in the skies over Sydney, posing potential danger to citizens and property below.

Next, Commodore Norman Lee, RAN (Retired), a junior Firefly pilot embarked aboard HMAS *Sydney* during the Korean War, treats us to a very detailed and thorough account by of the tactics employed in carrying out combat missions. Navy duty could also be dangerous aboard ship, as recounted by Thomas Henry, a young Able Seaman aboard *Sydney*, a chockman who found himself in peril when the pilot of a Sea Fury undertook a power run with his aircraft chocked, and lashed to ringbolts in the flight deck. As Henry remained in position, engine power dramatically increased, and the lashings started to part....

Ian Webster, apparently the first Sea Fury pilot to ditch at sea, did so successfully and was in his dinghy fishing, having already eaten all the food aboard, when *Sydney*'s rescue boat came to his aid. Conventional wisdom was that ditching was not possible, because the heavy engine nosing down would cause the aircraft to flip. Despite engine failure and his plane falling like a stone, Webster pulled off this seemingly impossible feat. Chapter 10 closes with an account of the first ejection in the RAN and the first such from a Sea Venom jet aircraft. Brian Dutch and Edward "Sandy" Sandberg also lived to tell others, with much exactness, of how this was possible.

POSTSCRIPT

Commodore Donohue's postscript provides a nice introduction to an individual whose career closely paralleled and, was in fact, intertwined with the RAN aircraft carrier program. During his lengthy military career, begun in 1940 with the New Zealand Waikato Mounted Rifles, Commander Guy Alexander Beange, DSC RAN (Retired) served as both a soldier and naval aviator in the New Zealand military, and later joined the Royal Australian Navy. Working his way up from junior enlisted man to commissioned officer over the course of World War II, he reported to HMS *Glory*, which joined the British Pacific Fleet in August 1945, too late to see combat. *Glory* was off Rabaul when Japanese forces there surrendered to the General Officer Commanding 1st Australian Army, on 6 September 1945.

Beange joined the RAN in 1948 as a Lieutenant (Pilot) (Acting) (on Probation) and over the next thirty-one years until his retirement in

1979, repeatedly validated Australia's decision to offer him an officer's commission, albeit a probationary opportunity. Beange would be one of only three RAN naval aviators to earn the Distinguished Service Cross in the Korean War. His came while embarked aboard HMAS *Sydney*. During the war, Beange also commanded 808 Squadron aboard HMAS *Vengeance*. Following the war, he took command of the corvette HMAS *Junee* in 1956. Built as a minesweeper in World War II, the still relatively-new, 13-year old *Junee* was then employed as a training ship.

Photo Preface-7

Corvette HMAS *Junee* (J362), date and location unknown.
RAN photograph

Returning to flying, Beange commanded 805 Squadron embarked aboard HMAS *Melbourne*. The remainder of his career was occupied with a series of shore assignments, including diplomatic duty as the Australian Service attaché to Manila. Late in his career, Beange served as Command Aviation Officer to Flag Officer commanding East Australia. He retired in 1979, and "crossed the bar" (passed away) in 2004. Little known today outside aviation circles, he gave much to the RAN and will always be closely linked to its aircraft carrier history.

USE OF QUEEN'S ENGLISH IN PARTS OF THE BOOK

American readers may have noticed the use in some forewords and the preface of what Rob Hoole (retired Royal Navy mine clearance diver) terms "English, English." Such involves the use of the letter "u" in certain words, creating, for example, harbour, honour, and colour in lieu of the American versions of harbor, honor, and color. Other differences involve the use of "c" and "s" in words non-citizens of Commonwealth countries would expect to find an "s" or a "z." Defence and minimise are two examples. These and similar words will be found in Chapters 4 and 5, penned by Canadian George Duddy, and Chapters 9 and 10 and the Postscript by Australian Hector Donohue.

EXPLANATION OF "STONE FRIGATES"

As most readers are aware, the acronyms HMS and HMAS mean "His or Her Majesty's Ship" or "His or Her Majesty's Australian Ship," respectively, depending on whether a king or queen is sitting on the throne. Ship names that follow HMS or HMAS are italicized to denote their connection to a vessel. So far so good. However, HMS or HMAS may also be associated with the names of shore establishments that provide, ashore, functions previously carried out by an afloat vessel.

Prior to the first of January 1959, the Naval Discipline Act only applied to those officers and men who were carried on the books of one of His or Her Majesty's ships of war. Thus, all personnel were allocated to a nominal ship when not actually serving in a proper seagoing warship. This peculiar ordinance even affected Naval Air Stations which were given names prefixed with HMS. This custom was a legacy from the days when anchored hulks served most of the Navy's accommodation, administrative, accounting, and training needs afloat; the only shore facilities were small outposts or the Royal Dockyards where ships were built and repaired.

To try to minimize confusion between real ships and non-ships, the names of the so-called "stone frigates" are not italicized in this book, although such is the convention in the Royal Australian Navy.

Photo Preface-8

Painting by Richard DeRosset of the rescue by a USAF air commando helicopter of a downed Marine fighter pilot from a frozen reservoir in North Korea, while under fire by enemy troops.

1

Downed Pilot Saved in Daring Rescue

Joe Barrett and Frank Fabijan picked a Marine Major named Cleeland off the ice on the Haiju Reservoir in a big daylight shootout.

All in all, we, six of us [pilots], put roughly one thousand hours on four H-19s. We did both the ARC [Air Resupply and Communications mission], and the Air Rescue mission, having never refused a single one. We earned a bunch of decorations, took our share of battle damage, yet never, as long as combat missions were flown in that theater, had an accident, a combat loss or a fatality.

—Excerpts from an article by Robert F. Sullivan, titled "The 581st's Helicopters at K-16"[1]

Photo 1-1

Light fleet carrier USS *Bataan*, location and date unknown.
USS *Bataan* (CVL-29) 1952-1953 Third Far Eastern cruise book

On 24 February 1953, USS *Bataan* (CVL-29), with Marine Attack Squadron VMA-312 (the renowned "Checkerboards") embarked, was operating in the Yellow Sea off the west coast of Korea. The ship's commanding officer, Capt. Harry R. Horney, was designated officer in charge, West Coast of Korea, and commander, Task Unit 95.1.1. The mission of the task unit, comprised of the light fleet carrier and escorting destroyers, was to "assist in enforcing the United Nations blockade in the defense of the friendly islands off the west coast of Korea."[2]

Photo 1-2

F4U Corsairs of VMA-312 with "checkerboard" pattern on engine cowlings, readied for flight operations above the waters and over the land along the west coast of Korea. USS *Bataan* (CVL-29) 1952-1953 Third Far Eastern cruise book

Recurring activities associated with this benign-sounding mission description, included providing:
- Armed reconnaissance of the coastal area between the Han River (near Seoul) and Taedong Estuary, and on alternate days, the coast north of the Taedong Estuary up to Hanchon
- Armed reconnaissance strikes and interdiction throughout assigned area (attacks on enemy supply lines, facilities, and troops as opportunity presented itself)

- Air strikes as requested by units of TG 95.1 (UN Blockading and Escort Force), guerilla organizations, and JOC (Joint Operations Center) Korea
- Shore bombardment spotting services as requested by naval units of the UN Blockading and Escort Force[3]

Map 1-1

Namp'o (formerly Chinnamp'o) is situated on the estuary of the Taedong River. Hanchon is located 47 miles southwest of Pyongyang, the capital of North Korea.
http://legacy.lib.utexas.edu/maps/middle_east_and_asia/korean_peninsula.gif

Flying over enemy territory brought with it the possibility of being shot down, particularly when low cloud cover forced pilots, committed to striking the enemy, to fly beneath it to search for targets. Planes flying just above the ground, sometimes slowed by dodging hills and snow squalls in winter, were fair game for Communist small arms and automatic weapons fire—no matter a pilot's experience.[4]

On the morning of 24 February 1953, Maj. David Cleeland, USMC, on his 101st mission, was hit at 1015 by enemy ground fire, ten miles north of Haeju. Leading his flight of four F4U Corsairs down, he had destroyed two bridges, and his fellow pilots had managed to smash three more. Cleeland was too far inland to make the open sea and, in attempting such, if he went down while proceeding over the mountains, his rescue would be difficult. He chose instead to crash land on nearby frozen Annyong Reservoir (38°3'N, 125°61'E) and "belly in."[5]

4   Chapter 1

Photo 1-3

F4U Corsair launching from the light fleet carrier *Bataan* in 1953.
USS *Bataan* (CVL-29) 1952-1953 Third Far Eastern cruise book

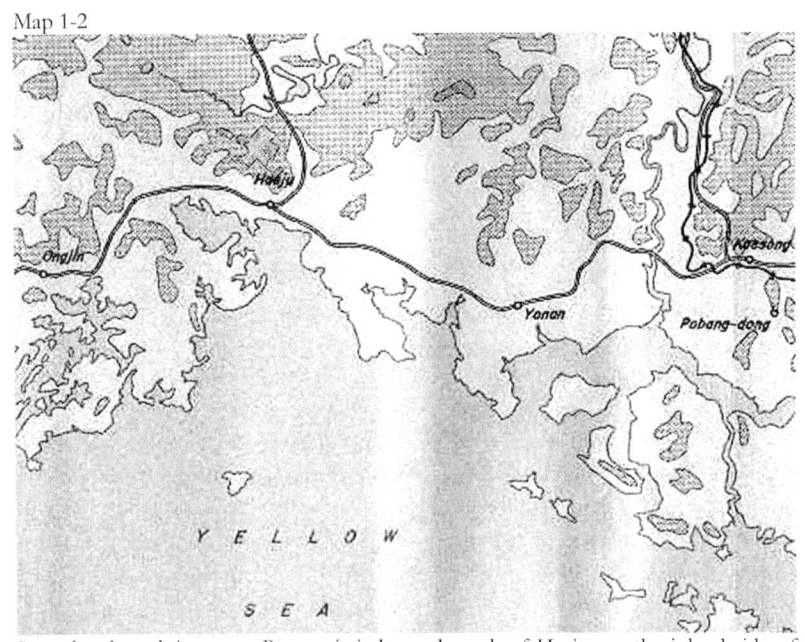

Map 1-2

Irregular-shaped Annyong Reservoir is located north of Haeju, on the inland side of mountainous terrain, in a low-lying area east of the road running NNW to SSE, before it makes a jag to the southwest near Haeju and intersects a coastal road.
https://history.army.mil/books/korea/maps/271151.jpg

The ice held up as he came down, but enemy troops began shooting at him from the perimeter of the reservoir. After sliding in, Cleeland used the plane's engine as a bunker. the other three F4Us held off other Communist forces in the area with strafing runs, and bombed and napalmed the hill from where the enemy was firing at their fellow pilot, who had, while landing, sustained a gunshot wound in his left leg.[6]

Bataan launched six additional Corsairs at 1035, as relief for those flying rescue combat air patrol (RESCAP) over Cleeland and his aircraft. This action proved timely, because the aircraft returning to *Bataan* landed with as little as fifteen gallons of fuel remaining. Fortunately, the relief RESCAP arrived on scene (at 1055) just as the Corsairs they were replacing ran out of ammunition. On the other hand, low cloud cover began to frustrate Cleeland's squadron mates attempting to strafe the enemy who were now massing on the reservoir's shore.[7]

After having been under fire for nearly an hour, wounded, and seemingly with few remaining options, salvation finally came to Cleeland. He was rescued by the courageous actions of a USAF Sikorsky H-19A Chickasaw helicopter pilot and crew. The Checkerboard pilots flying cover then took the crashed F4U Corsair under fire with rockets and destroyed it to prevent its capture, before it dropped through the ice.[8]

Photo 1-4

Drawing by Herbert C. Hahn of a F4U Corsair firing rockets, earlier in the war, in close air support of Allied ground forces, circa 1951.
Naval History and Heritage Command photograph #88-191-BG

HELICOPTER FLIGHT, 581ST ARCS (AIR RESUPPLY AND COMMUNICATIONS SQUADRON)

581st ARCS
17 April 1952 –
8 September 1953[9]

Helicopter Flight
Commanding Officer
Capt. Frank Westerman, USAF

The above brief account, based on *Bataan*'s Action Report for the period 15-26 February 1953, provides few details about the special operations helicopter and crew that picked up Cleeland. (It is unlikely such would have been known by *Bataan*'s commanding officer or, if so, he would have included it in his report.)

The Air Resupply and Communications Service (ARCS), of which the helicopter was a part, had been established by the US Air Force on 23 February 1951. The ARCS was charged with developing an unconventional warfare capability that included inserting, supplying, and extracting indigenous partisans (guerillas) and U.S. Special Forces personnel behind enemy lines. Another mission they were tasked with was the design, production, and airdropping of psychological warfare materials.[10]

The 581st AR&CS Wing (a component of the ARCS) was activated at Mountain Home AFB in July 1951, and posted to Clark Air Force Base in the Philippines. Combat operations by the Wing in Korea included basing a special H-19 Helicopter Flight at Seoul City Airbase (K-16). It was blended in with elements of the 2157th Air Rescue Squadron. By October 1952, six pilots, one NCO (senior enlisted), and twelve airmen comprised Helicopter Flight 581st ARCS Squadron. The unit was commanded by Capt. Frank Westerman. As they were a long way from the support of their parent wing in the Philippines, they learned early to fend for themselves in the operation and maintenance of the four brand-new helicopters for which they had responsibility.[11]

The primary task of the Helicopter Flight was to insert United Nations intelligence agents behind enemy lines by means of infiltration flights at night. These were flown at the lowest possible altitudes to avoid enemy radar. These flights invariably called for them to fly from Allied-controlled islands off Korea's west coast, skimming the waters of the Yellow Sea while flying to their blacked-out landing points on a—hopefully—deserted coast.[12]

Many of the night insertion missions began with one of the H-19 helicopters and its crew departing in darkness from Cho-do, a small island located only ten miles from the Korean coast, but sixty miles behind enemy lines. The island (described by one pilot as "acres and acres of nothing but acres and acres) was vulnerable to enemy attack but its proximity to the peninsula's rugged coastline and mudflats, proved an ideal jumping off point to carry out unconventional warfare missions.[13]

In one six-month period of their duty in Korea, the six pilots of the Flight logged over 1,100 hours of combat helicopter flying while carrying out in excess of 300 intelligence and rescue missions.[14]

Photo 1-5

Sikorsky H-19A Chickasaw rescue helicopter.
Courtesy of Woody Woodward

An expanded account of the rescue and recognition of the helicopter crew with awards for heroism follows:

As Major Cleeland lay wounded in freezing conditions, next to the fuselage of his crashed F4U Corsair in the middle of a frozen reservoir, watching Korean soldiers organizing on shore to come for him, an H-

19 Air Commando helicopter appeared. The Corsairs on scene were out of ammunition and, as the enemy heard or sighted the approaching H-19, some soldiers charged out of their positions in a last-ditch effort to capture or kill him. (Accounts vary as to whether the helicopter was scrambled from Seoul, or from Kimpo AFB (K-14) located just northwest of Seoul.)[15]

Fortunately, as the enemy rushed Cleeland, a combination of just-arrived Corsairs, and USAF F-80 jet fighters orbiting overhead, raked the exposed soldiers with 20mm cannon fire. In response, the entire rim of the reservoir seemed to explode with flashes of gunfire as the enemy took the low flying aircraft under fire. In the midst of this air-ground exchange, the H-19 swooped in while under fire and picked up the pilot. With several bullet holes—including one to the aircraft's tail rotor spar, one to a fuel cell, and one through the hand of Airman Second Class Thomas Thornton, the helicopter then sped away. On 21 May 1953, its Air Force pilots and crew—Capt. Joseph Barrett, 1st Lt. Frank Fabijan, and A2C Thomas Thornton—received the Silver Star Medal for their gallantry.[16]

2

Korean War, June 1950 - January 1952

> *We'll never have any more amphibious operations. That does away with the Marine Corps. And the Air Force can do anything the Navy can do nowadays, so that does away with the Navy.*
>
> —President Truman's Secretary of Defense, Louis A. Johnson to Admiral Richard L. Connally, USN, in 1949

Photo 2-1

HMS *Triumph* at Kure, Japan, with crew members topside in ranks. The light fleet carrier was in Far East waters when North Korea invaded South Korea, and went on to play a key role in the early stages of the war.
Australian War Memorial photograph HOBJ0627

On 25 June 1950, well before daylight on a Sunday morning, 135,000 North Korean troops launched an invasion of South Korea in an all-out surprise attack. Following 45 minutes of artillery bombardment, six North Korean infantry divisions and three Border Constabulary

Brigades, supported by Soviet-made T-34 tanks, heavy artillery, and the North Korean Air Force, swarmed across the 38th Parallel. Aimed at reuniting the country under Communist rule from the North, the hostile act touched off the Korean War.[1]

Map 2-1

Korean Peninsula

The Soviet-supported North Korean Army advanced rapidly overland against poorly-trained and ill-equipped Republic of Korea forces, while along South Korea's east coast, a Border Constabulary Brigade carried out amphibious landing at Kangnung and Samchok. On 26 June, following a demand by the UN Security Council that North Korea terminate its attack and return to its borders, two more North Korean divisions moved south across the 38th parallel. The following day, the UN Security Council approved a resolution, introduced by the U.S., asking member nations to provide such assistance as necessary to South Korea. The measure passed because the Soviet Union representative was absent, and thus unable to veto it.[2]

The first U.S. troops to fight in defense of South Korea engaged North Korean military forces at Osan, 30 miles south of Seoul with tragic results. Task Force Smith, which had been quickly dispatched from occupational duties in Japan to fight a delaying action against overwhelming odds, was crushed on 5 July by the North Korean 4th Division. The U.S. unit, comprised of only 540 men of the 24th Infantry Division, had been misinformed about its objective, undertrained for the mission, and poorly equipped with castoff gear from WWII.[3]

Photo 2-2

A member of the 24th Infantry Division mans a bazooka at the Battle of Osan. PFC Kenneth Shadrick (at right) was killed by enemy fire a few moments after this photo was taken, becoming the first U.S. soldier to die in the Korean War. US Army Center for Military History

In response to this devastating defeat, the United Nations Command was created on 7 July under the command of Gen. Douglas MacArthur, and the following week Lt. Gen. Walton Walker, the commander of the U.S. Eighth Army, was assigned responsibility for ground operations in Korea.[4]

Many books and articles about the Korean War exist. This chapter, and the following one, are devoted to contributions made by six light fleet aircraft carriers—four RN, one RAN, and one USN—to Allied ground, air, and sea operations on, over, and off the Korean Peninsula.

HMS *Triumph*
Battle Honour
Korea 1950

HMS *Theseus*
Battle Honour
Korea 1950-51

HMAS *Sydney*
Battle Honours
Korea 1951–52
Malaysia 1964
Vietnam 1965–72

HMS *Glory*
Battle Honour
Korea 1951-53

HMS *Ocean*
Battle Honour
Korea 1952-53

USS *Bataan*
7 Battle Stars

ROYAL NAVY AUGMENTS COMNAVFE FORCES

American forces in the Orient in 1950 were a part of the Far East Command under General MacArthur, who was also, as Supreme Commander for the Allied Powers, responsible for the occupation of Japan. Only a little over a third of the US Navy's active strength was in the Pacific, only a fifth of that was in the Far East, and the naval component under Vice Adm. C. Turner Joy, USN, was very small. Turner Joy, commander, Naval Forces Far East (ComNavFE), did control, in Task Force 96, a small amount of fighting strength, and in Task Force 90 the nucleus of an amphibious force.[5]

Fortunately, Task Forces 90 and 96 were not the only naval units in Asiatic waters. Based in the Philippines, under the command of Vice Adm. Arthur D. Struble, was the Seventh Fleet, the embodiment of American naval power in the Western Pacific. Considering the unpredictable responsibilities of Admiral Joy's situation, the transfer of Seventh Fleet forces to his operational control was all that could be done at the time.[6]

Photo 2-3

Vice Adm. Arthur D. Struble, USN, commander, Seventh Fleet, in his office aboard the battleship USS *Missouri* (BB-63).
National Archives photograph #80-G-430079

However, an important addition soon came in the form of British Commonwealth units commanded by Rear Adm. Sir William G. Andrewes, KBE, CB, DSO RN, who was Flag Officer Second in Command, Far Eastern Station. On 29 June, the British Admiralty placed Royal Navy units in Japanese waters at the disposal of ComNavFE. Answering the call, similar action was taken the following day by the Australian government; in Canada, three destroyers were ordered to prepare to sail; and from New Zealand came the promise of the early dispatch of two frigates.[7]

Commonwealth naval strength present in the Far East was still significant. Andrewes' Task Group 96.8, on 30 June 1950, included HMS *Triumph*, a 13,000-ton light carrier; two 6-inch gun cruisers, heavily armored *Belfast*, the largest cruiser in the Royal Navy, and *Jamaica*; three destroyers, and four frigates. Two of the ships, the destroyer *Bataan* and frigate *Shoalhaven*, were units of the Royal Australian Navy.

British Task Group 96.8

HMS *Triumph* (R16)	HMAS *Bataan* (D191)
HMS *Belfast* (C35) flagship	HMS *Black Swan* (F116)
HMS *Jamaica* (C44)	HMS *Alacrity* (F57)
HMS *Cossack* (D57)	HMS *Hart* (F58)
HMS *Consort* (D76)	HMAS *Shoalhaven* (F535)[8]

Photo 2-4

Formal portrait of Vice Adm. William G. Andrewes, RN, taken sometime between his 1 December 1950 promotion to Vice Admiral and mid-1952. Naval History and Heritage Command photograph #NH 97139

After they had been placed under U.S. command, Admiral Andrewes' ships were allocated between commander, Naval Forces Far East's Support Group (Task Group 96.5) and the Seventh Fleet Striking

Force, which had reached Okinawa on 30 June. Joined the next day by *Triumph*, *Belfast*, *Cossack*, and *Consort*, Task Force 77 was then poised between Korea and Formosa.[9]

INITIAL AIRSTRIKES ON ENEMY TARGETS

Photo 2-5

As part of the first Allied carrier air strikes, 3-4 July 1950, planes from USS *Valley Forge* (CV-45) and HMS *Triumph*, part of the joint U.S.-British Task Force 77, attacked a North Korean railroad train just south of Pyongyang on 4 July 1950. National Archives photograph #80-G-417148

It was decided that aircraft from the carrier USS *Valley Forge* (CV-45) and *Triumph* would initially strike objectives in the Pyongyang area. First priority would be given to the airfield complex of the North Korean capital, followed by the railroad yards and the bridges over the Taedong River. The prospect of operating this mixed carrier force presented some problems, owing to the differences between British and American aircraft types and the fact that *Triumph*'s maximum speed of 23 knots was 10 knots slower than that of *Valley Forge*. But the British were eager to go, many of their officers had participated in joint operations in World War II, and the two forces had recently held maneuvers together. Thus, the advantages outweighed the difficulties.[10]

At 0500 on 3 July, *Valley Forge* launched combat and anti-submarine patrols from a designated point in the Yellow Sea. Forty-five minutes later, *Triumph* flew off 12 Fireflies and 9 Seafires for an attack on the airfield at Haeju, and at 0600 *Valley Forge* began launching her strike group. After sixteen Corsairs and twelve Skyraiders carrying rockets and bombs, respectively, were airborne and headed toward the Pyongyang airfield, *Valley Forge* catapulted eight F9F-2 Panthers, whose higher speed would bring them in first over the target area. The fighters encountered little opposition over the North Korean capital. Two Soviet YAK fighter-bombers of the North Korean Air Force were destroyed in the air, another was damaged, and nine aircraft were reportedly destroyed on the ground. Enemy anti-aircraft opposition was also negligible at Haeju, and no plane suffered serious damage.[11]

That afternoon, aircraft from *Triumph* flew a second strike, and *Valley Forge* launched a second attack against the marshalling yards at Pyongyang and the bridges across the Taedong River. Considerable damage was reported done to locomotives and rolling stock, but the bridges survived this effort.[12]

Pyongyang was struck again on 4 July. One of the Taedong River bridges was damaged, some locomotives were destroyed, and some small ships in the river were attacked. Increased anti-aircraft opposition resulted in damage to four Skyraiders, and one, unable to lower its flaps, came in too fast when returning aboard *Valley Forge* and bounced over the barrier, destroying three planes and damaging six more. After flight operations were completed, the Striking Force retired southward.[13]

The following day, the three Canadian destroyers—HMCS *Cayuga*, *Athabaskan*, and *Sioux*—earlier alerted, sailed from the west coast of Canada on 5 July, bound for Korea. They arrived in the theater of operations on 25 July, and took up their assigned duties. These would include blockading the enemy coast, preventing amphibious landings by the enemy, protecting aircraft carriers from the threat of submarine and aerial attack, and bombarding enemy-held coastal areas.[14]

During the war, five other Canadian destroyers—HMCS *Crusader*, *Huron*, *Iroquois*, *Nootka*, and *Haida*—would also serve with Canadian Destroyer Division, Far East, as part of the United Nations fleet in the waters off Korea.[15]

Photo 2-6

Canadian destroyer HMCS *Crusader* under way off Korea, on 3 March 1954. National Archives photograph #80-G-642747

SUPPORT FOR AMPHIBIOUS LANDING AT POHANG, AND STRIKES ON NORTH KOREAN LAND TARGETS

The morning of 18 July found *Valley Forge*, *Triumph*, and their screening ships in the southern Sea of Japan, some 60 miles northeast of Pohang. The town of Pohang, where the US Army 1st Cavalry Division would come ashore later that day, lay about 65 miles north of Pusan on the western shore of Yongil Man, a bay about six miles wide. At dawn, *Triumph* launched local anti-submarine and combat air patrols for force protection, while *Valley Forge* sent off a target combat air patrol and a group of attack planes to cover the landing.[16]

The amphibious landing proved unopposed and, except for a requirement for a combat air patrol over Pohang, the *Valley Forge* air group was now available for attacks on North Korean targets. Strikes were flown on the 18th and 19th against railroad facilities, industrial plants, and airfields from Pyongyang and Wonsan northward through Hungnam and Hamhung. Of about fifty aircraft sighted on the ground, more than half were destroyed and the remainder damaged, while flights north along the railroad on 19 July struck four locomotives.[17]

18   Chapter 2

Map 2-2

Northeast coast of Korea
Navy Interdiction Korea Vol. II, Rear Adm. Combs

The destruction of grounded aircraft was the most important result of the two-day operation. Together with some similarly successful sorties by US Air Force jets on the 19th, it pretty well liquidated the North Korean Air Force. But the most spectacular results were achieved at Wonsan. An attack on an oil refinery at the seaport city, on the afternoon of 18 July, by a strike force of Skyraiders and Corsairs from the *Valley Forge*, destroyed 12,000 tons of petroleum products, and the installation itself was declared a total loss. (This information was gleaned that autumn during interrogation of refinery supervisory personnel by US Marine Corps officers.) Smoke rising from the resultant large fires was visible to the force at sea. In the 18-19 July 1950 strikes against North Korea, two aircraft were lost but both pilots were recovered.[18]

REASSIGNMENT OF *TRIUMPH* TO WEST COAST BLOCKADING FORCE

Near the end of July, HMS *Triumph* and destroyer HMS *Comus* (R43) were detached from Task Force 77 for further assignment to the West Coast Blockading Force. The availability of *Triumph* was of particular importance as the hydrography of the west coast restricted the movement of heavier ships and thus made aircraft attacks particularly valuable. Thor Thorgrimsson and E. C. Russell, described in their book, *Canadian Naval Operations in Korean Waters 1950-1955*, the prevailing conditions faced by Allied ships:

> The western coast-line, for instance, is ragged and heavily indented, and the water is extremely shallow and dotted with islands, low-water mud flats, rocks and shoals. High, strong tides, of over thirty feet in some places, scour the muddy bottom, and channels are formed, obliterated and reformed with remarkable frequency. There are few harbours worth the name, and those that exist must be continually dredged to prevent silting.[19]

Cruisers and destroyers could conduct shore bombardment, and monitor shipping passing around the headlands, but the inshore patrol had previously been largely left to the ROKN (Republic of Korea Navy). After *Triumph*'s arrival, their efforts were greatly enhanced by her air group. Because of the prevailing shoal water, utmost vigilance was required by surface ships and supporting carrier planes to prevent the infiltration of enemy agents by small craft, the movement of supplies and men, and even the transport of invading troops to and from the mainland and the many off-shore islands. The shallows also made it very difficult for even small ships to approach close enough to the shore to provide effective gunfire support for UN and guerilla forces and to attack the enemy's lines of communication.[20]

USS *Valley Forge* and her screen anchored in Buckner Bay, Okinawa, on 31 July, and the next day, Task Force 77 was strengthened by the arrival of the carrier USS *Philippine Sea* (CV-47).[21]

INCHON INVASION (OPERATION CHROMITE)

The best I can say about Inchon is it is not impossible.

—Rear Adm. James H. Doyle, commander, Assault Force (TF 90),
23 August 1950

Photo 2-7

Drawing by Herbert C. Hahn of American invasion fleet attacking Inchon, circa 1951. Naval History and Heritage Command accession #88-191-BB

In the early months of the war, as the North Korean Army drove UN ground forces southward, General MacArthur noted its over-extended supply lines, most of which passed through Seoul. If the city of Inchon, only fifteen miles south of the capital, could be seized by sea assault, the enemy's supply lines would be quickly severed, which would shorten the war, save countless casualties, and possibly eliminate the necessity for a winter campaign. The basis for the general's strategy was his belief in the importance of striking decisively and unexpectedly well behind enemy lines. In addition to preferring Inchon for its location, MacArthur believed that his forces would prevail in that improbable site because the North Koreans would consider a landing there impossible, even insane, and be taken by surprise.[22]

The basis for his belief was the myriad hazards to navigation imposed in the area by geography. The tides of Inchon (33 feet at their maximum) are among the highest in the world and reach their peak in approximately six hours, producing a 5-knot current. Vast mudbanks near Inchon extend at low water some 6,000 yards seaward. The approach channel to the port city, Flying Fish Channel, is narrow, tortuous, and difficult even for a daylight passage.[23]

In early September, and again in the days preceding the planned landing at Inchon on 15 September, the three carrier units of Joint Task Force 7—Rear Adm. Edward C. Ewen's, USN, fast carriers; Rear Adm. Richard W. Ruble's, USN, escort carriers, and the British light fleet carrier *Triumph*—were to work over the west coast with their efforts gradually converging toward Inchon. In support of the actual landing, cruisers and destroyers were to provide bombardment and fire support; and carrier aviation, air cover, air strikes, and close air support.[24]

HMS *Triumph*'s efforts in this regard had begun in mid-August. Screened by the destroyers HMS *Cornus* and HMCS *Athabaskan*, while operating off the west coast of Korea between the Mackau and Clifford Islands, her planes had struck the enemy in and around Inchon, Kunsan, and Mokpo. The operations against Inchon and Kunsan were of particular importance. Although plans in progress for a large-scale amphibious landing at Inchon—designed to cut off and destroy the enemy attacking a defensive perimeter around the city of Pusan—had not yet gained final approval, such was expected. Inchon was to be the site of the landing, and Kunsan the scene of deceptive operations intended to draw attention away from Inchon.[25]

An armada of Allied ships was assembled for the invasion of Inchon under the command of Vice Adm. Arthur Struble, USN. Designated Joint Task Force 7, the force of some 230 ships was comprised of the following task forces:

Task Force 90 (Attack Force): Rear Adm. James H. Doyle, USN

1-2 AGC, 1 AH, 1 AM, 6 AMS, 3 APD, 1 ARL, 1 ARS, 1 ATF, 2 CVE, 2 CA, 3 CL (1 USN, 2 RN), 1 DE, 12 DD, 5 LSD, 3 LSMR, 4 ROKN PC, 1 PCEC, 8 PF (3 USN, 2 RN, 2 RNZN, 1 French), 7 ROKN YMS, 47 LST (30 Scajap), plus transports, cargo ships, etc., for a total of approximately 180 ships

Note: Scajap (Shipping Control Authority for the Japanese Merchant Marine) ships were Japanese-manned and supported but operated under Allied occupation force control.

Task Force 91 (Blockade and Covering Force): Rear Adm. Sir William G. Andrewes, RN

1 CVL, 1 CL, 8 DD

Task Force 92 (Tenth Corps): Maj. Gen. Edward M. Almond, USA

1st Marine Division, Reinforced; 7th Infantry Division, Reinforced; Corps Troops

Task Force 99 (Patrol and Reconnaissance Force):
Rear Adm. George R. Henderson, USN

2 AV, 1 AVP, 3 USN and 2 RAF Patrol Squadrons

Task Force 77 (Fast Carrier Force): Rear Adm. Edward C. Ewen, USN

2-3 CV, 1 CL, 14 DD

Task Force 79 (Logistic Support Force)

2 AD, 1 AE, 2 AF, 1 AK, 3 AKA, 3 AKL, 4 AO, 1 AOG, 1 ARG, 1 ARH, 1 ARS, 1 ATF[26]

Admiral Andrewes' Task Force 91, the Blockade and Covering Force, consisted of the light fleet carrier HMS *Triumph*, the cruiser HMS *Ceylon*, and the eight destroyers identified below:
- British HMS *Cossack* and HMS *Consort*
- Australian HMAS *Bataan* and HMAS *Warramunga*
- Canadian HMCS *Cayuga*, HMCS *Athabaskan*, and HMCS *Sioux*
- Dutch HNLMS *Evertsen*[27]

This force was charged with several important duties: conducting special reconnaissance and covering missions prior to D-Day; providing cover for the ships of the attacking force en route to Inchon; maintaining a naval blockade of the Korean west coast south of 39°35' North; and performing interdiction missions as might be assigned.[28]

INCHON LANDING A GREAT SUCCESS

Putting assault troops ashore at Inchon posed great challenges owing to the geography. Because the approach channel was so narrow, if a ship foundered in the final approach to Inchon the vessels astern of it would be blocked and those ahead trapped, particularly at low tide. The tides also controlled the invasion date. The tank landing ships would require at least 29 feet of water beneath their keels, conditions that existed only a few days each month. Possible dates for such a landing in autumn 1950 were limited to 15 September, 11 October, or 3 November, give or take a day or so.[29]

Additionally, Wolmi Island provided defenders with a strong garrison flanking the harbor. In spite of intelligence warning of the attack, the overextended North Korean Army was unable to mount a strong defense. The US Marine Corps, for the first time in its history, had to scale seawalls with ladders before beginning an assault into the heart of a major city, against the prospect of heavy opposition from an enemy hidden in warehouses, buildings, and other cover. Inchon fell with Allied losses of only 20 dead and 179 wounded.[30]

Photo 2-8

Aboard the heavy cruiser USS *Rochester* (CA-124), Rear Adm. James H. Doyle, USN (commander, Task Force 90) congratulates four sailors who have just received the Silver Star Medal for service as coxwains of LCVP landing craft during the Inchon Invasion. The men are (left to right): Seaman Chancey H. Vogt, Seaman William H. Ragan, Engineman-Fireman Richard P. Vinson, and Seaman Apprentice Paul J. Gregory. National Archives photograph #80-G-423716

HMS *TRIUMPH* RELIEVED BY SISTER SHIP *THESEUS*

Triumph had arrived off Korea on 2 July 1950 with her embarked air group of twelve Seafire 47 and twelve Firefly 1 aircraft. Her combat service lasted until October when relieved by sister ship HMS *Theseus*. By that point, following operations with the US Navy on the west and east coasts of Korea and support for the Inchon landing, her Air Group had been reduced to three Seafires and six Fireflies.[31]

Theseus, with 17th Carrier Air Group embarked, had sailed from Spithead (a roadstead off Gilkicker Point in Hampshire, England) on 18 August to relieve *Triumph* in Far East waters. Following brief stops at Malta, Aden, and Singapore, she had reached Hong Kong on 24 September for a week's exercises with the British Army and RAF defence forces there. *Triumph* arrived at Hong Kong on 29 September, and after a quick take-over from her, *Theseus* proceeded to the UN Naval Base at Sasebo, Japan.[32]

24   Chapter 2

Photo 2-9

Light fleet carrier HMS *Theseus* at sea, circa 1952.
Australian War Memorial photograph 302489

Photo 2-10

Admirals rowing Lord Louis Mountbatten across Valetta Grand Harbor, Malta, to HMS *Surprise* on 15 December 1954, after he relinquished command of Allied Forces, Mediterranean, to become First Sea Lord of Britain. Mountbatten is seated in the stern of the boat; the admirals are, L to R: Louis Mornu of France, Marco Calamei of Italy, George Zepos of Greece, Sheres Karapiner of Turkey, Peter Cazalet of England, and James Fife of the United States.
Naval History and Heritage Command photograph #NH 62445

Earlier, on 12 September 1950, the various task groups operating under Vice Adm. C. Turner Joy, USN, commander, Naval Forces Far East, had been consolidated. Rear Adm. Allan E. Smith, USN, was assigned command of the United Nations Blockading and Escort Force; the West Coast Support Group, now Task Group 95.1, continued under the control of Rear Adm. William Gerrard Andrewes, RN; and East Coast operations under Rear Adm. Charles Clifford Hartman, USN. Smith's Task Force 95 (UN Blockading and Escort) was comprised of four subordinate task groups:

- Task Group 95.1: West Coast Group (British Commonwealth and other allied warships under Rear Admiral Andrewes)
- Task Group 95.2: East Coast Group
- Task Group 95.6: Minesweeping Group
- Task Group 95.7: Republic of Korea Navy[33]

Rear Adm. William Gerrard Andrewes' headquarters were in HMS *Ladybird*, a British converted Yangtze River steamer secured to the jetty at Sasebo. *Theseus*, and a screen of usually four destroyers, formed Task Element 95.11. Later, the light fleet carrier USS *Bataan* (CVL-29) and some USN destroyers were added to the group.[34]

Daily at first light, *Theseus* conducted armed-reconnaissance of the west coast to detect any enemy shipping movement or mining activity. As required, she also flew Combat Air Patrols and anti-submarine patrols over elements of the group, and provided shore bombardment spotting aircraft, and aircraft in indirect or close-air support of land forces along the battle-front. During her first operational period, 9-22 October, UN forces advanced to a line north of Pyongyang-Wonsan. Concurrently, *Theseus* attacked targets in the Wanchall Province and as far north as Pakchon and Chonju. Four days replenishment in Sasebo followed before her second operational period from 29 October-5 November.[35]

The course of the war had been reversed on 15 September by the Inchon landing, and following the recapture of Seoul on the 29th, the North Korean Army appeared broken and beaten. By September's end, the shattered North Korean Army was in full retreat and escape routes, except for mountainous areas, were in United Nations' hands. In their hurry to escape, enemy troops abandoned tanks, mortars, artillery, and small arms. UN ground troops advanced rapidly on all fronts. The Republic of Korea First Corps, on the east coast near the 38th Parallel, awaited orders to drive toward the ports of Wonsan and Hungnam while the 3rd, 6th, 8th, and Capital Divisions were similarly poised to worsen the enemy's dire straits as the U.S. Eighth Army reoccupied territory held by enemy troops since the war's beginning.[36]

MacArthur believed that his ultimate military objective was the destruction of the North Korean military forces, and he intended to extend ground operations beyond the 38th parallel as necessary to achieve this goal. His supporting operations plan made two important assumptions: first, that the bulk of the North Korean Army had already been destroyed, and second, that neither the USSR nor Red China would enter the conflict. The plan provided that Walker's Eighth Army attack across the 38th Parallel, directing its main effort along the Kaesong-Sariwon-Pyongyang axis, while Almond's Tenth Corps landed on the east coast at Wonsan. Almond would then move northward between the Sea of Japan and the Taebek Mountain Range, turning westward through passes in the mountains to link up with Walker's Army and thereby trap the remnants of the North Koreans.[37]

The plan envisioned that these two commands, after uniting, would advance north to the Chongju-Kunuri-Wongwon-Hamhung-Hungnam line, which stretched a mere fifty to one hundred miles south of the Yalu River marking the border between Korea and Red China. In recognition of probable Chinese concern for the nearness of Allied forces, only ROK troops would proceed north of the line.[38]

CHINA ENTERS THE WAR

The entry of Communist China forces (CCF) into the war vastly altered the strategic picture, forcing UN troops to retreat southward in early November. On 1 November 1950, a regiment of the US Army 1st Cavalry Division was hit by a strong CCF attack in the first encounter of the war between U.S. and Chinese forces. Two days later, in the face of continued heavy onslaughts, Walker was forced to order the bulk of the Eighth Army to withdraw to the Chongchon River, which flows south-southwest into the Korean Bay north of Chinnampo, to regroup and resupply.[39]

Simultaneously with the entry of Chinese ground forces into the war, Russian pilots, dressed in Chinese uniforms, entered the skies over the Yalu. The appearance of the Soviet MiG-15 came as a huge surprise to the UN coalition forces. The MiG-15 was 100 miles-an-hour faster that the fastest jet in the UN inventory and could fly higher. It was a "hot fighter" that outclassed anything the UN coalition had. But, according to American pilots who encountered the MiG, the Russian pilots had a lot to learn. American Navy jets shot down three of them in November 1950.[40]

On 9 November 1950, the first jet vs. jet air-to-air victory, which can be confirmed from both sides, occurred when Lt. Comdr. William T. Amen, USN, flying a F9F-2B Panther from the aircraft carrier USS *Philippine Sea* (CV-47), shot down a Soviet MiG-15. Amen, the CO of VF-111, "Sun Downers," was flying top cover with his squadron while AD Skyraiders were attacking bridges across the Yalu River. Captain Mikhail Fedorovich Grachev, 139th Guards Fighter Aviation Regiment, led a squadron of MiG-15 fighters from their base at Antung, China, to attack the Skyraiders. Amen led VF-111 to intercept the MiGs as they dove on the Skyraiders. Seeing the approaching Navy fighters, the Soviet fighters broke up into single aircraft, or pairs, but did not counterattack with any organization. Visibility was poor, and airplanes would disappear then reappear in the clouds.[41]

Photo 2-11

A Grumman F9F-2 Panther with wings folded up being moved by a flight deck tractor aboard USS *Philippine Sea* (CV-47), during operations off Korea, circa 19 October 1950. Other planes parked nearby are Vought F4U-4B Corsairs.
National Archives photograph #80-G-420925

Captain Grachev and two wingmen turned toward Amen. "I was coming head on at one of them and he didn't even try to get in a shot," Amen recalled. As the two jets closed on each other, with Amen firing, Grachev made a sharp left turn, rolled over, and went into a steep dive.

Bill Amen stayed on his tail and, followed him down, continuing to fire his four 20 mm cannon. "When I got on his tail, he tried to evade but he wasn't very sharp." Grachev did not pull out of the dive, and his smoking jet crashed into a wooded slope and burned. Grachev did not return from his mission and is presumed to have been killed in the crash, becoming the first Soviet pilot to die in the Korean War. It appears this was the world's first jet vs jet encounter and the first shot down.[42]

On 18 November, the carrier USS *Leyte* (CV-32) launched a strike at the bridge at Sinŭiju, North Korea, to cut the communist supply lines across the Yalu River. Twelve MiG-15 fighters jumped the VF-54 strike group that was made-up of F4U-4B Corsairs as they rendezvoused at 31,000 feet. Their top cover, F9F-2 and F9F-3 Panthers, led by Lt. Comdr. William E. Lamb, the VF-52 commanding officer, with his wingman, Lt. Robert E. Parker, flying F9F-2 Panthers, downed one MiG while Ens. Frederick C. Weber of VF-31, flying another F9F-2 Panther, shot down a second MiG-15 piloted by Senior Lieutenant A. Tarshinov, 139th Guards Fighter Aviation Regiment. The Russians listed Lieutenant Tarshinov as MIA. The Navy's score of three MiGs would remain for exactly two years.[43]

Failing to grasp the full meaning of events, MacArthur ordered a new offensive on 24 November to push right up to the Yalu River. He had already mistakenly concluded that the war was near an end and that when the troops reached the Yalu River they could go home. In the next few days, however, about 180,000 Chinese "volunteers" attacked, following which a shocked MacArthur told Washington, "We face an entirely new war," and ordered a long and humiliating retreat—one performed in sub-zero temperatures—which took the troops below the 38th Parallel by the end of December 1950.[44]

In early November, as the first elements of the Chinese "Volunteers" had crossed the border, the requirement for an aircraft carrier in the Yellow Sea had been deemed no longer necessary and *Theseus* was withdrawn to Hong Kong. She stayed there for just over a fortnight (two-week period), during which further exercises were carried out with the British Army and Royal Air Force. When Chinese Communist forces launched a major offensive, and UN forces went into full retreat, *Theseus* was hurriedly recalled to the west coast of Korea to provide badly needed air support to the UN Land Forces.[45]

From 5-26 December, HMS *Theseus* operated at a very high tempo in the Yellow Sea with a brief break of three days for replenishment. Operations taxed everyone on board to the fullest, particularly the aircrews. Thereafter, an alternating cycle of nine or ten days on station, and a similar-length period of replenishment at Sasebo or Kure was organized. The escort carriers USS *Badoeng Strait* (CVE-116) and *Sicily* (CVE-118) relieved *Theseus* in the Yellow Sea operating area on 27 December and began to fly missions in support of Eighth Army. The Marine fighter pilots embarked in the escort carriers flew in to provide protective patrols, strike the advancing enemy, and burn quantities of Allied supplies at the abandoned Kimpo Air Base.[46]

Map 2-3

Korea and relatively nearby ports of Sasebo and Kure, Japan (Sasebo and Kure are located in southwest Japan; the former in the Nagasaki Prefecture, and the latter (not shown on map) on the Inland Sea in Hiroshima Prefecture)

USS *BATAAN* TAKES UP KOREAN WAR DUTIES

On 16 January 1951, USS *Bataan*, with Marine Fighting Squadron VMF-212 embarked, and screened by Destroyer Division 72, relieved HMS *Theseus* and her screen, as Task Element 95.11. This began a pattern of the two light carriers, along with their escort ships, alternating ten-day periods of duty. Capt. Edgar T. Neal, USN, *Bataan*'s commanding officer, had reported to commander, Task Force 95, at Sasebo, one day earlier on 15 January, and further reported to Vice Admiral Andrewes, commander, Task Group 95.1. Andrewes had ordered him to sail from Sasebo to the west coast of Korea operating area and, on arrival, relieve the British light carrier.[47]

Of the nine USN *Independence*-class light fleet carriers, only *Bataan* served in Korea. Brought out of the Reserve Fleet and recommissioned on 13 May 1950 for war service, her commissioning pennant would be hauled down for the final time on 9 April 1954. Sister ships *Belleau Wood* and *Langley* served into the 1960s as the French carriers *Bois Belleau* (R97) and *Lafayette* (R96), respectively. *Dedalo* (R01)—the former *Cabot*—was a unit of the Spanish Navy from 1967 into 1988, before she was returned by Spain to the United States in August 1989.[48]

Photo 2-12

USS *Bataan* (CVL-29) under way in January 1952 with F4U-4B Corsair fighter-bombers of VMF-314 on board.
National Archives photograph #80-G-633888

Independence-class Light Fleet Aircraft Carriers

Ship	Commissioned	Decommissioned
Independence (CVL-22)	14 Jan 43	28 Aug 46
Princeton (CVL-23)	25 Feb 43	Sunk in Japanese aircraft attack on 24 Jul 44
Belleau Wood (CVL-24)	31 Mar 43	13 Jan 47
French *Bois Belleau* (R97)	9 Sept 53	Sep 60
Cowpens (CVL-25)	28 May 43	13 Jan 47
Monterey (CVL-26)	17 June 43	11 Feb 47
Training Carrier (AVT 2)	15 Sept 50	16 Jan 56
Langley (CVL-27)	31 Aug 43	11 Feb 47
French *Lafayette* (R96)	2 Jun 51	Mar 63
Cabot (CVL-28)	24 July 43	11 Feb 47
brought back into service	27 Oct 48	21 Jan 55
Spanish *Dedalo* (R01)	30 Aug 67	5 Aug 89 at New Orleans, LA
Bataan (CVL-29)	13 May 43	11 Feb 47
Service in Korea	13 May 50	9 Apr 54
San Jacinto (CVL-30)	15 Dec 43	1 Mar 47[49]

Bataan would do yeoman's work off Korea, earning nine battle stars for tours of combat duty between 16 December 1950 and 6 May 1953.

Dates	Battle Stars	Operation
16 Dec 50-24 Jan 51	★	Communist China Aggression 1951
25 Jan-21 Apr 51	★	First UN Counter Offensive 1951
22 Apr-3 Jun 51	★	Communist China Spring Offensive 1951
30 Apr 52	★	Second Korean Winter 1951-52
1 May-2 Aug 52	★	Korean Defense, Summer-Fall 1952
16 Feb-30 Apr 53	★	Third Korean Winter 1952-53
1-6 May 53	★	Korea, Summer-Fall 1953

BELIGERANTS STALEMATED IN JANUARY 1951

Early January 1951, witnessed the launching of another major Chinese Communist offensive which drove UN forces back to a line south of Suwon and Wonju by mid-month. The enemy was stopped and held there, then the Allied forces shifted to offense, steadily consolidating their gains. Lt. Gen. Mathew Ridgeway, who had taken over command of the Eighth Army after Lt. General Walker was killed in a road accident, described his current emphasis thus:

> The U.N. forces are now more concerned with killing the enemy and destroying his equipment than with acquiring real estate.[50]

BATAAN'S INITIAL TEN-DAY PATROL

> *When the loss of Capt. [Alfred H.] Agan [USMCR] is compared with the rescue of Capt. [Russell G.] Patterson [Jr., USMC] two days earlier, subsequent rescues effected during the period covered by this report, and others known to this command it is clear that it is better to risk a landing in enemy held territory than in cold water when it is in any way probable that rescue cannot be effected almost immediately.*
>
> —Excerpt from a USS *Bataan* Action Report, regarding a lesson learned by pilots of Marine Fighting Squadron VMF-212, embarked aboard the light fleet carrier, during their first few days of combat duty in Korea. If a pilot forced to ditch knew that rescue could not be accomplished at sea within ten minutes, and the choice existed, it was preferable to land behind enemy lines rather than in death-inducing, frigid 35°F water.[51]

During *Bataan*'s initial duty off Korea's west coast from 17-26 January, her flight operations in support of UN troops were conducted from sunrise to sunset. The daily air plan called for forty sorties, of which eight were defensive CAP (Combat Air Patrol) missions. The remainder were Close Air Support (CAS), Armed Reconnaissance (A/R), and Target CAP (TCAP) missions. The A/R missions had as their primary task, reconnaissance of the coast and off-lying waters from the bomb line north to the 39th Parallel, in implementation of the UN blockade of Korea. These missions also reconnoitered enemy airfields at Haeju, Onjin, Onjong-ni, and Seoul.[52]

Three pilots of VMF-212 were shot down in the first four days of operations from *Bataan*. On 18 January 1951, a F4U-4 Corsair fighter, piloted by Marine Captain Russell G. Patterson Jr., was hit by enemy anti-aircraft fire during a close air support mission. Patterson proceeded toward friendly territory, but was forced to make a crash landing behind enemy lines, near Suwon. He was uninjured and, upon clearing the aircraft, took cover, while other members of his flight formed a rescue combat air patrol to shield him from capture by enemy troops. An Air Force helicopter was summoned from Pyongtaek, about twenty miles to the south, which retrieved Patterson within thirty minutes.[53]

Photo 2-13

F4U-4 Corsair from the aircraft carrier USS *Boxer* (CV-21), about to make a rocket attack on a North Korean railway bridge, September 1951.
National Archives photograph #80-G-435115

The next day, 19 January, 1st Lt. Alfred Joseph Ward's, USMC, Corsair was hit by machine gun or rifle fire while making a strafing run on enemy troops near Kumchon. His plane exploded on impact near the target troops, and there was no chance of his survival. Another squadron fatality followed almost immediately. A Corsair piloted by Capt. Alfred Hiram Agan, USMCR, was hit by enemy anti-aircraft fire, or forced down by his own bomb blast, during recovery from a glide bombing attack on a target at Inchon.[54]

Agan chose to head for a nearby island believed to be friendly, to make a forced landing, as opposed to the alternative of landing on a beach in an enemy-held area south of Inchon. He was forced to land in the water before making the island, due to damage his plane had sustained, and was seen to leave the aircraft alive. However, this site was about sixty miles from *Bataan*, and forty miles from the nearest land-based rescue aircraft. Although aid was sent from both, the pilot died from exposure in the cold water before help arrived, but his body was returned to the *Bataan*.[55]

SUPPORT FOR CRUISERS AND DESTROYERS

Photo 2-14

USS *St. Paul* (CA-73) bombarding enemy installations at Wonsan, 20 April 1951.
National Archives photograph #80-G-428355

Following relief by *Theseus* and her escorts in the evening of 25 January 1951, *Bataan* and escorts proceeded to Sasebo for replenishment and upkeep, returning to the operating area off the west coast of Korea on 3 February, to take up the duties from *Theseus* once again. Air operations aboard *Bataan* commenced at sunrise the next day, with the same general plan as before.[56]

One distinct change was daily air-spotting and combat air patrol for the heavy gun cruiser USS *St. Paul* (CA-73), destroyer USS *Hank* (DD-702), and light cruiser HMS *Belfast*, providing gunfire support for the advance of Maj. Gen. Frank W. Milburn's, USA, First Corps in that area. (*St. Paul* would later gain some renown for firing the last salvo of the Korean War; at 2159 on 27 July 1953, one minute before the armistice came into effect.)[57]

Air-spot and CAP aircraft were loaded with the same ordnance as that used for close air support missions—it being practical to briefly divert these aircraft, while on station for their primary missions, to employ them against enemy positions in the shore bombardment area. In many instances, these aircraft were able to make attacks on reverse slopes, inaccessible to naval gunfire. (The term "reverse slope" refers to the landward side of coastal hills or mountains.)[58]

Theseus and escorts relieved *Bataan* and escorts on 13 February, and the latter again proceeded to Sasebo for replenishment and upkeep.[59]

BATAAN PATROLS, 23 FEBRUARY-6 APRIL 1951

Photo 2-15

The Han River, Korea, in 1871.
Naval History and Heritage Command photograph #NH 63673

Bataan and *Theseus* continued to alternate patrols, with *Bataan* on station off the west coast of Korea: 23 February-4 March, 13-22 March, and 1-6 April. New challenges during these periods included a request by the *St. Paul* for the squadron to map and take aerial photographs of the north bank of the Han River north of Seoul. In the absence of a photo-configured aircraft, an attempt was made on 25-26 February to fulfill this request, using a K-25 camera, vertically mounted in a makeshift stand for mapping and a hand-held K-20 for obliques. The results were only partly successful, but paved the way for future improvements. *Bataan* put into Pusan, Korea, on 5 March, disembarked Squadron VMF-212 (Corsair F4U-5s), and embarked Squadron VMF-312 ("The Checkerboards") before proceeding to Sasebo.[60]

During her next period of operations, Maj. Frank H. Prestley, USMCR, crash-landed on 15 March in the Han River, thirty miles northwest of Seoul, after engine failure due to AA fire. Prestley was uninjured and picked up by an Air Force helicopter. Six days later, 1st Lt. Harold R. Knowles, USMC, was forced down behind enemy lines owing to engine failure caused by a drop in oil pressure believed to be the result of enemy AA fire. He was rescued by the ship's helicopter. On 2 April, 1st Lt. D. H. Hauge was hit by AA fire in the Sariwon area. He was able to fly over friendly territory, until damage to his plane forced to him to bail out in the vicinity of Inchon. He landed offshore near Yongjondo Island, was recovered by boat from a dock landing ship in Inchon Harbor, and later returned to *Bataan* by helicopter.[61]

On 3 April, Capt. William Miller Jr., USN, was flown aboard *Bataan*. (Miller served as the ship's commanding officer from 17 April 1951-14 April 1952.) Misfortune struck the following day, when VMF-312 lost its squadron leader, Maj. Donald P. Frame. Struck by AA fire near Hwangju and with his plane on fire, he attempted to bail out. His parachute streamed immediately, causing him to strike the aircraft's tail. The chute eventually opened and he landed in enemy territory, ten miles south of Sariwon. Rescue CAP held enemy forces down until he was retrieved by Air Force helicopter, but Frame died of his injuries while en route to Seoul. On 6 April, *Bataan* and the task element departed for Sasebo.[62]

KOREAN EAST COAST OPERATIONS, FOLLOWED BY RETURN TO WEST COAST AND SHOOT DOWN OF YAKS

> *The enemy aircraft were first sighted about 0715. The dog-fight was over by about 0725. All the aerial action took place between 2000 and 3000 feet. This unexpected attack found both Capt. [Phillip C.] DeLong and 1st Lt. [Harold D.] Daigh's aircraft carrying a belly tank and a 500-pound bomb; or a napalm tank, which were not jettisoned until the combat was nearly over. Each plane, likewise, was carrying a wing load of six HVAR [high velocity aircraft rockets]… and two 100-pound bombs which were not jettisoned until the flight headed for the ship.*
>
> —Excerpt from USS *Bataan* Action Report, regarding combat action on 21 April 1951 in which two Marine Corps pilots from VMF-312, piloting F4U-4 Corsair fighters, shot down three of a group of four North Korean Air Force YAK-3 or YAK-9 fighter-bombers, which had "jumped them" off the west coast of Korea.[63]

At 0700 on 8 April 1951, Task Element 95.11—a two-carrier, truly United Nations naval group—comprised of USS *Bataan*, with VMF-312 embarked; HMS *Theseus* with the 17th Carrier Air Group; and screening destroyers USS *English* (DD-696), USS *Sperry* (DD-704), HMS *Consort*, HMAS *Bataan*, HMCS *Athabaskan*, and HMCS *Huron*, sortied from Sasebo. They were bound for the east coast of Korea, to conduct operations involving the stoppage of enemy traffic, especially trucks, on the enemy's main supply route along the coast in the vicinity of Wonsan, Hamhung, and Songjin. During these operations from 9 April through 15 April, five aircraft and one pilot were lost to enemy action.[64]

On 10 April, a Sea Fury from HMS *Theseus*, piloted by R. H. Johnson, was shot down by AA fire over enemy territory about thirty-five miles southwest of Wonsan. A thorough search failed to reveal any sign of the pilot and rescue efforts were abandoned. He was reported lost in action, presumed killed. The pilots of the other four downed aircraft were recovered by a helicopter from the light cruiser USS *Manchester* (CL-83), engaged in bombardment activities along the northeast coast of Korea, primarily at Wonsan and Songjin.[65]

In late afternoon on 15 April, the two light carriers split up. *Theseus* and her escorts assumed the duties of Task Element 95.11 and departed for the west coast operating area; whereas the *Bataan*, accompanied by HMAS *Bataan* and USS *Sperry*, set a course for Sasebo. Following their receipt of logistic support in Japan, *Bataan* and escorts relieved *Theseus* and her screen at 2000 on 19 April. Two days later, two F4U-4 Corsairs from *Bataan* on a reconnaissance and bombing mission, were waylaid by twice their number of North Korean Air Force YAK fighters.[66]

Photo 2-16

HMAS *Bataan* in company with USS *Bataan* off the Korean coast, April 1951. (RAN)

Marine Capt. Phillip DeLong and 1st Lt. Harold Daigh were climbing for altitude over Hojang-do in an open formation, with Daigh about 500 yards behind, and slightly to the left (7 o'clock position) of DeLong. Upon reaching 2,000 feet, Daigh sighted four aircraft above them approaching from the northwest.[67]

Flying at approximately 5,000 feet in a loose right echelon, the four planes made a right, then a left turn toward DeLong, apparently not yet aware of Daigh's presence. The first two aircraft opened fire on DeLong, putting a bullet into his plane aft of the cockpit. Daigh pulled in behind the attacking planes—all Soviet Yakovlev YAK-3s or YAK-9s—and was able to follow the number three plane, leaving the fourth to DeLong. Setting up for an attack ended when Daigh dove to the left and below the number four plane, which was firing at him.[68]

As all six planes jockeyed for position, Daigh made a climbing 360-degree turn and opened fire on two YAKs, with unobserved results. He then tailed in (slid in) at 4 o'clock on another, and opened fire, hitting the enemy plane's tail, fuselage and wing. The YAK's starboard wing broke off, and the plummeting plane crashed and burned.[69]

DeLong, upon being hit, performed a "Split S" to pick up speed, and made a climbing turn to the left. (The Split S is an air combat maneuver mostly used to disengage from combat. To execute a Split S, the pilot rolls inverted, then executes a descending half-loop, resulting in level flight in the opposite direction at a lower altitude.) Two YAKs made firing runs on DeLong from astern, but overshot and turned wide, upon which he pulled in behind them and returned fire with unobserved results. While DeLong was in his climbing left turn, a third YAK had crossed in front of him from right to left, as the remaining enemy plane crashed into the ground (Daigh's kill). DeLong took the crossing plane under fire, sending it into the ground, smoking.[70]

As DeLong turned to the left, and headed eastward, he observed three planes ahead of him, also flying east. Daigh was pursuing one of the two remaining YAKs; with the other following Daigh, positioned to his left, and turning right on to his tail. DeLong radioed Daigh and told him to pull up as the enemy was on his tail. Daigh turned hard to the left, and dropped under and astern the following YAK, opening fire on the fighter, as it overran him. His gunfire started the enemy smoking from both sides of the cockpit and wing roots (where the wings attached to the fuselage). The plane was last seen climbing east into the sun.[71]

During this action, DeLong tailing the lead plane, started it smoking with his opening fire. As this single remaining YAK attempted to evade by turning to the south, then west, DeLong's pursuing fire caused it to puff smoke. The enemy then did a "Split S" and headed west. DeLong in pursuit, continued to slide in on the YAK, while firing his guns. As the enemy plane emitted smoke from both wings and fuselage, and fragments of the plane continued to fall off, the pilot jettisoned his cockpit canopy and bailed out. The YAK crashed into the water, as the pilot's parachute opened and he descended into the Sea of Japan, apparently unhurt.[72]

Captain DeLong and First Lieutenant Daigh then joined up and climbed to 6,000 feet, with smoke in the cockpit of DeLong's plane and a rough engine in Daigh's, compelling them to return to *Bataan*, bombing mission uncompleted, at 0820.[73]

Phillip Cunliffe DeLong had become a Marine Corps Double Ace in World War II, credited with shooting down eleven enemy aircraft in aerial combat, and assisting in destruction of another. This day credited him with two additional aerial victories, for which he was awarded the Silver Star. A copy of the citation follows:

The President of the United States of America takes pleasure in presenting the Silver Star to Captain Phillip Cunliffe DeLong, United States Marine Corps, for conspicuous gallantry and intrepidity as a Section Leader and Pilot in Marine Fighter Squadron THREE HUNDRED TWELVE (VMF-312), in action against enemy aggressor forces in the vicinity of the Taedong-Gang Estuary, Korea, on 21 April 1951. Suddenly attacked from above by four enemy fighter aircraft while leading his section on a reconnaissance mission and carrying a full load of bombs, rockets and ammunition, Captain DeLong immediately jettisoned his external load and, although his plane was damaged during the initial aerial assault, effectively organized his flight to assume the offensive. Quickly attaining the advantage, he skillfully pressed an attack and, within a period of approximately three minutes, shot down two hostile planes. As a result of his skilled airmanship and tactical ability, his flight destroyed three of the enemy aircraft and severely damaged the fourth. By his marked courage, brilliant airmanship and steadfast devotion to duty, Captain DeLong upheld the highest traditions of the United States Naval Service.

Harold D. Daigh was awarded the Distinguished Flying Cross.

THESEUS RELIEVED BY *GLORY*, DEPARTS FOR UK

On the last day of *Theseus'* operations, 19 April 1951, the front line was, for the most part, north of the 38th Parallel. *Theseus* arrived in Sasebo on the 20th, having carried out nearly seven months of very intensive operations. Following her relief in the Japanese port by HMS *Glory*, which had arrived there from the UK, *Theseus* departed on 25 April, bound for the United Kingdom.[74]

HMS *Glory* would complete three tours of duty during the Korean War. The first began on 24 April 1951, following her relief of *Theseus*. Her second commenced in 1952, and the final one was from October 1952 to 8 November 1953.[75]

HMAS *SYDNEY* REPORTS FOR DUTY

In September 1951, the Australian light fleet carrier HMAS *Sydney* (R17) under the command of Capt. David Harries, RAN, relieved HMS *Glory* as the carrier representative of the British naval forces in the Korean Theater. It was an historic occasion, *Sydney* being the first, and only Dominion carrier to serve in the war. Comprising her Carrier Air Group were three Fleet Air Arm Squadrons—No. 805 (Sea Furies), 808 (Sea Furies) and 817 (Fireflies)—as well as a helicopter and its crew on loan from the United States Navy.[76]

40   Chapter 2

Photo 2-17

Hawker Sea Fury FB.11 fighter being catapulted from HMS *Glory*, circa June 1951. Allied aircraft in Korea were painted with "Invasion Stripes" to help aid in visual recognition and reduce 'friendly fire' incidents.
Naval History and Heritage Command photograph #NH 97044

Photo 2-18

A Sikorsky S-51 search and rescue helicopter, borrowed from the United States Navy, lands aboard HMAS *Sydney*, at the conclusion of the day's flying in 1951.
Australian War Memorial photograph 301426

Sydney, the first aircraft carrier of the Royal Australian Navy, had been laid down as HMS *Terrible*—one of six Royal Navy *Majestic*-class light fleet aircraft carriers whose construction had begun in 1943. These ships, originally of the *Colossus*-class, had been modified while under construction to handle larger and faster aircraft. Work on the *Majestic*-class ships had been suspended at the end of World War II. Five were eventually completed; *Sydney* was commissioned at Devonport, England, on 16 December 1948. Sailing from Devonport on 12 April 1949, she arrived in Australian waters the following month for RAN service.[77]

Photo 2-19

Launching of HMS *Terrible* at Devonport, England, on 30 September 1944. She would later be commissioned into the RAN as HMAS *Sydney*.
Australian War Memorial photograph 305532

Laid down as the same type light fleet carrier as the British ships with whom she would exchange duty in Korea, *Sydney* shared many of the same characteristics. Stretching 695 feet in length, with an 80-foot beam and 25-foot draught, her four Admiralty 3-drum boilers providing steam to Brown Curtis turbines could propel the 15,740-ton carrier to a top speed of 24 knots.[78]

HMAS *Sydney* began her first patrol of the Korean War on 4 October 1951 in the western theater, transferring four days later to the east coast for special operations on 10-11 October.[79]

SHORE BOMBARDMENT/STRIKES AGAINST KOJO

Photo 2-20

USS *New Jersey* (BB-62) during bombardment operations against enemy targets in Korea, 10 November 1951.
National Archives photograph #80-G-435681

On 8 October, Captain Harries announced that *Sydney* was heading for the east coast of Korea for special operations. Radio silence was to be maintained and no "gash" (food waste) was to be thrown over the side, as this could identify the ship's whereabouts to the enemy. In early morning darkness on 10 October, bombers could be heard passing overhead. At dawn, action stations (routine manning of battle stations in the event of an enemy air attack at first light), crewmen topside could see gun flashes from HMS *Belfast*, HMS *Comus*, and HMS *Cossack* as they conducted shore bombardment against the Kojo area of North Korea. Kojo was a coastal town located some forty miles south of Wonsan.[80]

Screened by British, Canadian, and American destroyers, HMAS *Sydney* launched her first aircraft at 0630. Throughout the day, her planes attacked any targets they could find. By mid-afternoon, after 58 sorties, the seas became very rough and flight operations were terminated. Results the following day, 11 October, were much better.[81]

At 0300, the battleship USS *New Jersey* (BB-62) began pounding enemy bunkers, stores, ammunition dumps, troop concentrations, and other targets with 16-inch rounds. As the thunder from *New Jersey*'s massive guns continued almost unabated, *Sydney* provided her with "spotter aircraft" to report whether her gun rounds were falling short, long, left or right of target, so that corrections could be made. Each 2,700 pound, 16-inch round could reach thirty miles. HMAS *Sydney*'s crew could see the destroyers firing at the enemy, and while operating close to the coast, landmarks and buildings were visible.[82]

Near the end of the day's operations, twelve of *Sydney*'s Sea Furies caught more than 1,000 enemy troops engaged in 'digging in' on the hills behind the beaches, and their ensuing air attacks killed or wounded approximately 200 of them. By dusk, the Aussie light fleet carrier had completed a record 89 sorties, and sailed for Sasebo at 20 knots, escorted by the light cruiser HMS *Belfast* and four destroyers.[83]

SYDNEY'S SECOND PATROL

Photo 2-21

A Fairey Firefly of the RAN. HMAS *Sydney*'s complement included one squadron of Fireflies (No. 817 Squadron) during her service in Korea.
Australian War Memorial photograph

On 18 October 1951, HMAS *Sydney* began her second patrol on the west coast of Korea in tactical command of Task Element 95.11. Subsequent operations included morning patrols up the coast to the Manchurian border—attacking junks, sampans, and shore targets such as buildings, bridges, railways, and tunnels—and providing close air support for the Commonwealth Division. Trafalgar Day was celebrated by air strikes against junks believed to be concentrating in the Yalu Estuary for an invasion of Taehwa-do Island.[84]

On 23 October, in addition to the normal days flying program, the carrier provided air search for downed American airmen in the northeast area of Korea Bay. A Sea Fury pilot detected a survivor and towards dusk a Firefly dropped a dinghy and supplies. The airman was eventually recovered by the frigate HMAS *Murchison*.[85]

During operations on 25-26 October, three of *Sydney*'s aircraft were shot down and a fourth badly damaged. A Sea Fury was hit on the 25th by light flak off Chinnampo and forced down. Happily, the pilot was promptly rescued by helicopter, and landed at Kimpo Air Field, which was back in the Allies' hands. Another Sea Fury was hit while operating over the front line but managed to reach Kimpo safely.[86]

The following day, 26 October, a Sea Fury from 805 Squadron engaged in the Han River area was hit by flak and crash-landed on a mudbank on the south side of the river. The aircraft broke in half on impact but the pilot, Sub Lt. Noel Knappstein, RAN, was unhurt. With opportunity to sell the wreckage to some local villagers, Knappstein did so for about 1,000 Won (recouping some value for the RAN). He was rescued by a boat from HMS *Amethyst*, together with salvageable items from the aircraft.[87]

HELICOPTER CREW EARN MEDALS FOR HEROISM

United States Navy Cross

Commonwealth Distinguished Service Medal

United States Navy Cross

A second aircraft (third overall during the two days of operations) was lost later that day during a strike by a flight of five Fireflies on a railway tunnel between Chaeryong and Haeju. The aircraft from 817 Squadron, piloted by Sub Lt. Neil D. MacMillan and Chief Petty Officer Phillip Hancox was hit by flak and forced down in a frozen rice paddy fifty miles behind enemy lines. A rescue attempt by *Sydney*'s US Navy Dragonfly helicopter in the brief remaining daylight was considered to be an extremely hazardous undertaking. Nevertheless, such effort was undertaken, and the Firefly air crew's recovery successfully carried out.[88]

The Sikorsky HO3S-1 (S-51) Dragonfly was the preeminent shipboard search and rescue helicopter during the late 1940s and early 1950s. Many downed aviators and injured ground troops from that era owed their lives to the small, four-seat helicopter's unique capabilities and the courage of its flight crews.[89]

The two downed aviators had resisted capture by the enemy with the aid of an Owen submachine gun and protection overhead provided by Sea Furies from *Sydney*, and Meteor jet fighters from the Royal Australian Air Force's 77 Squadron. The helicopter carried out the rescue at the very limit of its fuel endurance, having flown 172 km (106 miles) one way, to do so. Upon landing at the Kimpo Airfield, it was unable to taxi, having run out of fuel.[90]

The pilot, Chief Petty Officer Arlene (Dick) Babbit, USN, was awarded the Commonwealth Distinguished Service Medal as well as the United States Navy Cross for his efforts that day, earning the distinction of being one of the few, or perhaps only, Allied serviceman in Korea to receive the awards of two nations for the same action. His aircrewman, Aviation Machinist's Mate Third Callis C. Gooding, shot dead a North Korean soldier as MacMillan and Hancox scrambled into the helicopter.[91] Gooding's Navy Cross medal citation reads:

> The President of the United States of America takes pleasure in presenting the Navy Cross to Aviation Machinist's Mate Third Class Callis C. Gooding, United States Navy, for extraordinary heroism in connection with military operations against an armed enemy of the United Nations while serving as crewman of a helicopter in Helicopter Squadron ONE (HU-1), Unit FOURTEEN, attached to H.M.A.S. *Sydney*, during the rescue of two downed airmen behind enemy lines near Sariwon, Korea, on 26 October 1951. Despite grave hazards presented by the limited flying range of the rescue helicopter, approaching darkness, and the certainty of capture or possible death if the mission failed, Aviation Machinist's Mate Third Class Gooding voluntarily accompanied the helicopter pilot deep into enemy-held territory to assist in the rescue. Approaching the objective in the face of intense, hostile anti-aircraft and small arms fire, Aviation Machinist's Mate Third Class Gooding provided effective cover and fire support with a submachine gun, accounting for two enemy casualties during the period in which the helicopter landed, picked up the two airmen and departed to the safety of Kimpo airfield eighty miles away. By his great personal courage and

46   Chapter 2

inspiring devotion to duty, Aviation Machinist's Mate Third Class Gooding contributed in large measure to the successful rescue of the downed airmen. His actions reflect the highest credit upon himself and the United States Naval Service.

The escort carrier USS *Rendova* (CVE-114) relieved *Sydney* as CTE 95.11 on 27 October 1951, bringing to an end her second operational period. In company with HMCS *Athabaskan*, she proceeded to Kure, arriving the following day.[92]

THIRD PATROL

Sydney departed Kure on 3 November 1951 to renew west coast operations, assuming command of Task Element 95.11. Screened by the destroyers HMCS *Athabaskan* (G07), HMCS *Cayuga* (R04), HMCS *Sioux* (R64), USS *Hanna* (DE-449), and *Collett* (DD-730), she began operations early on 5 November. That day, she suffered her first combat casualty, a pilot of 805 Squadron. Lt. Keith Elwood Clarkson, RAN, was killed when his Sea Fury failed to pull out of a strafing dive against an enemy truck.[93]

Clarkson was one of the squadron's most experienced pilots, having served in World War II with the RAAF. The Squadron's diary entry for this sad day noted:

> '52 Flight were first airborne and once more the Han River was the target. Troop concentrations were rocketed and strafed followed by an Armed Recce heading north from Packichan. It was during this recce that 52 leader was hit while making a strafing run on a possible truck at BT.670155. The aircraft rolled over on its back and dived into the ground, breaking into many pieces. No sign of life or of fluorescent panels were seen. One aircraft returned to the ship and the remaining two carried out Rescap [Rescue Combat Air Patrol] over the area. Few enemy troops were seen and were strafed and some rockets put into a slit trench. Both aircraft were hit and soon had to land at Kimpo, being short on fuel.
>
> The Diary would like to record the courage and determination of Lieut Keith Clarkson and say how much he was admired and respected by all pilots in the Group. His loss will be felt very deeply.'[94]

The death of Lt. Clarkson was a tragic event in what was otherwise a relatively quiet patrol, notwithstanding the 401 sorties flown over the period. On 13 November, the single clear day of the patrol, *Sydney* was joined by the battleship USS *New Jersey* flying the flag of Vice Adm.

Harold M. Martin, USN, commanding the U.S. Seventh Fleet, who remarked, "I am pleased to be able to say that on 13 November no railway line was serviceable in the area covered by my aircraft." Ending her patrol, *Sydney* arrived at Sasebo on 14 November 1951.[95]

Photo 2-22

Battleship USS *New Jersey* (BB-62) bombarding targets near Hungnam on 5 October 1951. Hungnam city is visible at the extreme left.
National Archives photograph #80-G-434535

FOURTH PATROL

On 18 November, *Sydney* sailed from Sasebo to join Task Group 95.8, under the command of Rear Adm. Alan Kenneth Scott-Moncrieff, DSO RN, in HMS *Belfast*, for a coordinated strike against the industrial center of Hungnam on the east coast. Shortly after dawn on the 20th, shore bombardment by the light cruiser HMS *Belfast* and destroyers HMAS *Tobruk* and HMNS (His Majesty's Netherlands Ship) *Van Galen* commenced. The naval gunfire against known anti-aircraft positions was preliminary to the first of ten attacks by *Sydney*'s aircraft with barracks, industrial plants, stores, and rail communications targeted. More than 100 sorties were flown during the two-day operation in which the light fleet carrier was screened by the destroyers USS *Hyman*, HMCS *Sioux*, and HMS *Constance*.[96]

Sydney detached on the 21st and accompanied by *Constance* and *Van Galen*, proceeded to the west coast theater. Snow and high winds prevented the resumption of flying operations on 24 November, and continued to severely limit activity over the next few days. It was not until the 27th that conditions improved sufficiently to resume offensive operations, but *Sydney*'s patrol ended the following day.[97]

FIFTH PATROL

Sydney returned to the west coast from Kure on 7 December, again providing the carrier component to TE 95.11. Flying began shortly after first light but unfortunately, the success of the day's sorties was marred by the loss of a second Sea Fury pilot from 805 Squadron, when Sub Lt. Richard Sinclair, RAN, was hit by flak northwest of Chinnampo. His aircraft lost oil pressure and the engine caught fire forcing him to bail out. He died of injuries resulting from being struck by his falling aircraft's tail. A squadron diary entry described the fatality:

> Armed Recce No 2 for the day was 51 Flight and this turned out to be a milk run. After checking some junks at 951904 a strafing attack was made on some troops in trenches. The flight then headed for [untelligible] to check the rail yard [for] box cars. On leaving this area 51-4 (Sub/Lieut Sinclair) was hit by an explosive shell and called up to say there was a smell of burning in the cockpit. He then gained height and headed seaward. Directly over the coast flame appeared from forward and underneath the aircraft and very shortly afterwards the aircraft went into an apparently uncontrolled dive. Approx 300-400 feet from the deck the pilot was seen to bail out and the parachute open at 100 ft. On hitting the ground the pilot was not seen to move, and when the helicopter from Bromide-Baker [codeword for Allied-held Cho-do and Paengyong-do islands] picked the body off the mud bank there was no sign of life. Medical examination subsequently showed that he was hit by the tail surfaces and the parachute was broken open by the impact.[98]

Four other aircraft were hit that day and one Sea Fury was forced to land with its wheels up at the USAF airfield on Paengyong-do Island (designated K-53).[99]

Profiting from several days of fine weather through 14 December, *Sydney*'s aircraft maintained a high rate of attack. Troop concentrations in the Changyon-Hanchon areas, the Chinnampo waterfront, coastal small ships, and rail communications all received their attention. On the morning of 13 December, a Sea Fury was shot down to the west of Pyong-Gang and that afternoon a second Sea Fury off Ongjin. The pilot of the first plane was rescued by a U.S. helicopter from Paengyong and the latter by a friendly junk.[100]

The closing days of the patrol were occupied by providing air support for incoming convoys, and anti-invasion operations in the Cho-do-Sokto area, including a continuous daylight patrol over the ships in the vicinity. The first patrol ended on 18 December with *Sydney*'s Air Group having tallied 383 sorties. Twenty-five aircraft suffered flak damage including five lost, with the majority of hits sustained in the heavily-gunned Angag Peninsula area.[101]

Sydney arrived at Kure a little before noon on 19 December 1951, a particularly welcome event as she was to spend Christmas there.[102]

SIXTH AND SEVENTH PATROLS

> *Whilst the day had been something of an anti-climax, I was also somewhat relieved that the flyers had not been given that last dashing opportunity to get themselves shot down.*
>
> —HMAS *Sydney*'s commanding officer, Captain Harries, remarking on the cancellation on 25 January 1952, of planned air raids into the heart of north Korea's capital, Pyongyang. This action, on the ship's last operational day in Korean waters, was not under- undertaken owing to high winds and seas giving way to low cloud cover, heavy snow, and poor visibility.[103]

The light fleet carrier's brief respite at Kure ended on 27 December 1951, when *Sydney* sailed to relieve USS *Badoeng Strait* on the west coast. Operations began in bad flying conditions in the early morning of 29 December, and through month's end the main task was providing cover to outbound convoys from Inchon.[104]

Photo 2-23

Naval airmen (known as 'birdies') sweep the snow and ice from the flight deck of HMAS *Sydney* before flying could commence for the day. Clearing snow and ice from her decks became a common occurrence during *Sydney*'s sixth and seventh patrols in Korea. Australian War Memorial photograph P03815.007

Sydney resumed offensive missions on New Year's Day 1952, furnishing air cover for friendly guerilla forces evacuating Yongho-do, which had been invaded early that morning by North Korean forces. Aircraft were credited with saving ninety of those fleeing the island located near Ongjin Peninsula, which projected into the Yellow Sea below the 38th parallel. Although the peninsula was in the Southern zone, it was isolated and therefore difficult to defend. Surrounded by the sea, its only land route was through North Korean territory.[105]

On 2 January 1952, *Sydney* and embarked 805 Squadron suffered the third, and final combat casualty of the war when an aircraft piloted by Sub Lt. Ronald J. Coleman, RAN, disappeared over the Yellow Sea. During an otherwise uneventful combat air patrol, Coleman disappeared into a cloud and was not seen again. With weather conditions and visibility extremely poor, an arduous search mounted by *Sydney* proved fruitless.[106]

Photo 2-24

Rear Adm. Alan Kenneth Scott-Moncrieff, DSO RN, commander, West Coast Blockade Force, in the engine room of the destroyer HMAS *Warramunga* with Chief Engine Room Artificer A. L. McKinnon and Lt. M. McLachlan, RAN.
Australian War Memorial photograph 304835

Three days later on 5 January, Rear Admiral Scott-Moncrieff transferred to *Sydney* from *Belfast*. He authorized strikes on two targets in a zone in which her aircraft were not normally permitted to attack, and personally briefed the pilots. While taking part in an ensuing attack on gun positions along the Yesong River (on the north side of the Han River estuary, close to the neutral area around Panmunjom), Lt. Peter Goldrick, RAN, was wounded in the arm by a .303 round but managed to safely return aboard *Sydney*. The Sea Fury pilot (808 Squadron) was fortunate in that the energy of the bullet had largely dissipated passing through lead shot of a message bag on the starboard side of the cockpit. (Pilots forced to ditch in enemy waters could employ such weighted bags to drag classified documents to the bottom, helping prevent their capture by the enemy.) Goldrick's luck soon ran out when the RAN, informed of his wound, signaled that his flying pay had been stopped.[107]

Sydney assumed command of TE 95.11 for the last time on 16 January, when she took over the west coast patrol from USS *Badoeng Strait* and commenced her seventh patrol. Screened by the destroyers USS *Hanson* (DD-832), USS *Radford* (DD-446), HMCS *Sioux*, and HMAS *Tobruk*, her planes' last series of sorties began in bad weather the following day. *Sydney*'s last raids were scheduled for 25 January 1952, striking directly on the North Korean capital of Pyongyang. Extremely poor weather, however, meant that the mission was cancelled. She left Korean waters on 25 January and, following port visits to Sasebo, Hong Kong, and Singapore, arrived at Fremantle, Australia, on 22 February 1952—ending her participation in the Korean War.[108]

Signals of farewell included one from commander, Seventh Fleet:

> Departure of *Sydney* is met with mixed feelings of regret and joy. Setting records for getting planes into the air in all conditions of weather – striking troop concentrations and supply lines and furnishing air spots for United Nations ships are only a few of your many achievements. Fighting side by side with other United Nations units, *Sydney* has upheld highest traditions of Commonwealth Navy. With great respect for the proven fighting ability of this fine ship and its embarked air groups, I extend to all hands our heartfelt thanks for a job well done. May you all have a safe and happy journey to a well-deserved rest.

Vice Admiral Harold Martin, USN Com 7th Fleet[109]

HONOURS AND AWARDS FOR VALOUR

Twenty awards were made to officers and men of HMAS *Sydney*, which served in the Korean area from October 1951 until January 1952. Of note, Gordon Churchill Hughes was the only RAN observer in Korea to receive the Distinguished Service Medal for Gallantry. Six of the individuals listed below were Royal Navy personnel on loan to the Australian light fleet carrier.

CBE (Commander of the Military Division of the Most Excellent Order)
Commodore David Hugh Harries, ADC RAN

MBE (Member of the Military Division of the Most Excellent Order)
Lieut.-Commander (E) Robert Joseph Tunstall, RN

Bar to the Distinguished Service Cross (DSC)
Commander Michael Frampton Fell, DSO, DSC RN

Distinguished Service Cross (DSC)
Lieut.-Commander Walter George Bowles, RAN
Lieut. Harold Edwin Bailey, RAN
Lieut. Guy Alexander Beange, RAN

Distinguished Service Medal (DSM)
Observer II Gordon Churchill Hughes, RAN

Mention in Despatches (MID)
Commander Launcelot John Kiggell, DSC RN
Lieut.-Commander Brian Stewart Murray, RAN
Lieut. George Firth Spencer Brown, DFC RAN
Lieut. Edward Thomas Genge, RN
Lieut. Alexander Hughie Gordon, DFC RAN
Lieut. Peter William Seed, RAN
Lieut. (E) William John Rourke, RAN
Sub-Lieut. Armand John Roland, RAN
Chief Petty Officer Eugene Eljerfield Fernandes Sydney, RAN
Chief Airman Fitter (E) Clifford Frank Dubber, RN
Chief Airman Fitter (E) Arthur Winstanley, RN
Chief Electrical Artificer James Patrick Whelan, RAN
Acting Chief Airman William Daniel Gardner, RAN[110]

Three RAN Pilots Earned the DSC in the Korean War

- Lieut.-Commander Walter George Bowles, RAN
  Also received the USN Legion of Merit Medal

- Lieut. Harold Edwin Bailey, RAN

- Lieut. Guy Alexander Beange, RAN

3

Korean War, February 1952-July 1953

Photo 3-1

British light cruiser HMS *Belfast* coming alongside the light fleet carrier USS *Bataan* off the west coast of Korea on 27 May 1952. National Archives photograph #80-G-633883

Following the end of HMAS *Sydney*'s service in late January 1952, HMS *Glory* and USS *Bataan* alternated tours of duty off the west coast of Korea with HMS *Ocean*, the fourth British *Colossus*-class CVL ordered to combat duty in Korean. The tours of the six Allied light fleet carriers that participated in the Korean War are identified in the following table, along with the squadrons embarked aboard the ships. This chapter concerns itself with the middle portion of the table, covering the period from 27 January 1952 through 27 July 1953, when the Korean Armistice Agreement was signed.

The emblems of the Fleet Air Arm Squadrons embarked aboard the Royal Navy and Royal Australian Navy carriers during this period are depicted, as well as that of Marine Fighting Squadron VMF-312 (later VMA-312) carried aboard the USS *Bataan*. Although its mission remained the same, VMF-312's designation was changed to VMA-312 (Marine Attack Squadron) on 25 February 1952.[1]

The tour lengths associated with ships in the table refer to the periods they served in the Korean Theater. Each light fleet carrier (CVL) conducted several combat patrols, generally in the Yellow Sea off the west coast of Korea, during their tours. Time "off the line" was spent at Sasebo or Kure, Japan, to provide rest and replenishment for crew and ship, before returning to the Korean coast and taking up patrol duties from the CVL on station. In some cases, light fleet carriers and escort carriers shared alternating patrol periods.

**RN, RAN, and USN Light Fleet Aircraft Carriers
and Embarked FAA or VMF/VMA Squadrons**

802 Squadron 804 Squadron 807 Squadron 810 Squadron 812 Squadron 825 Squadron

**VMF-312 (the "Checkerboards")
1 June 1943-25 February 1952**

**VMA-312 (the "Checkerboards")
beginning 25 February 1952**

Light Carrier	Tour Length	Carrier Air Group	Squadrons
HMS *Triumph*	25 Jun-29 Sep 50	13th CAG	800, 827
USS *Bataan*	15 Jan-5 Mar 51	-------------	VMF-212
USS *Bataan*	5 Mar-13 Jun 51	-------------	VMF-312
HMS *Theseus*	29 Sep 50-23 Apr 51	17th CAG	807, 810
HMS *Glory*	23 Apr-30 Sep 51	14th CAG	804, 812
HMAS *Sydney*	20 Sep 51-27 Jan 52	21st CAG	805, 808, 817
HMS *Glory*	27 Jan-5 May 52	14th CAG	804, 812
USS *Bataan*	29 Apr-21 Jul 52	-------------	VMA-312
HMS *Ocean*	5 May-8 Nov 52	*Ocean* CAG	802, 825
HMS *Glory*	8 Nov 52-19 May 53	14th CAG	804, 812
USS *Bataan*	15 Feb-8 May 53	-------------	VMA-312
HMS *Ocean*	17 May-23 Jul 53	*Ocean* CAG	807, 810
HMAS *Sydney*	Nov 1953-1954	*Sydney* CAG	805, 817[2]

Following a four-month refit in Australia, HMS *Glory* sailed for the Far East in late January 1952. At Hong Kong, en route, she relieved HMAS *Sydney* of her duties, and arrived on station off the west coast of Korea on 6 February. Aboard her were No. 804 Squadron (Sea Furies) and No. 812 Squadron (Fireflies). Flying operations as opposed to earlier tasking described in the previous chapter, were expanded to include the defense of west coast islands occupied by Allied forces, as well as other duties. These other duties included: interdiction of enemy supply lines, spotting for shore bombardment, blockade enforcement, and close support of the 1st Commonwealth Division.[3]

Before taking up *Glory*'s air operations, a brief introduction of the 1st Commonwealth Division, and the 3rd Battalion, Royal Australian Regiment (a component of the division), as well as the state of ground warfare then existing, will help provide context for the eighteen months remaining in the Korean War.

The soldiers of the 1st Commonwealth Division then in a static position (as were the Allied forces in general) were engaged in an active defense of the front that spanned the breadth of the Korean Peninsula. This lull resulted from a belief by "top brass" that the cost of further major assaults on the enemy's defenses would exceed any benefits, and that possibly, peace might come out of the recently reopened armistice talks, which ruled out costly large-scale offensives by either side. Fighting had tapered off into a monotonous routine of patrol clashes, raids, and bitter small-unit struggles for key outpost positions. Throughout the spring and summer of 1952, Allied forces engaged in "outpost battles" with the Chinese, for control of various hills and other important terrain features, while concurrently fighting to hold ground already dearly won with spilled blood and loss of life.[4]

1ST COMMONWEALTH DIVISION

Division Commanders

Maj. Gen. James Halkett Cassels, BA
28 July 1951-7 September 1952

Maj. Gen. Michael Alston-Roberts-West, BA
7 September 1952-1953

Shoulder Patch

The 1st Commonwealth Division was a British-commanded, multi-national force formed on 28 July 1951. It replaced the British Army's 27th Infantry Brigade, the initial Commonwealth land forces in Korea, which had arrived in country, eleven months earlier on 28 August 1950. The division was formed by combining the 29th British Brigade, 28th British Commonwealth Brigade, and 25th Canadian Brigade. The 3rd Battalion, Royal Australian Regiment (3RAR) was also part of the division when formed, owing to it being assigned to the 28th British Commonwealth Brigade. Combat arms and service unit troops from

Britain, Canada, Australia, New Zealand, and India served with the 1st Commonwealth Division during the Korean War. The division was deactivated in 1954, following the end of hostilities and a period of occupation duty.[5]

FIRST BATTLE OF MARYANG SAN

> *In this action 3RAR had won one of the most impressive victories achieved by any Australian battalion. In five days of heavy fighting 3RAR dislodged a numerically superior enemy from a position of great strength. The Australians were successful in achieving surprise on 3 and 5 October [1951], the company and platoon commanders responded skillfully to [Lt. Col. Francis George] Hassett's directions, and the individual soldiers showed high courage, tenacity and morale despite some very difficult situations, such as that of D company when the mist rose on 5 October and those of B and C Companies when the weight of enemy fire threatened their isolation of Hill 317 on 7 October .... The victory of Maryang San is probably the greatest single feat of the Australian Army during the Korean War.*
>
> —Australian historian and academic Robert O'Neill, Australia's official historian for the Korean War.[6]

Photo 3-2

Korea, 23 March 1952. View of imposing Hill 355, a part of the terrain in which the 3rd Battalion, Royal Australian Regiment, (3RAR), 1st Commonwealth Division, had been operating around and over since early November 1951. This hill (Kowang San in Korean, but referred to by soldiers as "Little Gibraltar"), which dominated the country for miles around, was captured by "C" Company, 3RAR, and the King's Own Scottish Borderers in early October 1951.
Australian War Memorial photograph 042310

The experiences of the 3rd Battalion, Royal Australian Regiment (3RAR), during bitter fighting in concert with Operation COMMANDO (5-8 October 1951), and subsequent duty on the front lines, were representative of those of the Allied ground forces. It is worth noting that 3RAR was battle hardened. Less than six months earlier, in the Battle of Kapyong (23-25 April 1951), vastly outnumbered United Nations forces had checked the Communist advance on the South Korean capital of Seoul. Two Commonwealth battalions—the 2nd Battalion of the Princess Patricia's Canadian Light Infantry Regiment (2PPCLI) and the 3rd Battalion of the Royal Australian Regiment (3RAR)—bore the brunt of the attack. Their defense of the Kapyong River Valley against an entire Chinese division helped halt the Chinese Spring Offensive, for which both regiments were awarded the United States Presidential Unit Citation.[7]

In late 1951, Chinese People's Volunteer Army forces held a group of hills overlooking the Imjin River and Commonwealth forces positioned below the high ground. The largest of these features, Maryang San (Hill 317), rose steeply above the valley, with ridges running east and west. As long as the Chinese held Maryang San, they could dominate the terrain and Commonwealth forces to the south.[8]

Earlier attempts by U.S. forces to cross the valley in front of Maryang San, and attack the hill had failed. In late September, the 1st Commonwealth Division was ordered to prepare for a general advance, termed COMMANDO, designed to push the Chinese forces back farther north of the 38th parallel. Lt. Col. Francis Hassett, commander of the 3RAR, planned to draw on the Australians' experience in New Guinea during World War II by "running the ridges." Gaining additional ground would also give the UN more leverage in the continuing armistice negotiations.[9]

On 5 October, while British regiments attacked farther west, 3RAR's A Company advanced along a difficult route up a spur southeast of the summit. Their attack was not expected to succeed, but drew Chinese defenders away from the main ridgeline, up which B and D Companies advanced from the east. In a series of bitter fights in heavy mist, D Company captured four knolls leading up the ridgeline. In the late afternoon, C Company rejoining the battalion after assisting a British attack on Kowang San (Little Gibraltar), captured a feature called "Baldy," then moved quickly to occupy the summit, which had been abandoned by the Chinese.[10]

Throughout the following day, 6 October, the Australians held the summit against heavy Chinese fire and repeated attempts to infiltrate the position. Early on 7 October, B Company captured "the Hinge," a high

58   Chapter 3

point on the ridge west of the summit, after a fierce action highlighted by a number of acts of great bravery. All next day and night the Chinese bombarded the Australian positions, making resupplies of ammunition and the evacuation of casualties difficult. That evening, 8 October, the bombardment, the heaviest yet, preceded a series of desperate and courageous Australian counter-attacks during the night. The enemy was forced to withdraw with heavy losses after each attack until, on the morning of the 9th, the Chinese gave up and the Australians' hold on Maryang San was secured.[11]

Twenty Australians were killed, and 89 wounded, in some of the heaviest fighting the Australians were to see in Korea. With the support of New Zealand and British artillery and British tanks, the Australians had succeeded in capturing Maryang San. Lieutenant Colonel Hassett (who would retire as Gen. Sir Francis George Hassett AC, KBE, CB, DSO, LVO) was awarded the Distinguished Service Order for his exemplary leadership throughout the long and bloody fight.[12]

Photo 3-3

Korea, 11 April 1952. Lt. Col. Frank G. Hassett (left) celebrates his 34th birthday with Maj. Jeffrey J. (Jim) Shelton (right) and Maj. Bill Finlayson (behind birthday cake). Australian War Memorial photograph 147774

Sadly, by 5 November 1951, after the Australians were withdrawn to recuperate, and British troops had taken over, Maryang San was recaptured by the Chinese and remained in their hands for the rest of the war. Following the loss of Maryang San and the country beyond the hill, 1st Commonwealth Division, because of exhaustion, handed over defense of most of Hill 355 ("Little Gibraltar") to the Americans who were in a position to their right. The Chinese continued their assault and, for a brief period, recaptured the hill at the end of November. The Americans took back Hill 355 and held the main portion of it, with 3RAR holding the lower left-hand part (see photograph at beginning of this section).[13]

From late autumn 1951, until the ceasefire on 27 July 1953, 3RAR's main activity was patrolling "no man's land" between the two opposing trench lines that ran along the 38th Parallel. This duty included patrols, reconnaissance, and some trench raids and minor skirmishes, which resulted in small gains or losses of territory. Overall, the front line altered very little in this time. Living conditions remained difficult. In winter it was not uncommon for temperatures to be below zero, with the risk to troops of frost-bite and trench foot. Summers were humid, and brought heavy rain that often flooded the trenches. These hardships were in addition to enemy shell and mortar fire. Following the armistice, 3RAR was involved in training and border patrols until its return to Australia in November 1954.[14]

HMS *GLORY*'S FIRST PATROL (6-15 February 1952)

HMS *Glory* (Capt. Kenneth Stewart Colquhoun, DSO RN) arrived on station off the west coast of Korea on 6 February 1952. The first sorties launched from her were over snow-covered terrain which made navigation difficult. While Sea Furies were strafing and rocketing any moving targets that were visible, Fireflies were hitting fixed targets. The first such were railroad tunnel mouths at Changyon, which they skip-bombed with 500 pounders with short-timed fuses, causing a landslide that damaged the rails. Other targets over the next couple of days included a bridge and railway tunnels at Haeju. During the middle portion of the patrol, Sea Furies carried out armed reconnaissance of the Yonan area, involving the destruction of buildings, followed by a strafing run along the beach at Paengyong-do where enemy troops were foraging and training.[15]

On 13 February, Sea Furies struck warehouses near the Koho-ri Peninsula, one of which blew up spectacularly. Fireflies attacking enemy positions near Ongjin, made a direct hit on an ammunition dump. Despite inclement weather near patrol's end, which restricted flying, Sea Furies found work along the coast, destroying vessels secreted at various points. After completing her first patrol, *Glory* set a course for Sasebo, arriving on 15 February 1952. While at anchor, replacement aircraft were transferred to her from HMS *Unicorn*.[16]

Purpose-built as an aircraft maintenance vessel, *Unicorn* had a full-length flight deck to enable the exchange of airworthy aircraft, and to allow her to function as a carrier if operationally necessary. Underneath were two hangar decks, which could accommodate up to 48 aircraft with folded wings and an additional 8 with wings spread. She had extensive workshop facilities for provision of up to depot-level maintenance. Her stern was squared off to allow aircraft engines to be moved below decks, and she carried extensive stocks of spare parts for both the Sea Fury and the Firefly. In addition to acting as an aircraft repair ship, she ferried troops, supplies, and replacement aircraft, and in 1953, she actually used her four-inch guns to bombard targets in North Korea.[17]

Photo 3-4

British aircraft maintenance carrier HMS *Unicorn* lying at anchor in a Japanese port (probably Sasebo) during the Korean War.
National Archives photograph #80-G-427411

SECOND PATROL (25 FEBRUARY-4 MARCH 1952)

Glory departed Sasebo on 24 February to relieve her counterpart, the escort carrier USS *Barioko*, and resumed flying operations the following day. Space restrictions in this book do not allow for coverage of the service of *Barioko* and other escort carriers in Korea.[18]

The focus of this patrol for *Glory*'s Sea Furies and Fireflies was targets in the Sogang-ni, Chinnampo, Changyon, Ongjin, and Koho-ri areas. These included troop concentrations, oxcarts suspected of carrying supplies, and railroad infrastructure. Marshalling yards at Sinchon, and locomotive sheds at Haeju were also hit. On 4 March,

Glory handed over patrol responsibility to *Barioko*, and departed for Kure. During her time on station, eight pilots aboard *Glory* had celebrated the completion of their 100th sortie flown from the light fleet carrier.[19]

Photo 3-5

Escort carrier USS *Barioko* (CVE-115) off San Diego, California.
Naval History and Heritage Command photograph #NH 97320

THIRD PATROL (13-23 MARCH 1952)

Glory arrived back on station on 13 March and began flying operations the following day. The targets were as before, with greater success achieved this time. On 15 March, Lt. Richard James Overton's Sea Fury was hit southwest of Punchon. Ditching off Cho-do Island, his aircraft exploded. Overton was rescued by the South Korean Navy Auxiliary Motor Minesweeper 501, but died of his wounds.[20]

A change in the normal target set occurred on 21 March, when some Sea Furies were launched to support a landing by South Korean forces at Ponghwa-ri, a village situated at the mouth of the Han River. The Han River Estuary marked the western border of the 38th Parallel.[21]

Glory returned to Sasebo on 23 March following the completion of her patrol. There, her Sea Furies were modified to carry 500lb bombs, requiring the pilots to undergoing training in their use. The first lesson involved a steep, 45-degree dive from 4,000 feet and releasing at 2,000. Experience and refinement of this technique proved that dropping from 1,500 feet, led to more accurate results.[22]

FOURTH PATROL (1-9 APRIL 1952)

When *Glory* returned to station and commenced flying on 1 April, her Sea Furies were carrying 500lb bombs fused for 30 seconds instead of rockets, joining the Fireflies as bombers. Over the next several days, pilots of both squadrons struck enemy positions and supply lines with no losses. Deviation from bombing occurred on 4 April, when Sea Furies were launched fitted with rockets instead of bombs, their targets being an enemy-held ridge north of the Imjin River. Although met with extensive anti-aircraft fire, they hit most of the specified area. On a subsequent mission, Sea Furies hit enemy barracks at Chinnampo with bombs, while Fireflies bombed villages at Yuchon-in and Changyon. On 9 April, *Glory* departed her station and headed for Kure. While berthed across the jetty from *Unicorn*, she received replacement aircraft and stores from the maintenance carrier.[23]

Photo 3-6

A Marine Corps F4U Corsair dropping napalm on enemy positions in the Imjin River sector of the Korean front lines, October 1952. The position had been captured by the enemy from South Korean Marines.
National Archives photograph #80-G-447567

FINAL PATROL OF COMMISSION (18-29 APRIL)

With personnel and ship rested and replenished, *Glory* departed Kure on 18 April on the final patrol of her tour of duty. Low cloud cover and poor visibility limited the number of sorties flown the first four days to twenty-two. Even so, Sea Furies found and destroyed three junks near Haeju, and Fireflies attacked the railways at Chinnampo. On 23 April, a US Navy Avenger delivered Captain T. A. K. Maunsell, RN, aboard. He was Captain Colquhoun's relief as commanding officer. While the change of command was taking place, the airwing's planes were attacking troop positions and T-34 tanks found hidden at Chinnampo.[24]

The following day, *Glory* replenished from the fleet oiler RFA *Green Ranger* and Colquhoun departed the ship. USS *Bataan* relieved *Glory* on station on 29 April, and the British carrier set a course for Hong Kong.[25]

USS *BATAAN*'S SECOND PATROL

Photo 3-7

Members of the famed "Checkerboards" on board USS *Bataan*.
USS *Bataan* (CVL-29) 1952-1953 Third Far Eastern cruise book

USS *Bataan*, under Capt. Harry R. Horney, USN, with Marine Attack Squadron VMA-312 (the renowned "Checkerboards") embarked, began combat sorties on 30 April 1952. This marked her second deployment to the Korean Theater for combat duty, the first having been from 15 January to 13 June 1951. The war in Korea was bogged down, with both sides heavily dug in along the 38th Parallel. Tasked with interdicting enemy supply routes between Hanchon and Yonan, the squadron's pilots flew an average of thirty sorties a day, bombing supply dumps, railway tracks, bridges, and road traffic.[26]

Three destroyers—HMCS *Cayuga* (DDE218), HMS *Constant* (DD71), and USS *Lowry* (DD-770)—served as screening vessels for *Bataan*. Late each afternoon, the screen was reduced to two ships when, one destroyer was detached to conduct a patrol of the islands south of Haeju. This area was characterized by a mass of islands, most of them very small, and an even more confused mass of peninsulas, so heavily indented that one had to look closely at a chart to distinguish between island and peninsula (mainland). A destroyer, upon completion of her patrol (codenamed Worthington), would resume screening duties the following morning after refueling from a tanker at Taochon Do.[27]

The "Worthington patrol" had been instituted when the problem of island defense became acute. It involved using screening destroyers, in rotation, to assist a ship assigned to maintain anti-invasion patrols in the area from Choppeki Point to Sunwido. Such duties provided more excitement to destroyer sailors than operating with a carrier as described by Thor Thorgrimsson and E. C. Russell in *Canadian Naval Operations in Korean Waters 1950-1955*:

> Thus once every three days a destroyer could count on relief from her monotonous screening duties and on getting the opportunity of carrying out shore bombardments, supporting guerilla raids, repelling enemy invasions and engaging in the many interesting operations that fell to the lot of the inshore patrol ships.[28]

Bataan and her screen were operating in the Korean Coastal Area "Nan" in the vicinity of 37°30'N, 124°30'E. Tasking for her F4U Corsairs included: armed air reconnaissance of the west coast of Korea from the UN front lines northward to 39°15'N, and surveillance of enemy airfields in the Haeju-Chinnampo region. Depending on their mission (armed reconnaissance, combat air patrol, target combat air control, strike, or naval gunfire support), the planes dropped or fired some combination of 500lb GB bombs, HVAR rockets, 3.25" rockets, napalm, and .50-caliber machine gun rounds.[29]

Korean War, February 1952-July 1953   65

On the evening of 10 May, following her relief on station by HMS *Ocean* (Capt. Charles Evans, DSC, DSO RN), USS *Bataan* set a course for Sasebo, accompanied by HMS *Constant*, who would later detach and proceed to Kure, Japan.[30]

HMS *OCEAN* ARRIVES IN THE KOREAN THEATER

Photo 3-8

British light fleet aircraft carrier HMS *Ocean* at anchor, location and date unknown. Australian War Memorial photograph 302467

HMS *Ocean* had departed Valetta, Malta, in April 1952, bound for Korea, ceremoniously piped out of Grand Harbour by the Pipes and Drums of the Highland Light Infantry. Following her arrival at Hong Kong, and handover with HMS *Glory*, she had proceeded to Korea to relieve *Bataan*, and take up her first war patrol. Aboard the British light fleet carrier were two Fleet Air Arm squadrons, No. 825 with a dozen Fairy Fireflies and No. 802 with twenty Hawker Sea Furies.[31]

Having a full complement of aircraft onboard, and associated personnel to operate and maintain them, created a major problem in accommodation. *Ocean* didn't have sufficient berths for the numbers of crewmen and airmen aboard. Sleeping space was at a premium, even for slinging hammocks. Additionally, *Ocean* operating in the Far East in summer was not equipped with air conditioning. By comparison, the

American carriers she met up with in Sasebo, offered ice cream, bunks and associated personal space for everyone.[32]

As had long been the practice, the British and Australian carriers operated in the Yellow Sea off Korea's west coast, alternating duty with the light fleet carrier *Bataan* (CVL-29), or escort carrier USS *Badoeng Strait* (CVE-116), USS *Barioko* (CVE-115), USS *Rendova* (CVE-114), or USS *Sicily* (CVE-118). All four of these escort carriers served in Korea. Two-week operational periods were followed by return to Sasebo, Kure, or Kobe, Japan, for a fortnight period of re-supply, rest, and maintenance. The much larger American 7th Fleet aircraft carriers kept to the east coast in the Sea of Japan.[33]

The several British and the one Australian carrier operating off Korea's west coast were usually stationed about sixty miles southwest of Haeju and operated with a screen of six destroyers and similar ships that alternated with other duties. The destroyers included HM Canadian Ship *Iroquois* and HM Australian ships *Bataan* (same name as USS *Bataan*) and *Kimberley*. All of the islands off the coast were in Allied hands, so the primary role of carrier aircraft was to provide air support for them, and to quiet enemy guns shelling them from the mainland. In addition to employing bombs and rockets to do so, *Ocean*'s planes also spotted the gunfire of ships shelling targets ashore. Among the beneficiaries of their reports were the light cruiser HMS *Belfast*, and battleship USS *Missouri* (BB-63).[34]

The preceding information is from an article by Russ Mallace, about *Ocean*'s deployment to Korean waters from May to October 1952. The Hawker Sea Fury pilot summarized other duties of the British light carrier's embarked squadrons, including air strikes on land targets and defense of Allied troops:

> Role 2 was to carry out armed reconnaissance flights over all of our patch [operating area] to knock out road and rail bridges, transport and in general to prevent the build-up of troops and supplies that had provided the means for previous, offensive actions. This activity amounted to about two thirds of our operations.
>
> Role 3 was close air support for the [1st] Commonwealth Division NE of Seoul and on occasions for a US Marine Brigade.[35]

Mallace also described the necessity at times to use rocket-assisted take off from *Ocean*, owing to the ship's inability, when the prevailing winds were calm, to develop enough speed to produce sufficient relative wind across her flight deck to get aircraft aloft:

The Light Fleet carriers had a design speed of 25 knots but at 22 knots, with the ship vibrating to bits and the engine room becoming hotter and hotter, that was our practical maximum. The usual way of launching aircraft was by means of the catapult.... It had a track length of just under 50 yards and could accelerate the aircraft to 66 knots. The lack of ship's speed was a problem.

To fly, a Sea Fury needs 90 knots of airflow over the wings. So with the ship doing 22 knots in calm air you would just about have enough airflow over the wings to get airborne. The ship always turned into wind to launch and recover aircraft, but the name Korea means "Land of the Morning Calm" so windless mornings were not uncommon. With 1000lb bombs mounted more like 95 knots was needed so... rocket assisted take off ... was used instead of the catapult. Rockets were attached to the underside of the aircraft and the take-off run was started from the stern of the ship. At a predetermined point on the take-off run you would fire the rockets and heigh-ho you hopefully found yourself up in the air.... The rocket carriers were jettisoned after take-off.[36]

During *Ocean*'s six-month deployment to Korea from 5 May to 8 November 1952, No. 802 squadron, to which Mallace was assigned, flew 3,964 sorties. Seven hundred thirty-five of these involved RATOG (Rocket-Assisted Take Off Gear). After the light fleet carrier had returned to Britain, at Lee on Solent, in early 1953, both 802 and 825 squadrons were awarded the Boyd Trophy for their combat operations in Korea. The trophy was a silver model of a Fairey Swordfish, mounted on the upturned tail of a swordfish, which was presented by the Fairey Aviation Company Limited in 1946, in commemoration of the work for Naval Aviation of Adm. Sir Denis Boyd, KCB, CBE, DSC RN. The coveted trophy was awarded annually to the naval pilot(s) or aircrew who, in the opinion of the flag officer, Naval Air Command, had achieved the finest feat of aviation during the previous year.[37]

BATAAN'S SECOND PATROL (18-28 MAY 1952)

Bataan relieved *Ocean* on 18 May 1952, and took up her second patrol. In addition to commanding Task Element 95.11, Captain Horney was officer in tactical command, West Coast of Korea, for a few days until Rear Adm. Alan Kenneth Scott-Moncrieff, RN, entered the area aboard HMS *Constant* (DD71) on the 21st. (Scott-Moncrieff was commander, West Coast Blockade Force.) As before, *Bataan* operated in Area Nan, screened by three destroyers—HMS *Conus* (DD20), HMNS *Piet Hein* (DD-805), and USS *Marsh* (DE-699)—except when, one at a time, in rotation, they engaged in Worthington patrols.[38]

During *Bataan*'s nine-day patrol, Squadron VMA-312 aircraft flew 296 combat sorties and 1 photo sortie, while carrying out armed reconnaissance, target combat air patrol, combat air patrol, pre-briefed strikes, and photo and air spots for naval gunfire missions. On 22 May, a F4U-4 Corsair, piloted by Capt. William J. Barbanes, USMC, was shot down behind enemy lines near Sukchon, North Korea, while flying an armed recon mission. After landing his plane in a rice paddy and taking cover, the downed pilot's wingmates protected him from the enemy by strafing, and directing an Air Force helicopter to the scene. The rescue aircraft picked up Barbanes while under heavy fire, and returned him aboard *Bataan* for duty the following day.[39]

Photo 3-9

View of *Bataan*'s flight deck, island structure, and flight deck personnel.
USS *Bataan* (CVL-29) 1952-1953 Third Far Eastern cruise book

HMS *Ocean* relieved *Bataan* on 28 May 1952, upon which *Bataan* proceeded to Yokosuka for repairs to her flight deck. Six days earlier, shortly after Barbanes had been shot down, a VMA-312 Corsair had landed aboard the light fleet carrier with three hung rockets—one dangling by an attaching lug. As the plane set down, all three rockets came loose and continued up the flight deck. One came to rest on the cargo net rocket barrier, the second struck a cross deck pendant and was deflected aft to a position near the LSO (Landing Signal Officer) platform. The third continued to bounce end-over-end, until its nose struck the deck directly above No. 5 arresting gear engine and exploded. Resultant damage included: plane towing tractors set afire, a three-foot hole in the flight deck, major damage to the arresting gear engine, with injuries to three crewmen by the rocket fragments.[40]

BATAAN'S THIRD PATROL (5-16 JUNE 1952)

Following repairs in Yokosuka, *Bataan* conducted three more Yellow Sea patrols in June and July, continuing the slow and frustrating task of attacking enemy supply lines. As before, she was screened at any given time by a maximum of three destroyers, and Worthington patrols continued. The destroyers were HMAS *Warramunga* (D123), HMS *Comus* (D20), HMS *Consort* (D76), and USS *Arnold J. Isbell* (DD869).[41]

During the carrier's nine days on station, VMA-312 aircraft flew 377 combat sorties; highlights of damage inflicted follow:

- 7 June: Damage included 65 troops killed in action, hitting of supply dumps, and attacking junk shipping
- 10 June: Armed recon in the Chinnampo-Chacryong-Yonan area with principal target being the destruction of 40 boats
- 11 June: Destruction of one large factory
- 12 June: Forty-five troops killed; eight gun-positions damaged
- 13 June: Armed recon attacked 200 troops with unassessed damage, one observation post destroyed, and seven gun-positions damaged
- 14 June: Primary targets were destruction of 95 buildings, two gun-positions, and killing of 34 enemy troops[42]

On 9 June, Marine Capt. James J. Kraus Jr. was shot down west of Chinnampo. After his F4U caught fire in mid-air, he was able to parachute to safety after having suffered second and third degree burns to his hands and face. Picked up by a helicopter in less than an hour, he was taken to a hospital in Seoul.[43]

BATAAN'S FOURTH PATROL (25 JUNE-3 JULY 1952)

Bataan, heading seaward from Sasebo in company with HMCS *Iroquois* (DDE217), on 23 June, to take up another patrol, experienced the effects of Typhoon DINAH before leaving the channel. After encountering heavy seas and high winds, the aircraft that were to fly aboard, were ordered to remain at the airbase at Itazuko, Japan.

Typhoon Condition I was set aboard the two ships, and they proceeded along the lee (westward side) of the Tsushima Islands in the Korean Strait. The weather abated somewhat that evening. Typhoon Condition III was set aboard ship at 1840, and *Bataan* with escort proceeded southward toward a permitted area for carrier flying operations near Iki Shima.[44]

On 24 June, the following morning, fourteen VMA-312 aircraft flew aboard *Bataan*, bringing the squadron total to twenty-four Corsairs. Of the 400 sorties scheduled during the nine-day operating period, forty percent were cancelled due to the weather. As a result of the 236 combat sorties flown, damage wrought by strikes on enemy forces, their supporting infrastructure, and logistics lines included:

- 25 June: Destruction of 103 buildings and 3 gun-positions, and seven railroad cuts (breeches of railroad tracks)
- 26 June: One hundred seven buildings destroyed
- 27 June: Flight of four aircraft discovered 1,000 troops, killing and wounding over 300 enemy combatants
- 28 June: Twenty-four troops killed and railroad tunnel closed (bombed)
- 30 June: Three railroad bridges and one transformer station damaged
- 1 July: Eight railroad cars destroyed and nine boats damaged
- 3 July: Principal damage inflicted on final day of operating period was eight rail cuts[45]

Following handoff to HMS *Ocean* at 2100 on 3 July, *Bataan* set a course for Sasebo.[46]

BATAAN'S FIFTH PATROL (12-21 JULY)

On the evening of 12 July 1952, *Bataan*'s commanding officer, Captain Horney, assumed command of Task Element 95.11 in Korean Coastal Area Nan. During her patrol, destroyers USS *John R. Craig* (DD-885), USS *Nicholas* (DDE-449), HMAS *Bataan* (D191), HMAS *Warramunga* (D123), and HMCS *Iroquois* (DDE217) acted as screening vessels. No more than four of these ships were assigned at a given time and, as was the convention, one unit of the screen was released daily for night patrol.[47]

These patrols were not pleasure jaunts. *Iroquois*, for example, engaged in daytime screening of aircraft carriers off the west coast of Korea in late June and July. At night she patrolled off Pengyong-do and Cho-do, usually with HMS *Belfast*. While operating with HMS *Ceylon* and HMS *Amethyst*, she shelled the southern tip of the Ongjin Peninsula where enemy forces were moving in by land, and on coastal defenses in the approaches to Haeju, a city located near Haeju Bay in North Korea. In August, *Iroquois* took up a patrol of the bay, which included the bombardment of Mu-do Island.[48]

Photo 3-10

Iroquois's commanding officer, Comdr. William Landymore (viewer's left), and principal armament control officer, Lt. George MacFarlane (left and forward of Landymore), search for and select gunnery targets during action on the Korean coast.
Courtesy of John MacFarlane

Marine Attack Squadron VMA-312 began flying combat sorties the morning of the 13th. Primary F4U Corsair targets included buildings, 113 of which were destroyed. Twenty-six sorties launched the following morning resulted in 172 enemy troops killed, and the destruction of a command post.[49]

DEFENSE OF CHANGNIN-DO ISLAND

> For limited offensives up to a few thousand meters [inland], the [guerrillas] were very good offensive fighters, because they all knew how to use the bayonet, rifle and hand grenade. Therefore, we were able to carry out some creditable military operations.
>
> —Lt. Col. Jay D. Vanderpool, commander of the U.S. Eighth Army's guerrilla unit in Korea.[50]

At 0944 on 15 July, *Bataan* received a report from Marine Col. James T. Wilbur, commander, West Coast Island Defense Element (CTE 95.15), of an amphibious invasion of Changnin-do by North Korean forces. This report was accompanied by a request for strike and target combat air patrol support. Squadron VMA-312 aircraft assigned to other missions were immediately diverted, and the remainder of the day's schedule was revised to provide all possible assistance.[51]

Changnin-do was one of many islands in the Yalu River Estuary, part of a long string of islands originating off northwest Korea that extended down around the peninsula to Pusan in the southeast. Some of these islands were of great tactical importance to Allied forces. Friendly, guerrilla-held islands were ideally suited for radar units and signal intercept stations, and also served as bases for other elements. They offered safe haven for helicopter teams and boat crews dedicated to rescuing downed airmen. Islands behind enemy lines, in particular, served as springboards for guerrilla actions and agent insertions.[52]

Additionally, guerrillas occupied key terrain that controlled several Yellow Sea choke points. Their control of these friendly islands limited enemy movements around the mouth of the Yalu River, into the port cities of Chinnampo and Haeju, and within the important Han River Estuary. Allied control of the sea, gained with guerrilla assistance, forced all supply support for the enemy front lines to move overland or by rail, making them vulnerable to air attacks.[53]

U.S. Eighth Army involvement with guerrilla activities had begun on 23 January 1951. On this date, an ad hoc command (titled the Attrition Section, Miscellaneous Division) was formed in an effort to administer and direct the operations of "partisans" occupying relatively secure enclaves on both coasts of the Korean Peninsula. The "guerrilla command" underwent several name changes. At this point in the war, it was titled the 8240th AU (Army Unit). On the West Coast, US Army Task Force LEOPARD personnel provided instruction and training for its guerrilla units in weapons proficiency, demolitions, infantry small unit tactics, ambush techniques, and communications.[54]

In November 1951, Communist forces had seized western islands near the mouth of the Yalu, when the 1,000 defenders on the islands were unable to stem the assault. In recognition of the vulnerability of critical islands to amphibious assault, additional support for the Republic of Korea (ROK) Marines and guerrillas holding the outposts was forthcoming. On 6 January 1952, commander, Blockading and Escort Force (CTF 95) became responsible for the defense of all islands north of the 38th Parallel along both coasts. Total responsibility for the sea, air, and land elements of northern island defense was now vested, for the first time, in a single commander.[55]

Returning to our account of the defense of Changnin-do, on 15 July 1952, the friendly, guerrilla-held island was invaded by 156 North Korean Army (NKA) soldiers in two sail junks and four wooden folding boats equipped with outboard motors. The light cruiser HMS *Belfast* (C35), sloop HMS *Amethyst* (F116) and aircraft from *Bataan* assisted friendlies by engaging targets of opportunity. *Amethyst* was taken under fire by a 75/76mm battery but was not hit. The Allied surface ships, after engaging in counterbattery fire, which caused secondary explosions, and silenced enemy guns, surrounded the island and awaited counterattack by friendly forces. (*Amethyst* later took part in the 1957 film *Yangtse Incident: The Story of HMS Amethyst*, depicting the heroics of her crew on the Yangtse River during the Chinese Civil War in the summer of 1949.)[56]

Bataan's contributions continued on 16 July, when forty-four VMA-312 aircraft were launched with their main effort directed toward the retaking of Changnin-do. That morning, a Corsair piloted by Marine Capt. Charles L. Duncan, was damaged by gunfire at Changnin-do and forced to ditch off the island. A small boat from *Amethyst* later retrieved Duncan from his life raft, and he was returned by the Worthington Patrol destroyer to *Bataan* two days later.[57]

Friendly guerrillas recaptured the island on the 17th, supported by the *Belfast*, *Amethyst*, and South Korean submarine chaser *Kum Kang San* (PC-702). Of the 156-man NKA invasion force, 60 enemy soldiers were killed, 30 drowned while trying to escape, 41 were taken prisoner, and five went missing. Friendly losses were eight killed, and 12 wounded.[58]

Photo 3-11

Kum Kang San (formerly USS *PC-799*) off the Mare Island Naval Shipyard In California, 17 June 1950, following transfer to the South Korean Navy. Naval History and Heritage Command photograph #NH 85482

RETURN TO USUAL/RECURRING AIR OPERATIONS

With the securing of Changnin-do on the morning of 17 July 1952, Corsairs from *Bataan* returned to a normal schedule of combat air patrol, target combat air patrol, and reconnaissance flights. Over the few remaining days, aircraft attacked buildings, a railroad station and tracks, a radio-radar station, and a power plant and substations. At 2100 on 21 July, HMS *Ocean* relieved *Bataan*. She then set course for Inchon Harbor. There, after offloading VMA-312 gear and personnel, *Bataan* got under way for Sasebo. She arrived there on 23 July, having completed her second tour (consisting of five patrols) in Korean waters. *Bataan* would next return to the theater in February 1953.[59]

HMS *OCEAN* COMBAT AIR OPERATIONS IN KOREA

> *In August on our sixth patrol we unexpectedly found a major new hazard in the form of enemy MiG15 jet fighters. Out of the blue, literally, we found ourselves being bounced by Migs. Over the next few days three of our planes were hit but not shot down and a flight led by Lt. Hoagy Carmichael shot down a Mig and so became the first and I believe only piston engine aircraft to shoot down a jet fighter. Hoagy was awarded the DSC. We had blithely assumed that the US Air Force Sabre jet fighters were keeping the Migs busy but due to restricted engine hours the Sabres were only flying fighter sweeps up to the Yalu River on Tuesday and Thursday afternoons. We restricted how far north we flew until the normal pattern resumed.*
>
> —Russ Mallace describing Lt. Peter (Hoagy) Carmichael, a fellow 802 Squadron fighter pilot, shooting down an enemy MiG-15 on 9 August 1952 in the vicinity of Chinnampo. Carmichael, flying a Hawker Sea Fury, was leading a four-aircraft formation to attack railway facilities between Manchon and Pyongyang.[60]

A highlight of HMS *Ocean*'s first tour of duty in the Korean Theater (5 May to 8 November 1952), occurred on 9 August. On that date, Lt. Peter "Hoagy" Carmichael was leading a flight of No. 802 Squadron Sea Furies toward a transportation nerve center between Pyongyang and Manchon, used by North Korean and Chinese forces to move around materiel, supplies, and troops. The four planes were flying in a combat formation, about one mile wide, which would allow them to spot enemy aircraft quicker and made them feel less vulnerable to ground fire. To Carmichael's left was his wingman, Sub Lt. Carl Haines, known to have the "sharpest eyes" in the fleet, and to his right, were Sub Lt. Peter Davis and his wingman, Sub Lt. Brian Ellis.[61]

The British flight encountered enemy MiGs at around 0600, when Haines sighted aircraft diving out of the sun over his right shoulder, and called out over the radio, "MiGs four o'clock high." Ellis, who was nearest the fast-approaching enemy, called a break in formation. The Sea Furies crossed over, the right pair taking the lead, then increased to maximum speed in a climbing turn toward the enemy. Each Royal Navy pilot tried to get into position for a high deflection shot if the opportunity presented itself. Carmichael later described the situation:

> Eight MiGs came at us out of the sun. I did not see them at first, and my No. 4, 'Smoo' Ellis, gave a break when he noticed tracer streaming past his fuselage. We all turned towards the MiGs and commenced a 'scissors.' It soon became apparent that four MiGs were after each section of two Furies, but by continuing our breaking turns, we presented impossible targets. They made no attempt to bracket us.[62]

Photo 3-12

Mikoyan Gurevich MiG-15B fighter aircraft in a hangar at Kimpo air base, South Korea, 21 September 1953. North Korean Senior Lt. No Kum-Sok (today Kenneth Rowe), deciding to defect to South Korea, had suddenly landed at the airbase near Seoul. The plane is, today, on display at the US Air Force Museum in Dayton, Ohio.
USAF photograph

In the ensuing four minutes of air combat, one MiG broke away from his wingman and screamed toward Carmichael. Reacting quickly to a split-second opportunity to engage it, Hoagy loosed a burst of cannon fire in the MiG's direction as it rushed past. As Carmichael banked, then jinked (dodged) away, radio chatter indicated that Haines had gotten a hit on the same fighter. After the third and fourth Royal Navy pilots, Lt. Pete Davis and Sub Lt. Brian Ellis, fired in the direction of the retreating MiG, the stricken aircraft began spewing smoke, veered sharply off course, and crashed into the ground. With one MiG "killed" and two or three others damaged, the survivors disengaged from the action, and left the area.[63]

As their adversaries retired, the Sea Furies returned to the carrier. Being the flight leader, Hoagy was awarded the kill. However, he felt that the MiG's downing was the result of a team effort from his wingman, Haines, and Davis and Ellis.[64]

HMS *GLORY* RELIEVES HMS *OCEAN* IN THEATER

On 8 November 1952, *Glory* returned to Korea waters to begin her third and last tour, relieved sister ship *Ocean*, and took up patrol duties. Her operations in Korean waters lasted through 19 May 1953, during which she received a new commanding officer; a flight of her Sea Furies was attacked by MiG-15s; and she lost to combat action or other causes, several pilots of Squadrons No. 801 (Sea Furies) and No. 821 (Fireflies), as well as her search and rescue helicopter with crew. The downed airmen, listed here, were all designated, "Missing, Presumed Killed."

Date	Sqd	Name(s)	Aircraft Loss Cause
18 Nov 52	801	Lt. Richard Nevile-Jones, MPK	Plane hit by flak at Sinwon Railway, caught fire and went into spin
16 Dec 52	SAR helo	Lt. Alan P. Daniels, MPK A1C Ernest R. Ripley, MPK	Helicopter crew, air crash
20 Dec 52	821	Lt. Peter D. Fogden, MPK	Starboard wing caught fire while attacking junk south of Haeju, plane exploded
25 Dec 52	821	Lt. Robert E. Barrett, MPK	Hit by flak west of Haeju, failed to recover from dive
5 Jan 53	801	Sub Lt. Brian E. Rayner, MPK; Sub Lt. James M. Simonds, RNVR, MPK	Air crash
11 Feb 53	801	Lt. Cedric MacPherson, MPK; Sub Lt. Richard D. Bradley, MPK	Air crash
25 Apr 53	801	Lt. John T. McGregor, MPK; Sub Lt. Walter J. B. Keates, MPK[65]	Air crash

On 14 December, Royal Navy Captain Edgar D. G. Lewin (holder of the DSO, DSC & Bar) took command of *Glory*. Highly decorated, in World War II he'd been a pilot aboard the light cruiser HMS *Ajax* during the Battle of the River Plate, on 13 December 1939, in which he reported the movements of the *Admiral Graf Spee*. Later in the war, he had taken part in attacks on the German battleship *Tirpitz*, ultimately sunk by Royal Air Force bombers, on 12 November 1944.[66]

The biggest concern of the pilots of propeller-driven Sea Furies and Fireflies were possible encounters with enemy MiG jet aircraft, particularly when operating near "MiG Alley." This moniker referred to a wedge-shaped area in northwestern North Korea between the Chongchon and the Yalu rivers, where the Yalu dumped into the Yellow Sea. In August 1950, a Soviet air division with 122 MiG-15 jet fighters had set up headquarters at Antung, in northeastern China on the Yalu River, the boundary between Chinese Manchuria and North Korea.[67]

The MiG-15, which was primarily designed as a bomber interceptor, included armor protection for the pilot, a bullet-resistant windscreen, self-sealing fuel tanks, a rugged structural design, and heavy armament, including two 23-mm and one 37-mm cannon. The MiG-15 was superior in performance to all Allied fighter aircraft with the exception of the F-86 Sabre. In addition, the MiG-15 had the advantage of a more lethal cannon armament compared to the F-86, F-84, and F-80C .50-caliber machine gun armament.[68]

In February 1953, during *Glory*'s patrol, a group of MiGs dove down from a great altitude on a flight from No. 801 Squadron. The MiGs took the Sea Furies under fire, but the enemy passed so rapidly through their formation, no hits were scored.[69]

Of the five Commonwealth light fleet aircraft carriers, HMS *Glory* saw the most action in the Korean War. During her service, she equaled HMS *Ocean*'s record of 123 sorties in a single day. This accomplishment required that every pilot, including "Commander Air" (the embarked wing commander) fly four sorties. That day's activity resulted in the destruction of seven bridges, twenty-eight buildings, and five oxcarts. During *Glory*'s three tours of duty in Korea, total losses to the enemy inflicted by her aircraft included: 70 bridges, 392 vehicles, and 49 railway trucks. The damage wrought to North Korean supply lines cost *Glory* the lives of twenty pilots and aircrewmen.[70]

BATAAN'S THIRD DEPLOYMENT TO KOREA

At 2100 on 15 February 1953, following her arrival in Korean Coastal Area Nan, USS *Bataan* relieved HMS *Glory* of command of Task Unit 95.1.1, beginning her third deployment of the war to Korean waters.

Over the next eighty days or so, she would make five patrols—the last one ending on 5 May 1953. During the first one through 25 February, she was screened by a maximum of five vessels at any particular time. These ships were: USS *McCord* (DD-534), USS *Hanson* (DDR-832), USS *Hanna* (DE-449), HMS *Cockade* (DD34), HMCS *Haida* (DD215), HMCS *Crusader*, and HMAS *Azac* (DD37).[71]

An average day "on the line," in the Yellow Sea off the west coast of Korea, began at a pre-dawn hour. Preparation by the Air Department, for launch of the first flight of the day, began with hot cups of coffee from the mess decks. Half an hour before dawn, other men hustled to their gun and lookout stations for "dawn alert"—an increased state of combat readiness as the sun rose. During this period, lookouts scanned the pre-dawn skies in search of possible enemy aircraft.[72]

Photo 3-13

USS *Bataan* sailors manning a gun mount during a daily "cold dawn alert."
USS *Bataan* (CVL-29) 1952-1953 Third Far Eastern cruise book

Concurrently, *Bataan*'s flight deck and hanger deck became a bustling airfield, and soon the noise of F4U Corsairs starting engines split the early morning silence. Upon signal, the first plane's engine of VMA-312 roared to a higher pitch, then it soared into the pre-dawn darkness to commence, with the other joined planes of its flight, the day's hostilities against the enemy. The strength of the embarked Marine Attack Squadron was 34 officers, 170 enlisted men, and a mixture of 13 F4U-4 and 11 F4U-4B Corsairs. In carrying out their various missions, the "Checkboards" now had another strike weapon, the 11.75-inch Tiny Tim air-to-ground rocket, at their disposal.[73]

ENCOUNTER WITH NORTH KOREAN MIGS

On 17 February 1953, sudden and heavy snow showers with visibility of less than a mile at sea, forced the cancellation of the morning Han River reconnaissance flight. Ten planes of Squadron VMA-312, airborne at the time, were diverted to K-6, a USAF base, for landing. The United States Air Force had numerous air bases in Korea, many former Japanese airfields. Because the spelling of Korean locations on maps varied greatly, and villages had both a Korean and a Japanese name, the USAF used "K" numbers to identify air bases, to thereby prevent confusion among locations. Airbase K-6 was at Pyongtaek.[74]

The weather cleared later in the day, and air operations resumed. F4U Corsairs damaged six buildings and one gun position, and were responsible for three "road cuts" (reference to the destruction of sections of roads). On the final flight of the day, five F4Us exchanged head-on firing runs with six MiGs encountered. No hits were observed for either side. Occasional sightings of enemy MiGs in the months ahead would keep the VMA-312 pilots watchful, but only a few combat actions occurred. Despite performance advantages that jet aircraft held over piston driven-planes, the Communist pilots seemed reluctant to attack. However, this may have been dependent on the nationality of the enemy pilots.[75]

The U.S. Fifth Air Force believed that many of the MiG pilots its F-86 Sabre fighters engaged in combat were Russian, not Chinese or Korean. This belief was based on sightings of Russians in the cockpits of MiGs, and U.S. intelligence intercepts of radio transmissions. It was decades later, before the Soviet Union publicly admitted the participation of its pilots in the Korean War. In order to keep secret their involvement, Russian pilots had been ordered to speak only Korean or Chinese language on the radio. This proved untenable as fighter ace Col. Yevgeny G. Pepelyayev later explained:

> It was impossible psychologically in the heat of battle to use a foreign language you hardly knew. So after a week or two we just decided to ignore the order. The top brass started complaining, so I told them: 'Go and fight yourselves!'[76]

Pepelyayev was Russia's top ace in the Korean War. He flew 109 combat sorties, participated in 38 aerial combats, and was credited with 19 victories against American aircraft (14 F-86s, two F-84s, one F-80, and two F-94s).[77]

Time has revealed that North Korean and Chinese pilots flew Chinese-built MiGs, and the Russians flew the Soviet-built version. The Soviets were first encountered in combat, on 1 November 1950, with the Soviet pilots wearing Chinese uniforms. The Soviets operated from Chinese air bases where they were safe from UN attacks. Basically, Soviet pilots could operate down to a roughly East-West line stretching from Wonsan to Pyongyang, just as UN airmen were restricted from crossing the Yalu River. While Soviet MiG-15 pilots could hold their own in a fight, Chinese and North Korean pilots fared poorly without Soviet assistance. This became evident when Chinese and North Korean pilots crossed the Wonsan-Pyongyang line and entered areas where the Soviet airmen couldn't fly.[78]

MARINE ATTACK SQUADRON VMA-312 MISSIONS

VMA-312's activities during this and ensuing patrols mostly involved combat air patrol, armed reconnaissance, prebriefed strikes, photo and weather reconnaissance, and air spotting for naval gunfire. As was usual in striking enemy positions and interdicting supply lines, Corsair pilots damaged or destroyed barracks areas, gun positions, buildings, railroad bridges, and road bridges, and cut railway lines and roads. On 21 February, the prize target was an enemy artillery field piece which the Checkerboard Marine pilots destroyed with 500lb bombs and napalm. Twenty-seven buildings were destroyed in a troop housing area, and twenty-five damaged.[79]

The following day, 22 February, Corsair pilots took advantage of perfect flying weather by holding a "field day" with the destruction of fifty-nine buildings in a Communist troop housing area. Capt. Malcolm A. Hill, USMC, had a close call, when small arms fire passed under his seat and emerged from the right side of the cockpit of his plane. Flying activities, the following day climaxed with brilliant teamwork between an air-spotting flight and HMCS *Crusader*, whose shore bombardment made direct hits on enemy troops and coastal gun positions. *Crusader* held the record for the Trainbuster Club (TBC).[80]

The TBC came into existence in July 1952, when the destroyer USS *Orleck* (DD-886) destroyed two trains during a two-week period. Commander, Task Force 95, recognizing a morale booster when he saw one, declared *Orleck* the train busting champion and issued a challenge to the other American ships involved in shore bombardment to beat that score. Although an ad hoc US Navy club, in the spirit of fairness and competition, the challenge to destroy trains was eventually extended to the ships of other navies. Membership in the club required that the train's engine be destroyed. However, southbound trains running the gauntlet in the Taeback Mountain range and laden with war materiel, were considered much more valuable targets than northbound trains which were essentially empty.[81]

Korean train engineers soon appreciated what "hell on earth" meant. During daylight, they hid in tunnels hoping that the entrances and exits did not get blocked by the persistent and accurate shelling of the naval guns, or skip-bombing by carrier aircraft. Out of the twenty-eight kills officially tallied by the TBC, the RCN accounted for eight, compliments of HMCS *Crusader*, *Haida*, and *Athabaskan*. The individual champion among Allied ships was *Crusader*, which bagged four trains, three of them in a single twenty-four-hour period. Trainbusting required great patience, a bit of luck, and superb gunnery. Targets were often elusive and, if present, poor weather might keep ships well out to sea, requiring the guns to perform at maximum range and hit a speeding target. Fog or rain also made verification of damage very difficult.[82]

DOWNED PILOT SAVED BY FELLOW F4U PILOTS AND AIR COMMANDO RESCUE HELICOPTER CREW

In late morning on 24 February 1953, David Cleeland, USMC, leader of a flight of four VMA-312 Corsairs, was hit by enemy ground fire ten miles north of Haeju, and crash-landed on the frozen Annyong reservoir. Heroic actions by a US Air Force special operations helicopter to save him, while U.S. planes overhead and enemy ground troops exchanged fire, is the subject of the first chapter of this book.

TURNOVER OF PATROL DUTIES TO HMS *GLORY*

On 25 February 1953, the day following the rescue of Major Cleeland, his squadron mates destroyed twenty-two buildings and a warehouse in a strike thirteen miles south of Haeju. After the last flight of the day, five F4Us proceeded from the target area to K-3 (Pohang-dong) to receive maintenance and compass corrections. That evening, *Bataan* departed the area for Sasebo, following her relief by HMS *Glory* as flag ship, Task Unit 95.1.1.[83]

BATAAN'S SECOND PATROL

On 6 March 1953, Captain Horney took command of Task Unit 95.1.1 at 2100, commencing *Bataan*'s second patrol in Coastal Area Nan. Squadron VMA-312 personnel and aircraft were embarked and a maximum of five destroyers comprised her screen. Serving in this role at various times, were the American USS *McCord* (DD-534), *Higbee* (DDR-806), and *Hanson* (DDR-832), Canadian HMCS *Haida* (DD-215) and *Crusader* (DD228), and Australian HMAS *Anzac* (DD37).[84]

The type of targets hit by aircraft over the next several days were much the same as during *Bataan*'s first patrol. Losses inflicted on the enemy included damaged or destroyed gun positions, buildings, troop billeting, a petroleum dump, railroad bridges, rail cuts, and a few strafed troops. On 10 March, in a Change of Command ceremony aboard ship, Capt. Shirley Snow Miller relieved Capt. Harry Ray Horney as commanding officer, USS *Bataan*. Miller, whose nickname at the Naval Academy had been Steamship (presumably because of his initials, S.S.), would end his career as a rear admiral.[85]

Photo 3-14

At left: Capt. Harry Ray Horney, USN; and at right, Capt. Shirley Snow Miller, USN. USS *Bataan* (CVL-29) 1952-1953 Third Far Eastern cruise book

In perfect flying weather, on 15 March, Marine pilots of VMA-312 inflicted the heaviest damage of the patrol. Eight enemy railroad cars were destroyed three miles northeast of Haeju, when they were sighted four miles from a tunnel entrance. Additionally, two railroad bridges were knocked out, one rail cut was made, and 1/4 mile of track was destroyed. Two possible radar towers, and one transformer were destroyed. Finally, three medium automatic weapons positions were neutralized, and an estimated twenty troops killed when trenches were strafed. At 2100, HMS *Glory* assumed the duties of CTU 95.1.1, and *Bataan* departed for Sasebo.[86]

Over the next several weeks, *Bataan* conducted three more "line tours" (patrols) between 25 March and 5 May 1953, before departing the west coast of Korea for the last time:

- 25 March-4 April 1953
- 11-20 April 1953
- 27 April-5 May 1953[87]

Despite poor flying weather associated with the spring thaw, VMA-312 continued to attack enemy troop concentrations and supply dumps reported by friendly partisans. The "Checkerboard" pilots also worked over roads, railways, and especially bridges, as flood waters hampered North Korean repair efforts.[88]

LAST CVL ON COMBAT DUTY IN KOREAN WATERS

HMS *Ocean* (Capt. Brian E. W. Logan, RN) was the last Allied light fleet carrier to serve in the war zone. Her second tour in the Korean Theater began near war's end on 17 May 1953, and lasted nine weeks, ending on 23 July. *Ocean* arrived at Sasebo from Malta, on 17 May, with No. 807 (21 Sea Furies XI) and No. 810 Squadrons (12 Fireflies V) embarked. She sailed from Sasebo on the 21st, and relieved the escort carrier USS *Barioko* as CTU 95.1.1 off the west coast of Korea.[89]

Operations during *Ocean*'s first patrol were directed largely against enemy communications, stores, troops, guns, and buildings. She provided close air support for the 1st Commonwealth Division and for partisans as requested, and naval gunfire spotting for the battleship USS *New Jersey* (BB-62), and light cruiser HMS *Newcastle* (C76). On 30 May, Rear Adm. Eric George Anderson Clifford, RN (Flag Officer Second-in-Command Far East Fleet) transferred from *Newcastle* to *Ocean* for passage to Sasebo, and she left the area. Clifford had become the final senior British naval officer in the Korean Theater when he took command of the Commonwealth forces in September 1952.[90]

Ocean relieved *Barioko* on station on 8 June 1953, the day United Nations Command and Communist delegates at Panmunjom signed an agreement for the repatriation of prisoners of war. During *Ocean*'s patrol, the Chinese were exercising increased pressure on sections of the front lines and, as a result, her aircraft devoted much of their effort to providing close support for the troops. *Ocean* also flew more sorties than usual for target CAP (combat air patrol over a strike force) to cover the withdrawal of personnel from inshore islands, or assist in silencing shore batteries.[91]

On 17 June, *Ocean* turned over her duties as CTU 95.1.1 to *Barioko* and proceeded to Kure. She sailed from there, on 25 June, and after a very foggy passage, resumed task unit command duties two days later. Fog, rain, and low cloud cover reduced the number of sorties on four days of the patrol, and on three other days targets were obscured. Considerable effort was again expended on close air support over the front lines, and efforts continued against the usual targets. *Barioko* took over on 5 July, and *Ocean* proceeded to Sasebo.[92]

Ocean carried out her last patrol from 15-23 July, once again in unfavorable weather. During this patrol, the thousandth landing was made and, by its completion, 1,197 had been achieved. In addition to support provided for the United States 8th Army, and the usual sorties flown against enemy troops, supply lines, weapons positions, and so on, a new commitment was undertaken at the request of the U.S. 5th Air Force. A small unit of three Firefly aircraft with seven officers and sixteen ratings were disembarked, on 17 July, to K-6 airfield at Pyongtaek (forty miles south of Seoul) for use as night fighters against slow, low-flying enemy aircraft. Twenty-one hours of day training, and eight of night training, preceded twenty-six hours of night operational flying. No "kills" were achieved during the period before the signing of the armistice.[93]

USS *Barioko* took over the duties of CTU 95.1.1 on the evening of 23 July, and *Ocean* proceeded to Kure, her combat duty finished.[94]

WAR'S END

The Korean War: No Victors, No Vanished.

—Title of a book by Stanley Sandler

As peace talks in Panmunjom were reaching a conclusion, the Chinese were eager to wrest strategically important territory from UN forces before the official signing of Korean Armistice on 27 July 1953. The final enemy offensive of the war, which began on the evening of 24 July 1953, was against the Hook, a position on the Samichon River held by the 2nd Battalion, Royal Australian Regiment (2RAR), and on American positions to their left, held by the 7th Regiment, 1st Division of the United States Marine Corps.⁹⁵

Photo 3-15

Unidentified members of A Company, 2nd Battalion, The Royal Australian Regiment (2RAR), and two New Zealand soldiers, celebrate the signing of the cease fire with a few bottles of beer around a 60mm mortar position.
Australian War Memorial photograph HOBJ4509

In early morning darkness on 26 July, the Chinese senior command called off their offensive. The Chinese 137th Division had suffered heavy casualties. Sunrise revealed the valley below littered with between 2,000 and 3,000 bodies, largely due to the gunners of the 16th Field Regiment, Royal New Zealand Artillery (RNZA), combined with the defensive fire from Australian and American positions.⁹⁶

The Armistice was signed at Panmunjom, at 1000 on 27 July 1953, ending the Korean War.

At the end of the hostilities, the forces manning forward hill positions were amazed to realize the enormity of the opposition they had been facing. At first light on 28 July, Canadian soldiers on the "Jamestown" line (a series of defensive positions just north of the 38th Parallel, and only 30 miles from Seoul) witnessed an astonishing scene. The Chinese hills on the other side of the line were crawling with men. Captain C. A. Kemsley of the 3rd PPCLI (Princess Patricia's Canadian Light Infantry) recalled:

> In the valley immediately below us the Chinese had set up a platform, with loud speakers and banners announcing "the peace." On the platform men and women were dancing and singing. But what impressed the troops was what looked like millions of Chinese [who had been] opposing them. No one will ever forget the psychological impact of seeing for the first time "the human sea."[97]

Among the Canadians, the Armistice had been celebrated casually and briefly the previous night, when the guns and mortars along the "Jamestown" line fell silent, at 2200 on 27 July. There was much to be accomplished in the seventy-two hours given each side to withdraw from the demilitarized zone.[98]

The next two chapters take us back in history to cover the Royal Canadian Naval Air Service from its inception in 1918 through WWII, and the service of its last carrier ending in 1970.

4

Royal Canadian Naval Air Service

Some fields of human endeavour endure and become routine, while others are cut off before their time but live on in the memory to become legendary. Such was the fate of Canadian Carrier-borne Aviation. In 25 years, aircraft of the Royal Canadian Navy reached their peak of efficiency, flying from HMCS BONAVENTURE. Their achievements were equaled by few, if any, Navies of the world.

—Vice Adm. John Charles (Scruffy) O'Brien, OC, CD RCN.[1]

HMS *Nabob*
5 September 1943-
30 September 1944

Royal Canadian
Naval Air Service
pilot wings 1918

HMS *Puncher*
5 February 1944-
16 January 1946

HMCS *Warrior*
24 January 1946-
23 March 1948

HMCS *Magnificent*
7 April 1948-
14 June 1957

HMCS *Bonaventure*
17 January 1957-
3 July 1970

Three light fleet aircraft carriers in succession proudly flew the Canadian naval ensign between 24 January 1946 and 3 July 1970. Despite its vast size, Canada's population is relatively small compared to other industrial nations and funding scarce. Accordingly, at the end of WWII, HMCS *Warrior* and HMCS *Magnificent*, the first two capital ships and centerpieces of the Royal Canadian Navy, were acquired on loan from the Royal Navy. The Canadian government purchased its third and final aircraft carrier, HMCS *Bonaventure*, outright from Britain in 1957.

The Royal Canadian Navy (RCN) first gained experience with aircraft carriers in World War II, when its personnel commanded, and provided most of the manning for two Royal Navy escort carriers, HMS *Nabob* and HMS *Puncher*. However, Canadian interest in acquiring its own Naval Air Service stretched back to the closing months of World War I, when a fledgling program was begun and then abandoned following the end of war. This terminating action resulted from a dearth of funding, and a belief that Canadian flyers returning home from combat duty with the Royal Air Force were sufficient for future national requirements.[2]

ROYAL CANADIAN NAVAL AIR SERVICE IN 1918

The organization of a naval air arm on 5 September 1918 was spurred by a German submarine offensive near the end of World War I, carried out by five U-boats off the east coast of Canada and the United States. The Canadian government had previously been unenthusiastic about developing such a capability, despite the Minister of the Canadian Naval Service, the Honourable John Douglas Hazen, having warned that "an air service is necessary for the adequate defence of the Atlantic coast."[3]

Part of the reluctance of the Canadian government probably stemmed from activities in Britain. As early as 1916, a bitter private war had been waging between the British Admiralty and the War Office over the competing demands of the RNAS (Royal Naval Air Service) and RFC (Royal Flying Corps). To help resolve the issue, the British Government appointed a committee under Gen. Jan Christian Smuts, the South African statesman, to study the whole question of air command. Its findings, published in 1917, recommended that the two services be consolidated under a new Air Ministry. Prime Minister David Lloyd George promptly made Smuts the minister of air. He organized the Royal Air Force, formed from the RFC and RNAS after the latter was taken from naval control on 1 April 1918.[4]

Across the Atlantic, events in August 1918 off the east coast of Canada, assisted those trying to establish an air arm. On 20 August, *U-156* captured the 236-ton Canadian fishing trawler *Triumph* about twenty miles from Cranberry Island in Maine, the northernmost state on America's Eastern Seaboard. Within twenty-five minutes of boarding, the Germans had equipped her with a wireless radio, two light guns with three or four boxes of 3-pound shells, and twenty-five depth charges. The trawler, based at Port Hawkesbury, north-northeast of Halifax, was known by sight to almost the entire fishing fleet but at the time they were unaware she was no longer friendly.[5]

Over a three-day period while *U-156* remained hull awash three or more miles away, *Triumph* preyed on unsuspecting vessels. She stopped and destroyed the American schooners *A. Piatt Andrew*, *Francis J. O'Hara Jr.*, *Sylvania*, and the Canadian schooners *Lucille M. Schnare*, and *Pasadena*. *Uda A. Saunders*, another Canadian schooner, was sunk by the submarine. The Royal Canadian Naval Air Service was formed two weeks after Canadians learned that a surface raider had sunk six vessels.[6]

By the beginning of November, Lt. Col. John T. Cull of the Royal Air Force, director of the RCNAS, was headquartered at Ottawa with a small staff. The plan was to recruit 92 flight cadets, send 80 of them to the Massachusetts Institute of Technology for ground school training, and send 12 to England for combined ground and air training in dirigible airships. (Ultimately only 60 cadets were chosen for training at MIT.)[7]

When the Armistice ending World War I was signed, on 11 November 1918, the process of demobilization and return to peacetime conditions began. Since the flight cadets in England had only completed their first three weeks of ground school, they were invited to become balloon pilots instead of undertaking the much longer dirigible airship program. They were also asked to transfer service to the RCN, as the RCNAS was being discontinued on 31 December 1918.[8]

By late January 1919, eight of the candidates had qualified to obtain balloon pilot licenses and, in spring 1919, the RCN retroactively awarded RCNAS wings to these individuals. Only Harry James Jackson would wear his wings proudly in World War II. Born on 28 January 1899 in a log cabin in Purbrook, Ontario, his nickname was "professor." Before his war service, he had graduated from Hamilton College at age 16. After World War I, he earned BA, MA, and Bachelor of Pedagogy degrees while becoming a very successful teacher.[9]

In March 1941, Jackson volunteered to serve as a RCAF Flying Officer with the British Commonwealth Air Training Program, and did so until his discharge in 1944, due to diabetes. He passed away on 4 June 1971, but will be remembered by aviation buffs as one of the RCN's first eight naval air pilots.[10]

CANADIANS TO THE FORE

Although Canada entered World War II in September 1939, and by 1942, its government could no longer afford to ignore the fact that naval air forces were essential for the conduct of war at sea, no action was taken to pursue this capability until March 1943. Moreover, this only happened because of Britain's critical need, after three years of war and associated casualties, for additional aviators in the skies over Europe.[11]

The British Admiralty made a proposal in December 1942 to Vice Adm. Percy Walker Nelles, Chief of Naval Staff (Royal Canadian Navy), that Canadian officers receive instruction as pilots or observers with the Royal Navy, but remain members of the Royal Canadian Naval Volunteer Reserve. On 2 March 1943, the Admiralty was informed that the RCN was agreeable to providing personnel for training with the Royal Navy's Fleet Air Arm (FAA).[12]

In autumn 1943, as the Royal Navy's resources became even more strained, the Admiralty cut its escort ship construction program, and implored the RCN to man two new America-built escort carriers (CVEs) that were then coming into service with the RN. The Canadian Naval Service, having decided to follow the Royal Navy's lead in cutting back on escorts and, with the easing of its own manpower situation, agreed to provide as many officers and ratings as possible to man one CVE, HMS *Nabob*. Commissioned at Seattle, on 7 September 1943, she was then at Burrard Drydock and Shipbuilding Company in Vancouver for modifications to British requirements.[13]

On 5 January 1944, the Cabinet reviewed and rejected the proposal. A week later, the Honorable Angus Lewis McDonald, Minister of National Defence for Naval Services (Canada), raised the matter again, and it was finally agreed that the RCN would furnish the ship's complement for HMS *Nabob* and *Puncher*, while the RN contributed the aircraft and associated personnel. The reason that the ships could not be commissioned directly into the RCN related to the fact that the ships were being acquired from the United States by Britain under lend-lease, and that a term of the agreement prohibited them being transferred to a third power.[14]

HMS *NABOB* JOINS THE FLEET

Nabob left Vancouver, on 8 February 1944, to make passage to England. Following stops at San Francisco, where she embarked her twelve Avengers of RN 852 Squadron; San Diego; transit of the Panama Canal; stops at Norfolk; and at New York City, she joined Convoy UT-10, on 23 March, to make the Atlantic crossing after embarking a ferry cargo of P51 Mustangs for the RAF. Arriving in the UK, *Nabob* called briefly at Liverpool to land passengers, then made her way up to the Clyde, where, on 6 April, the aircraft of No. 852 Squadron were flown off to Royal Naval Air Station Machrihanish. The escort carrier then returned to Liverpool for a refit, and later underwent work-up trials, 852

Squadron having rejoined. The training programme ended at Tail-of-the-Bank, an anchorage in the upper Firth of Clyde, immediately north of Greenock, a town in Scotland.[15]

HMS *Nabob*, and sister ship HMS *Trumpeter*, left the anchorage, on 31 July, and, making their way to Scapa Flow, joined the Home Fleet, assigned to Rear Adm. Rhoderick McGrigor's 1st Cruiser Squadron.[16]

Nabob would participate in her first wartime operation a week later. Enemy shipping transporting vital Swedish iron ore, from the port of Narvik, was taking advantage of natural protection by using channels running between the coast of German-occupied Norway and outlying islands. To thwart this practice, it was decided to mine these waters, forcing vessels out into the open sea, where they could be attacked by land-based fighters.[17]

OPERATION OFFSPRING

On 9 August 1944, Force 4, with Rear Admiral McGrigor flying his flag in the fleet aircraft carrier HMS *Indefatigable*, sailed for the Norwegian coast. In addition to the flagship, the force included the escort carriers HMS *Nabob* and *Trumpeter*, heavy cruisers HMS *Devonshire* and *Kent*, and eight destroyers of the 26th Destroyer Flotilla. The flotilla was made up of British (HMS *Myngs*, *Scourge*, *Verulam*, *Vigilant*, *Virago*, *Volage*) and Canadian destroyers (HMCS *Algonquin* and *Sioux*). Late the following morning, *Nabob* put up two Grumman F4F Wildcats to provide air cover for the fleet. (This carrier-based fighter aircraft had begun service in 1940 with the Royal Navy. Because Fleet Air Arm fighters were named after sea birds, this plane was initially called the Martlet.) Early that afternoon, twelve Grumman TBF Avengers of 852 Squadron, carrying a mine apiece, took flight from *Nabob*. (Similarly, these torpedo bombers were initially known as the Tarpon.)[18]

In the air, *Nabob*'s Avengers were joined by those of 846 Squadron launched from *Trumpeter*. Accompanied by Seafires, Fireflies, and Hellcats provided by *Indefatigable* as fighter protection, the minelaying aircraft sped on in the grey afternoon toward Lepsorev Channel and Haarhamsfjord. In addition to offensive mining, OFFSPRING's objectives also included her fighter aircraft attacking the airfield at Gossen near Kristiansand North and enemy shipping off the Norwegian coast.[19]

After making landfall on Stornholm Light, the two Avenger squadrons began their mining runs in sub-flights of three. This activity took the Germans by surprise; all mines were laid without the loss of aircraft. The two squadrons returned to their carriers to refuel and rearm, then carried out a second strike. This time the enemy was better prepared, but 23 of 24 mines were sowed (bringing to 47 the day's total), ending OFFSPRING—which would prove to be largest aircraft minelaying operation by elements of the Home Fleet in WWII.[20]

Force 4 withdrew that evening, having lost an Avenger, a Firefly, and three Seafires. While the Avengers were laying mines, the fighters had destroyed six Messerschmitt Bf 110 heavy fighters on the ground and ruined another; they damaged three freighters, as well as the mine clearance boat *R89* (which was later destroyed by an ammunition explosion); and left two hangars and some warehouses burning at Gossen. Subsidiary targets in the Lepsoy area included three radar and two radio stations, one dredger, gun positions, and three ships of which two were left burning, and one oil tank left smoking.[21]

OPERATION GOODWOOD

Photo 4-1

German battleship *Tirpitz* in a Norwegian fjord, circa 1942-44.
Naval History and Heritage Command photograph #NH 71388

Later in August, *Nabob* participated in Operation GOODWOOD, a series of British carrier air raids against the German battleship *Tirpitz*, which lay in Kaa Fjord, Norway. The behemoth 823-foot warship, by her mere presence, constituted a potential threat to the Atlantic and North Russian convoy routes, forcing the basing of a heavy concentration of ships at Scapa Flow in case she put to sea.

> **German Battleship *Tirpitz***
> Armament:
> - 8 x 38cm SK C/34 guns in four double turrets
> - 12 x 15cm SK C/28 guns in six double turrets
> - 16 x 10.5cm SK C/33 guns in eight double mounts
> - 16 x 3.7cm SK C/30 guns in eight double mounts
> - 20 x 2cm guns (78 in 1944)
> - 8 x 53.3cm torpedo tubes in two quadruple mounts[22]

Force 2, consisting of *Nabob*, *Trumpeter*, and five frigates—HMS *Bickerton*, *Aylmer*, *Bligh*, *Kempthorne*, and *Keats*—of the Fifth Escort Squadron, cleared the defences of Scapa Flow, on 18 August 1944. The carriers reached the designated launch position inside the Arctic Circle, north of Tromso, two days later. Fourteen Avengers aboard *Nabob* were armed with mines that afternoon, but rough seas precluded air operations. The force then steamed westward and refueled, before returning to the attack-launching position on the 22nd.[23]

Preparations were begun aboard *Nabob* for the mining operation, but a signal from the Admiralty cancelled the participation of No. 852 Squadron owing to a low cloud ceiling. Few mines were available, but the Avengers could not safely land while still carrying these weapons if unable to locate *Tirpitz*, and would have had to jettison their valuable loads into the sea. Action stations were ordered aboard *Nabob* at 1000, and later, her aircraft flew a protective patrol over the fleet while planes from the fleet carriers of the main force—HMS *Indefatigable*, *Formidable*, and *Furious*—flew two strikes against the German battleship.[24]

The first attack on the morning of 22 August failed, and a smaller evening raid also did little damage. *Tirpitz* survived continued efforts on 24 and 29 August, despite being hit with two bombs on the 24th. During the course of the operation, the Royal Navy lost 17 aircraft, a frigate sunk by a submarine, and the escort carrier *Nabob* was badly damaged. Despite German forces suffering the loss of 12 aircraft and damage to seven ships, the failure of the operation was attributed to the Fleet Air Arm of the Royal Navy and, as a consequence, responsibility for attacking *Tirpitz* was transferred to the Royal Air Force. In three heavy bomber raids, in September and October 1944, the battleship was first crippled and then sunk.[25]

HMS *NABOB* KNOCKED OUT OF THE WAR

Looking at her from a distance of seven miles, I never expected her to survive.

—Rear Adm. Rhoderick McGrigor, RN, quoted in a 2010 article by Shawn Cafferky in *Canadian Military History*.[26]

Photo 4-2

Escort carrier HMS *Nabob* proceeding homeward under her own power, with stern low in the water, after being torpedoed by *U-354* while participating in an operation involving air strikes on the German battleship *Tirpitz*.
Imperial War Museums photograph A25368

Force 2 withdrew on the afternoon of 22 August. That evening, *Nabob* was about 120 miles west-northwest of North Cape, in the Barents Sea, preparing to transfer fuel to the frigates. At 1716 there was a heavy explosion on her starboard side aft. She immediately developed a list, and settled fifteen feet by the stern to a draught of 42 feet.[27]

"Up Spirits" had just been piped before the escort carrier was struck by a torpedo fired by the German submarine *U-354* (commanded by Oblt. Hans-Jurgen Sthamer). The torpedo strike opened a large hole aft of *Nabob*'s engine room and below the waterline. Members of the supply staff, messmen, and others were gathered outside the spirit room to collect rations for distribution, and it was among them that most of the casualties occurred. The officer supervising the rum ration was carried up two decks through ladder wells by water pouring into the ship after the explosion.[28]

At 1723, as damage control parties aboard *Nabob* worked to shore up the hole and stem the flooding, *U-354* fired a second G7esT5 acoustic torpedo, intended to finish off the carrier, but it unintentionally struck the frigate *Bickerton*. (This is believed to have occurred because the torpedo was attracted to the frigate whose machinery was working, whereas the carrier had lost all power and was silent.) Extensive damage to *Bickerton*'s stern resulted with 38 of her crew killed, and many others seriously wounded. After *Bligh* and *Aylmer* took off survivors, *Vigilant* scuttled her squadron mate with a torpedo.[29]

Aboard the immobile *Nabob*, damage control efforts continued until flooding was under control. At 2140, after electricity was restored and steam raised, the escort carrier began the long 1,100-mile passage back to Scotland. Before she left, two hundred and fourteen men, of whom ten were wounded, were transferred to *Kempthorne*. Throughout 23 August, crewmen remaining aboard *Nabob* struggled on her canted, rolling decks, to jettison or move forward all portable heavy gear, and to strengthen decks and bulkheads in the after part of the carrier with timber. The next day brought 43 knot winds, and heavy seas which, although steep, were short, resulting in less rolling. On the morning of 27 August, *Nabob* entered Scapa Flow and moored to a buoy.[30]

Following emergency repairs, the escort carrier proceeded to Rosyth where she entered dry-dock. Here the remains of fourteen of her dead were removed from the damaged compartments, bringing her total casualties to 30 fatalities and 40 men injured. Determined to be beyond economical repair, *Nabob* was beached, on 30 September 1944, to spend the remainder of the war on a sandbank. Some of her machinery was taken to support sister ships. Her main reduction gear was installed in the other Canadian-manned CVE, after HMS *Puncher*'s MRG failed, on 27 November 1944.[31]

Her commanding officer, Capt. Horatio Nelson Lay, OBE RCN, and (chief engineer) Commander (E), Cecil I. Hinchcliffe, RD RCN, were awarded a Mention in Despatches "For good service when his ship HMS *NABOB* was damaged."[32]

HMC *PUNCHER*

With the paying off of *Nabob*, on 30 September 1944, the only remaining Canadian personnel involved in the manning of aircraft carriers were those on HMS *Puncher*, under Capt. Roger E. S. Bidwell, RCN, who had been in command since 10 April 1944. Although also built by Seattle-Tacoma Shipbuilding Corporation, and of the same class as *Nabob*, she had slightly smaller dimensions. Following completion of a British-specified refit at Burrard's yard and dry docking in Esquimalt, she cleared Duntze Head (a headland in British Columbia situated west of Esquimalt), on 8 June, bound for the eastern seaboard of the United States. Accompanying her was the frigate HMCS *Beacon Hill*.[33]

Stops were made by the two ships at San Francisco and San Diego, where the British fleet minesweeper HMS *Foam* joined. Making a steady 16 knots, the three ships reached Balboa on 23 June, passed through the Panama Canal, and continued on to New Orleans. Four 72-foot harbour defence motor launches were deck-loaded aboard the CVE there, and delivered to New York. *Puncher* then made her way back down the coast to Portsmouth Navy Yard for the installation of mounts for Bofors anti-aircraft guns, before returning to New York.[34]

Photo 4-3

Escort carrier HMS *Puncher* off the Chesapeake Bay, on 27 August 1944, while en route to Norfolk, Virginia, from Casablanca, Morocco.
Naval History and Heritage Command photograph #NH 106583

Preparations for the invasion of France were under way, and forty US Army planes, including some P-61 night-fighters ("Black Widows") were brought aboard for service in the Mediterranean. Convoy UGF-13 began forming up off Norfolk, Virginia, on 28 July, and *Puncher* took station in her assigned column. There was no action during the Atlantic crossing. Off the African coast, *Puncher* and the escort carrier USS *Shamrock Bay* (CVE-84) were detached and escorted by four French subchasers into Casablanca to offload cargo. After four days spent in the harbour, *Puncher* put to sea and joined Convoy GUS-48 for transit back to Norfolk. We will skip details of additional trips back and forth across the Atlantic ferrying aircraft, stores, and ammunition to the UK, and progress to operations with the Home Fleet in Norwegian waters.[35]

OPERATIONS SELENIUM I AND II

On 11 February 1945, Force 2—escort carriers HMS *Puncher* and *Premier*, cruiser HMS *Devonshire*, and four destroyers—left Scapa Flow, bound for Norway across the North Sea, to take part in Operation SELENIUM I. Embarked aboard *Puncher* were fourteen F4F Wildcat fighter aircraft of No. 881 Squadron and four Fairey Barracuda torpedo/dive bombers of 821 Squadron. The following morning, Force 1—the cruisers HMS *Norfolk* and *Dido*, and three destroyers—patrolled within gun range of the enemy shipping route between Bud and Kvitholm, looking for prey. In support, Wildcats from the two carriers flew fighter protection for a possible attack on shipping in Hustadviken Lead near Haugesund. No vessels were sighted, and Force 2 took up its next tasking.[36]

Photo 4-4

US Navy F4F Wildcats flying in formation, circa 1943.
National Archives photograph #USN 42969

SELENIUM II involved aerial minelaying in the Skatestrommen (a narrow channel between the eastern end of Bremanger and Rug-sundoy to the northward), abreast Skaten Lighthouse. While fighter planes from *Puncher* flew top cover, seven Avengers from *Premier* set out with one mine apiece, escorted by four Wildcats of 856 Squadron. One of the Avengers was forced to return with a heavy oil leak, but the remainder made landfall on Vaagso Island and, continuing up Faa Fjord, laid five mines at Skatestrommen; one aircraft was unable to release its mine and jettisoned it later set to "safe." The force then withdrew, and returned to Scapa Flow on 13 February.[37]

Map 4-1

Portion of Scandinavia, including the west coast of Norway

OPERATIONS SHRED AND GROUNDSHEET

Puncher's next operation in Norwegian waters also comprised two parts. The first, codenamed SHRED, was a minesweeping run (single pass by minesweepers working in concert) through Salhusstrommen Channel, off Stavanger in southwestern Norway, suspected to have been mined by the Germans. In the early hours of 21 February, six minesweepers of the 10th Minesweeping Flotilla—*Courier, Jewel, Serene, Wave, Hare,* and *Golden Fleece*—put to sea, followed by a support force of *Dido, Puncher, Premier,* and three destroyers. Heavy seas were running off the enemy coast, and it required great seamanship to stream gear. The operation was carried out as planned, but not rewarded by any evidence of mines bobbing to the surface from cut moors.[38]

Shortly before noon the following day, *Puncher* turned in to the wind, and launched nine Barracudas, with an escort of eight Wildcats, to carry out an aerial mining strike. Eight Wildcats from *Premier* flew top cover, as the mine-laden Barracudas and fighter escort shaped a course toward the coast to carry out Operation GROUNDSHEET.[39]

Photo 4-5

Fairey Barracuda taking off from an aircraft carrier deck under the control of a landing signal officer, also informally known as batsman (Royal Navy) or paddles (US Navy). Australian War Memorial photograph AC0009

Unfortunately, the Barracudas made landfall over the heavily defended town of Stavanger, Norway, instead of their intended waypoint, the solitary island of Utsire. As a result of this navigation error, the minelayers and fighter planes lost contact with each other. At Stavanger intense and accurate anti-aircraft fire was encountered, with the result that two of the Barracudas were shot down. The remaining seven were able to lay their mines in Karmoy Channel near Stavanger, while the fighters destroyed a Dornier 24 flying boat at its moorings, and strafed two silo-type buildings on the waterfront at Stavanger. The force then returned to base.[40]

OPERATION PREFIX

On 24 March 1945, four escort carriers—HMS *Puncher, Searcher, Nairana*, and *Queen*—cruisers HMS *Bellona* and *Dido*, and an escort of six destroyers sailed to carry out Operation PREFIX, a raid on enemy shipping in Norwegian waters. Although weather was not cooperative, on the morning of the 26th, a strike from *Searcher* and *Queen* was launched to attack shipping in Trondheim Leads and toward Kristiansand North. Nearer the coastline, visibility was better and aircraft attacked two ships proceeding up Tustna/Stablen Fjord.[41]

While this was occurring, two flights of Wildcats sighted and engaged eight or ten Messerschmitt fighters, shooting down three and damaging two others. The Avenger strike aircraft were not so lucky. Finding no suitable targets, they had to jettison their bombs and return to their CVEs. The last strike of PREFIX was by fighters on enemy shipping at Aalesund. Two vessels alongside a jetty were attacked, and a wireless radio station at Vikeroy Island was taken under fire. Missing one Barracuda, which failed to return from an anti-submarine patrol, the force returned to Scapa Flow.[42]

OPERATION NEWMARKET

Puncher's last operation of the war took place in early April. She was part of a powerful force sent to sea to attack the U-boat depot at Kilbotn, Norway. As the ships crossed the Arctic Circle, on 7 April, amid squalls and mountainous seas, the destroyers were hard pressed to keep up with the larger warships. For five days, the force steamed back and forth. The operation was first postponed, and then finally aborted.[43]

Back in the Orkneys, *Puncher* flew off all her aircraft, as her service was drawing to a close. She was escorted by the destroyers HMS *Savage* and *Scourge* to the Clyde for boiler cleaning, and subsequently entered drydock near Glasgow, where war's end found her on 8 May 1945. *Puncher* was transferred to the administration of Flag Officer, Carrier

Training on 15 May. A complimentary signal marking the occasion was received from Vice Adm. Rhoderick McGrigor, under whose orders the escort carrier had been operating.[44]

EXPERIENCE WITH THE BRITISH PACIFIC FLEET

> *When a kamikaze hits a US carrier it means six months of repair at Pearl [Harbor]. When a kamikaze hits a Limey carrier it's just a case of 'Sweepers, man your brooms.'*
>
> —Comment made by the USN liaison officer aboard the British fleet aircraft carrier HMS *Indefatigable*.[45]

Photo 4-6

Port side view of the aircraft carrier HMS *Formidable* with a Wildcat fighter about to land, circa 1943.
Australian War Memorial photograph 302388

While Canadian shipboard officers and men manning HMS *Nabob* and HMS *Puncher* were gaining valuable experience operating escort carriers, so too were Canadians flying combat missions with the Royal Navy. Canada did not have naval aviators in the ranks of the RCN during WWII, but like other members of the British Commonwealth and other allies, such as the Dutch, it did have considerable numbers of aviators RCNVR (Royal Canadian Navy Volunteer Reserve) and RCNR (Royal Canadian Navy Reserve) embedded in Royal Navy ships throughout the war. A list of Canadian aviators compiled by John MacFarlane (which includes WWI and the inter-war period, as well as WWII) tallies over 2,200 names. Most of the WWII service of Canadian flyers was in the

European Theater, but some also included duty late in the war with the British Pacific Fleet.[46]

As the invasion in Europe was well advanced in late 1944, and aircraft carriers were no longer required there in great numbers, the Royal Navy offered to assist the U.S. forces by supplying a fleet of carriers and other vessels to battle the Japanese in the Pacific. Initial U.S. opposition to this offer was overcome when it was established that the British force would be largely self-sufficient and would not put additional pressure on an already stretched America supply system. The British Pacific Fleet (BPF), ultimately mobilized to aid in the potential invasion of Japan, was the most powerful strike force ever assembled by the Royal Navy. It included 6 fleet carriers and their squadrons, 4 light carriers, 2 maintenance carriers, 9 escort carriers, 4 battleships, and dozens of cruisers, destroyers and lesser combat ships, as well as a huge train of supply and maintenance ships, oilers and assorted auxiliaries.[47]

Under Royal Navy command, ships and/or personnel of Canada, Australia, New Zealand, and the Netherlands participated in the British Pacific Force that was formed, on 22 November 1944, under Adm. Bruce Fraser, based at Sydney, Australia. In January 1945, while still under independent Royal Navy operating command as British Task Force 63, en route to Sydney, it successfully attacked Japanese oil refineries in Sumatra, eliminating the bulk of their supply of aviation fuel. Operation MERIDIAN significantly reduced production at Pladjoe, and completely stopped it at Soengei Gerong, until the end of March. The combined production of both refineries was returned to no more than thirty-five percent of their previous capability, by the end of May, and the Japanese never achieved full production before their surrender. The attacks on the refineries resulted in the enemy being desperately short of oil, and this incalculable effect on the war, may well have been the British Pacific Fleet's greatest contribution to Allied victory.[48]

From 26 March to 20 April 1945, while supporting the invasion of Okinawa, the British Pacific Force was responsible for neutralizing Japanese air bases in the Sakishima Islands and on Formosa (Taiwan), which were a constant threat from the southwest. Gunfire and air attack were used against potential kamikaze staging airfields that might otherwise be used to support attacks against US Navy ships at Okinawa. The Sakishimas, southwest of Okinawa, are a part of the same Ryukyu island chain previously mentioned.[49]

The BPF (Task Force 57) began operations attached to the U.S. Fifth Fleet at the end of March 1945—initially consisting of some twenty-five surface combatants, including four fleet carriers and a Fleet

Train of some thirty ships. The fighting core of the task force was the 1st Aircraft Carrier Squadron, under Rear Adm. Philip Vian, RN, which included HMS *Indomitable*, HMS *Victorious*, HMS *Illustrious*, HMS *Indefatigable*, HMS *Implacable*, and HMS *Formidable* (the latter two were still en route). The British fleet carriers were subjected to heavy and repeated kamikaze attacks off the Sakishimas. However, boasting armored flight decks, they were quite resilient and returned to action relatively quickly.[50]

Embarked aboard the six carriers were twenty Royal Navy Fleet Air Arm Squadrons. Comprising their collective 354 British and American aircraft were: 105 Avenger torpedo-bombers, 109 Corsair fighters, 29 Hellcat fighters, 88 Supermarine Seafire fighters, 21 Fairey Firefly fighters, and 2 Walrus air-sea rescue aircraft.

RN Aircraft Carrier	RNFAA Squadrons	RN/USN Aircraft
HMS *Indomitable*	857 Squadron	15 Avengers
	1839, 1844 Squadrons	29 Hellcats
HMS *Victorious*	849 Squadron	14 Avengers
	1834, 1836 Squadrons	37 Corsairs, 2 Walrus ASR
HMS *Indefatigable*	820 Squadron	20 Avengers
	887, 894 Squadrons	40 Seafires
	1770 Squadron	9 Fireflies
HMS *Illustrious*	854 Squadron	16 Avengers
	1830, 1833 Squadrons	36 Corsairs
HMS *Formidable*	848 Squadron	19 Avengers
	1841, 1842 Squadrons	36 Corsairs
HMS *Implacable*	828 Squadron	21 Avengers
	801, 880 Squadrons	48 Seafires
	1771 Squadron	12 Fireflies[51]

HMS *Formidable* joined the British Pacific Fleet late in April 1945. Her first major action was strikes against Japanese air bases supporting Japan's defense of Okinawa. Aircrew losses were heavy: the British carriers lost forty-seven aircraft to enemy anti-aircraft fire and operational causes.[52]

CANADA'S LAST VICTORIA CROSS WINNER

Aboard *Formidable* was Lt. Robert Hampton Gray, RCNVR. Gray, a Corsair fighter pilot assigned to 1841 Squadron, and a member of the Royal Canadian Navy Volunteer Reserve (RCNVR), colloquially known as "The Wavy Navy."[53]

The preceding year, Gray had received a Mention in Despatches (MID) on 29 August 1944, for his participation in an attack on three German destroyers, during which his plane's rudder was shot off. On

16 January 1945, he received a second MID for "undaunted courage, skill and determination in carrying out daring attacks on the [German battleship] ... *Tirpitz*" in August 1944.[54]

By July 1945, the combined Allied fleets were attacking the Japanese mainland, striking any targets found. On 9 August, while leading a strike against the Japanese naval base at Maisuru (located on an inlet of the Sea of Japan on northern Honshu), Gray made a direct hit on a Japanese destroyer, setting it afire and ultimately sinking it. Admiral Vian sent a congratulatory message to HMS *Formidable*, praising Gray's "resolute and professional manner" and recommended him for the immediate award of the Distinguished Service Cross. However, the valiant Canadian would not live to receive this award.[55]

On the day of Gray's attack, as the second atomic bomb fell on Nagasaki, three days after the one was dropped on Hiroshima, air strikes against Japanese targets continued unabated. Leading two flights of Corsairs against airfields in the Matsushima area, northern Honshu, Gray found little enemy activity, an earlier strike from *Formidable* having left the targets in ruins. This being the case, he decided to hit the secondary target of naval ships at nearby Onagawa Wan (Bay).[56]

Photo 4-7

Japanese escort ship *Etorofu*, May 1943, the same class ship as the *Amakusa*.
写真日本の軍艦第7巻 p. 198 (photographer unknown)

There, the flight found a number of Japanese ships and dove down to attack. Furious fire was opened on the carrier aircraft from army shore batteries and from warships in the bay. Gray selected for his target a Japanese destroyer. As he leveled out and made straight for it, his Corsair was hit with cannon and machine gun fire, set aflame, and one of his 500lb. bombs was shot off. Gray steadied the aircraft, and released his remaining bomb, which struck *Amakusa* below her after gun turret. The munition detonated the ammunition locker, blowing out the starboard side of the escort vessel, which then rolled over and sank.[57]

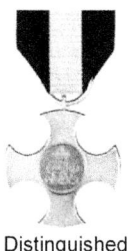

| Victoria Cross | Distinguished Service Cross | Mention in Despatches (oak leaf device worn) |

Lt. Robert Hampton Gray, RCNVR, did not return from this mission, having given his life at the very end of his fearless bombing run. One of the last Canadians to die in the war, he was posthumously awarded the Victoria Cross, the highest medal for valor in the British Commonwealth, on 13 November 1945. (This award followed that of the Distinguished Service Cross, on 31 August 1945.) This citation for the Victoria Cross (which remains today the last one issued to a Canadian) reads as follows:

> For great bravery in leading an attack to within 50 feet of a Japanese destroyer in the face of intense anti-aircraft fire, thereby sinking the destroyer although he was hit and his own aircraft on fire and finally himself killed. He was one of the gallant company of Naval Airmen who, from December 1944, fought and beat the Japanese from Palembang to Tokyo. The actual incident took place in the Onagawa Wan on the 9th of August 1945. Gray was leader of the attack, which he pressed home in the face of fire from shore batteries and at least eight warships. With his aircraft in flames he nevertheless obtained at least one direct hit which sank its objective.[58]

Gray's was only the second Victoria Cross earned by the Fleet Air Arm in WWII. The other was earned by Lt. Comdr. Eugene Esmonde, RN, posthumously, after leading an attack on German battle cruisers *Scharnhorst* and *Gneisenau*, and the cruiser *Prince Eugen* as they dashed from Brest, France, up the English Channel to the safety of the North German port of Brunsbuttel, in 1942.[59]

RCNVR flier Lt. Arthur William Sutton was killed, on 24 January 1945, when his Corsair of 1830 RN Squadron aboard HMS *Illustrious*, crashed into a hanger full of Japanese aircraft in Palembang, Sumatra (today Indonesia). He was recommended for the VC, but the award was denied because it could not be determined that he was still alive in the final moments of the attack, and had purposefully, and heroically carried out this action.[60]

GRAY'S SQUADRON MATES CARRY ON ATTACK

When Gray's aircraft rolled inverted and crashed into the waters of Onagawa Bay, his squadron mates took out their anger at the loss of their leader on the other ships in the bay by repeatedly strafing them. Having vented their frustration and reeling from the loss of Gray, the Corsairs returned to *Formidable* off the coast. Once recovered, flight deck crews armed and spotted the planes for another attack on Onagawa, while the pilots hurriedly grabbed some food.[61]

Among the pilots of the planes launched for the second strike were Canadians Lt. Charles Edgar Butterworth, RCNVR, and Lt. Gerald Arthur Anderson, RCNVR. As this flight hammered away at the remaining ships in the bay, they were joined by forty Hellcats from nearby American carriers. By the time the Corsairs from *Formidable* were heading back to the carrier mid-afternoon, there was total devastation at Onagawa Bay. Only the auxiliary minesweeper *Kongo Maru No. 2* remained afloat. The day's combat operations had been successful, but the loss of much-liked Robert Gray was a bitter pill to swallow, particularly because the war was winding down.[62]

Anderson's aircraft had been hit by anti-aircraft fire during the second attack and was leaking fuel rapidly during the 150-mile return flight. He had two options. He could ditch his damaged Corsair or try to make the carrier. Anderson may have been wounded and believed that extraction from the aircraft after ditching might prove difficult. He chose to land aboard and made an approach from the port rear quarter. It looked like he was going to make it when, just feet from the flight deck rounddown (deck edge), Anderson's engine quit on him. The 9,000-pound aircraft slammed hard and flat into the rounddown, angled toward the sky. The aft section of the Corsair behind the pilot then broke away and fell downward into *Formidable*'s turbulent wake, created by her three churning propellers.[63]

For several long seconds, the forward part of the Corsair lay precariously at the back of the ship. The 22-year-old Anderson was slumped forward, unconscious, his head resting against the control panel. Flight deck personnel were momentarily stunned, and before any action could be taken, Anderson and his wrecked plane slid back, pitched up, and toppled over the stern of the ship and disappeared into the deep. One can only hope that Anderson, in his sealed cockpit, did not regain consciousness as his Corsair settled to the sea floor. (It has been stated that just another pint of fuel would have saved the day for Anderson, the last Canadian combat casualty in the war.)[64]

Of the seven Canadian pilots attached to *Formidable*'s air group, only two, Lieutenants William Atkinson and Charles Butterworth, survived. Atkinson was the last Canadian to become an "ace" during the war. The seven pilots are identified below, along with the date of their death (if killed during the war), and awards for valor they earned.

Canadian RCNVR Pilots aboard HMS *Formidable*

Name	Killed	Awards
Lt. Gerald Arthur Anderson, RCNVR	9 Aug 45	
Lt. William Bell Asbridge, RCNVR	18 Jul 45	
Lt. William Henry Isaac Atkinson, RCNVR	Survivor	DSC, MID
Lt Charles Edgar Butterworth, RCNVR	Survivor	DSC
Lt Robert Hampton Gray, RCNVR	9 Aug 45	VC, DSC, 2 MID
Lt. James Finlay Ross, RCNVR	30 Jul 45	2 MID
Lt. Robert Ross Sheppard, RCNVR	22 Mar 45[65]	

Robert Sheppard was the brother of Donald John Sheppard, a pilot aboard HMS *Victorious* and the only other Canadian naval flyer to become a Pacific "ace" during the war. He and Atkinson were two of only sixteen WWII Fleet Air Arm pilots to achieve five or more air victories.[66]

The above tabulation is an example of participation for one country aboard only one fleet carrier, between 22 March and 10 August 1945. In addition to five Canadians, other Fleet Air Arm squadron losses aboard *Formidable* included ten British (eight officers and two petty officer airmen), and a Royal Netherlands Naval Air Service (RNNAS) pilot. These losses resulted from a variety of causes associated with war:

- Commander of 1842 Squadron missing in action (16 April)
- Loss of 848 Squadron Avenger aircraft (17 April)
- Kamikaze attack off Okinawa (4 May); two of the four victims perished that day, the remaining two died of their wounds on 7 and 16 May, respectively
- Loss of aircraft to combat action (18 July)
- Aircraft losses off Tukushima (24 July)
- Aircraft losses during attack on Japanese shipping at Onagawa Wan (9 August)
- A/Sub Lt. Leslie Alan Maitland, RNVR, lost (details unknown)

RN Fleet Air Arm Squadron Losses aboard HMS *Formidable* (22 March-10 August 1945)

Name	Killed	Squad	Awards
Lt. Robert Ross Sheppard, RCNVR	22 Mar 45	1845	
A/Lt. Comdr. Anthony M. Garland, RNVR	16 Apr 45	1842	DSC & Bar
T/A/PO Airman Charles W. Irwin	17 Apr 45	848	
Sub Lt. Douglas R. Whitehead, RNVR	17 Apr 45	848	
A/Sub Lt. John F. Bell, RNVR	4 May 45	1842	
A/Lt. Alan D. Burger, RNVR	4 May 45	1842	
A/Sub Lt. Donald G. Jupp, RNVR	16 May 45	848	DSC
Lt. William Bell Asbridge, RCNVR	18 Jul 45	1845	
Sub Lt. Walter Thomas Stradwick, RNVR	18 Jul 45	1842	MID
A/Lt. Alfred Cecil Francis, RNVR	24 Jul 45	848	MID
T/A/PO Airman Gordon C. Rawlinson	24 Jul 45	848	
Sub Lt. Bouke K. Swart, RNNAS	24 Jul 45	1842	
Lt. James Finlay Ross, RCNVR	30 Jul 45	1842	2 MID
Lt. Gerald Arthur Anderson, RCNVR	9 Aug 45	1845	
Lt. Robert Hampton Gray, RCNVR	9 Aug 45	1845	VC, DSC, 2 MID
A/Sub Lt. Leslie Alan Maitland, RNVR	10 Aug 45	1841	2 MID[67]

CANADIAN CONTRIBUTIONS TO THE WAR IN THE PACIFIC, AND PREPARATIONS FOR THE FUTURE

Even before, the cessation of hostilities in Europe, on VE day, 8 May 1945, Canada was re-focusing its naval planning to aid its allies in the Pacific as they made the final drive toward the Japanese homeland with its perceived drastic invasion casualties. Her new cruiser HMCS *Uganda* was active with the British Pacific Fleet and other units (such as the cruiser HMCS *Ontario*, the auxiliary cruiser HMCS *Prince Robert* and the destroyer HMCS *Algonquin*) were on their way to the Pacific, when hostilities were suddenly halted with the dropping of two atomic bombs.

Ironically, the civilian miners working on the shore of the pristine Great Bear Lake (in the Northwest Territories, on the Arctic Circle) and bush pilot aviators, inland navigators, and railway workers, who produced and transported the cancer-causing nuclear material for the Manhattan Project along the "Highway of the Atom," may have made Canada's greatest contribution to ending the war in the Pacific. (*Highway of the Atom*, the name of a book by Peter C. Van Wyck, exposing the pollution caused by these actions, refers to the transportation path of this these materials.)

5

Acquisition/Service of RCN Aircraft Carriers

Photo 5-1

HMCS *Warrior* passing under the Lions Gate Bridge, 10 February 1947.
City of Vancouver Archives photograph CVA 1184-3461

HMCS *Warrior*, a newly built *Colossus*-class RN light fleet carrier, was commissioned into the Royal Canadian Navy, on 25 January 1946, at Belfast, Northern Ireland. Under the command of Capt. Frank Llewellyn Houghton, she was the RCN's first aircraft carrier, although on loan from the Royal Navy. Following completion of ship and flying trials over the next three months, *Warrior* sailed from Portsmouth, England, on 23 March. Turning in to the wind off the Isle of Wright, she received No. 803 and 825 Squadrons and began her voyage to Canada. She experienced gale force winds on a portion of the Atlantic crossing, but arrived at Halifax, on 31 March, in fine, sunny conditions with large crowds along the whole length of the harbour to greet her as she entered port.[1]

During the latter part of World War II, having gained experience in the manning of carriers, Canada's Naval Board approved, on 31 March 1944, the formation of an air section under a Director of Air Division. The RCN then pursued the acquisition of its own air squadrons, which would involve support from the Royal Navy. On 15 June 1945, No. 803 Squadron, equipped with Seafire fighters, was re-formed at Royal Naval Air Station, Arbroath, Scotland, for eventual service in a Canadian carrier. The Royal Navy re-formed a second squadron destined for Canadian service, No. 825, at RNAS Rattray in Scotland, on 1 July 1945. When transferred after the war to the RCN, on 24 January 1946, it was equipped with twelve Fairey Fireflies.[2]

Photo 5-2

HMS *Magnificent* (left) and HMS *Powerful* under construction at Harland and Wolff's Musgrave Shipyard, Belfast, Northern Ireland (UK). Both carriers would serve with the Royal Canadian Navy (*Powerful* as HMCS *Bonaventure*).
Imperial War Museums collection photograph A 28022

When laid down at her builder's yard, Harland and Wolff in Belfast, during World War II, *Warrior* had been intended for employment in the Indian Ocean. Consequently, she was not equipped with proper heating for colder environments. A few months of operation in North Atlantic waters, off the east coast of Canada, demonstrated that she was not compatible with frigid, winter conditions. Accordingly, HMCS *Warrior* departed Halifax Harbour, 5 November, for passage to Esquimalt on the west coast of Canada. She was escorted as far as the Atlantic entrance to the Panama Canal, by the destroyer HMCS *Nootka*.[3]

Departing the canal, *Warrior* was accompanied by the destroyer HMCS *Crescent*. (She was the lead ship in an eight-ship flotilla proposed for loan to Canada by the RN—the only other acquired by Canada was HMCS *Crusader*, which served in Korea.) Proceeding up America's west coast, following calls at Acapulco, Mexico, and San Diego, California, the weather became progressively worse. During passage through the Strait of Juan de Fuca, on the final leg to Esquimalt, a series of snowstorms brought back memories of Halifax. Entering harbor, *Warrior* fired a salute to flag officer, Pacific Coast, Rear Adm. Edmond R. Mainguy, OBE RCN.[4]

On 18 January 1947, while *Warrior* was drydocking in Esquimalt, Commodore Harry G. DeWolf, CBE, DSO, DSC RCN, assumed command of the ship. During this refit, important decisions were being made in Ottawa regarding her future. Discussions with the Royal Navy resulted in agreement for her return to Britain, in exchange for a new light fleet carrier, *Magnificent*, when available. This action stemmed from *Warrior* being unsuitable for year-round duty in Canadian waters.[5]

HMCS *Warrior* steamed into Belfast Lough, on the east coast of Northern Ireland, on 20 February 1948, and work immediately began to transfer her stores to *Magnificent*. Following completion of this task, a week later, *Warrior* passed through the Needles passage, on 1 March, and anchored off Spithead. Her aviation fuel was offloaded and, on St. Patrick's Day, she moved into drydock. On 23 March, the Broad Pennant of Commodore DeWolf was struck and, with the hoisting of the Colours of the Royal Navy, she became HMS *Warrior*.[6]

Her later service with the RN included transporting troops and aircraft to the Far East during the Korean War; and participation in Operation GRAPPLE, a series of British nuclear weapons tests at Malden Island and Christmas Island (today Kiritimati) in the Central Pacific, in 1957 and 1958.

THE RCN FLEET THAT NEVER CAME TO FRUITION

After WWII Canada struggled with the future role of the RCN. A majority of its citizens, and government wanted a "peace dividend," a sharp decrease in previous wartime funding of the military. However, despite the fact its huge "Sheep Dog" (referring to convoy escort) fleet was laid up in disposal anchorages and its "for-the-duration" reservist crews returned to civilian life, the Royal Canadian Navy's RN-indoctrinated professional officers yearned for a two-ocean balanced naval force. Aircraft carriers featured predominantly in this vision as well as cruisers, fleet destroyers, and support vessels. However, events and conflicting priorities soon changed this vision. There were many uncompromising agendas and interests.

Many senior officers favored continuation of close association with the Royal Navy, with which they had trained or had served, while others favoured closer alignment with U.S. forces. On the eve of the Cold War, it was essential, at least, for the common defence of North America, that integration of military capabilities and communications be established. Countering this direction, Canada remained wary of the U.S. failure to recognize Canada's proclamation of sovereignty rights in the Arctic. There also was a unique need for the Canadian Navy to make space for, and to integrate, its French speaking citizens into what had formerly been almost an exclusively English-speaking force. To a French speaking citizen of the Province of Quebec, Royal Navy traditions meant little and, to some, were probably abhorrent in the extreme. Canadian prime minster Mackenzie King, a liberal, was opposed to close association with the Royal Navy, as he viewed it as support for the return of British Imperialism, which he detested.

The answer to the naval planning dilemma was soon provided by the onset of the Cold War, the threat of Russian submarines, and the subsequent formation of NATO, in 1949. Writer Marc Millar in his book, *Canada's Navy, The First Century*, sums up Canada's return to its WWII routes with the following words:

> In no small way, the decision to concentrate on anti-submarine warfare in 1947 was the most important event in Canadian naval history.

In this new arrangement, as a commitment to NATO, Canada would become a specialist in anti-submarine warfare centered in the North Atlantic. For a time, an aircraft carrier was a part of this effort. However, with the development of modern destroyer escorts and frigates with helicopters and missile batteries, and necessity for support ships to sustain them at sea, it eventually became too expensive to support even one carrier and its screening and supplying vessels. Further, the RCAF, with successive generations of long-range land-based patrol aircraft such as the Neptune, the Argus, and the Aurora, began to take-on increasing ant-submarine activities.

This reality did not diminish the critical importance of aircraft carriers and fixed-wing aircraft to national defence. Limited finances precluded RCN continued support of this warfare capability, and Canada benefited from the presence of the powerful U.S. Second Fleet to the south along the Eastern Seaboard, and the Third Fleet based on America's Pacific coast—both of which boasted large fleet aircraft carriers and associated squadrons of fighter and attack aircraft.

During the combined, sequential service of HMCS *Magnificent* and *Bonaventure* from 7 April 1948 to 3 July 1973, Canada's last two carriers provided valuable service to her defence, "showed the flag" proudly in numerous foreign ports, and participated in NATO exercises and UN Peace Keeping missions. This was in the Atlantic and Mediterranean; the *Warrior* was the only one of the three Canadian light carriers to be based in the Pacific, while operating for a time from Esquimalt.

HMCS *MAGNIFICENT* ("MAGGIE")

> *To the group of Canadian sailors from H.M.C.S.* Magnificent *and* Micmac: *Your vocation enables you to see a large part of the world. An old proverb has it that he who travels far knows much. This should be true. It is not always so. May this thought be with you in all places at all times. All men form the one great human family. It should be your ambition to unite these more closely with the bonds of love and kindness. We also send our blessing to your dear ones at home with the prayer that God's love and mercy may be with them always. We bless all religious articles you may have with you.*
>
> —Portion of an address made by Pope Pius XII, on 6 October 1951, from a balcony in Vatican City, Rome, to a large group of visitors, which included two hundred and thirty-four Canadian officers and men from the carrier HMCS *Magnificent* and destroyer HMCS *Micmac*, assembled in the courtyard below.[7]

On 7 April 1948, Commodore DeWolf, who had just relinquished his command of *Warrior*, assumed that of *Magnificent* at Belfast. With the hoisting of her colours, the new *Majestic*-class carrier joined the Royal Canadian Navy. Following ship acceptance trials and flying tests, and with the planes of the 19th Carrier Air Group and those of 806 Squadron, RN, aboard, she departed the UK on 25 May and began her westward journey to Canada. While in England, the 19th Group's 803 Squadron had been re-equipped with Sea Fury XI and its 825 Squadron with Firefly IV (later replaced with US Avengers) aircraft. *Magnificent* arrived at Halifax, on 1 June, to be greeted by low clouds and rain, permitting only two aircraft to be flown off to the Dartmouth air station on the eastern shore of the harbour. The Navy later took over the Air Force facility, whereupon its name changed to Royal Canadian Naval Air Station Shearwater.[8]

Photo 5-3

HMCS *Magnificent* (CVL 21) under way, circa 1950.
US Navy National Museum of Naval Aviation photograph 1996.488.037.040

"Maggie" was greatly beloved by Canadians as an important symbol of their nation during her RCN fleet service, and showing of her Naval Ensign overseas. During this period (7 April 1948-14 June 1957), eight officers were honoured to command HMCS *Magnificent* (CVL21).

Tour	Commanding Officer
7 Apr-29 Aug 48	Cdre. Harry George DeWolf, CBE, DSO, DSC RCN
30 Aug 48-28 Jun 49	Cdre. George Ralph Miles, OBE RCN
29 Jun-6 Sep 49	Comdr. Angus George Boulton, DSC RCN
7 Sep 49-28 Oct 51	Cdre. Kenneth Frederick Adams, RCN
29 Oct 51-10 Mar 53	Capt. Kenneth Lloyd Dyer, DSC RCN
11 Mar 53-29 Jan 55	Cdre. Herbert Sharples Rayner, DSC & Bar RCN
30 Jan 55-2 Aug 56	Capt. Anthony H. G. Storrs, DSC & Bar RCN
3 Aug 56-14 Jun 57	Capt. Alexander B. F. Fraser-Harris, DSC & Bar RCN[9]

Magnificent had no war service; when the Korean War broke out, commitments to NATO duties precluded her service in that theatre. In Europe with the Berlin Blockade starting in 1948 and the Cold War growing, a common strategy was required to counter Soviet-led expansion and to strengthen defences. As a result, the North Atlantic Treaty Organization (NATO) was created in 1949. The situation became even more dire, in 1950, when some NATO members also had to redirect resources to the Korean War, which some planners thought to be a diversionary tactic of the Soviet Union to its larger plans in Europe.

In October and November 1951, while her RN sister ships flew missions in Korea, *Magnificent* transported Sabre jets and RCAF personnel to Glasgow, the first elements of 1 Wing, Canada's first NATO fighter wing, comprising three squadrons of Candair CL-13 Sabre jets. Her cargo included all aircraft for Squadrons No. 410 and No. 441, as well as personnel for No. 410.

Photo 5-4

Cocooned RCAF Sabres on the deck of the HMCS *Magnificent* en route to Glasgow, Scotland, November 1951.
Courtesy of National Archives of Canada

Personnel for No. 441 Squadron arrived by ocean liner at Glasgow, in February 1952. In May-June that year, No. 439 Squadron flew from

RCAF Station Uplands in Ottawa, Ontario, to Scotland via Bagotville, Quebec; Goose Bay, Newfoundland; Greenland; and Iceland, in a process known as Operation Leapfrog. The rapid deployment of Canadian jets, for bases still under construction in Europe was of critical importance at the time. There were USAF shortages arising from the necessity to divert their squadrons to Korea to meet the increasing threat of Soviet MiGs that were becoming a grave threat to the UN Mission there.

Because of problems of loading the 35 Sabers in Halifax, they were ferried to Norfolk, Virginia, where US Navy personnel assisted in cocooning those for deck passage and loading the full complement on board. After returning to Halifax, where she had previously disembarked her fighting aircraft, *Magnificent* embarked 401 personnel and set off on a very difficult and rough North Atlantic crossing. After arriving in Glasgow, the aircraft were unloaded and towed along roads to a nearby airfield at Renfrew. After making them air ready, they were flown to their temporary home at North Luffenham, Rutland, in England.

As an aside, it is noted, that although the RCAF did not fly combat missions in Korea, twenty-two of their Sabre pilots on short-time postings with the USAF did distinguish themselves by shooting down a number of MiGs. Further, Canadian manufacturer Candair supplied sixty of their models of Sabre jets to the USAF to help deficiencies in the Korean theatre.

LIFE ABOARD MAGGIE, AND OTHER OPERATIONS

This section begins with some anecdotes of life aboard *Magnificent* (called "sea stories" by USN sailors, and "dits" by members of Commonwealth navies), followed by descriptions of a deployment to the Caribbean, a much-enjoyed "cocktail cruise" to Europe in 1952, and her participation in the Spithead Naval Review the following year. Other activities follow, including her role as a transport, during the Suez Crisis, delivering a large part of the Canadian peacekeeping force to Egypt, in early 1957.[10]

If HMCS *Magnificent* did not entirely live up to her name, she was nonetheless as comfortable a ship as any other in the Royal Canadian Navy in 1951, and at least had steam heat and some cold-weather engineering. Though to be fair, when scrubbing out the gallery deck mess during winter in the higher latitudes, soap and water would freeze to the deck. Moreover, on more than one occasion, long-handled scrapers were used to remove the ice. But, the light fleet carrier frequently ventured south to waters off Bermuda for exercises with the

Royal Navy and, less frequently, even further south to the Caribbean for interaction with other nations, and to show the flag. This created other problems, owing to unwanted ship visitors in warm climates.[11]

Photo 5-5

A Grumman Avenger torpedo bomber flying past HMCS *Magnificent*, circa 1953. US Navy National Museum of Naval Aviation photograph 1996.253.1746

Photo 5-6

Hawker Sea Fury FB Mk. 11 with HMCS *Magnificent* in the background. DND photograph

In 1951, "Maggie" was on a deployment to the Caribbean Sea. She berthed alongside the jetty in Port of Spain, Trinidad, and rat guards were affixed to mooring lines. During her three-day stay, the carrier offered local citizens shipboard tours. Leaving there, she proceeded to Bridgetown, Barbados, and anchored out. Soon, her crew began noticing rats around the ship. During the day, they were seen around the upper decks; at night while the crew was in their micks (hammocks), they were scurrying above them in the deck head (bathroom) duct work. About this time, opportunity presented itself for sailors to augment their pay, as former crewmember Gerald Sullivan recounted:

> A bounty was put on the rats; a dollar a rat. Produce the body to the MO [medical officer] in Sick Bay and receive the reward. Not bad when a carton of cigarettes was a dollar. An electrician's mate, while checking the main deck submersible pumps came across a nest of about ten of them. By this time, we had returned to Halifax. Some hands were getting dead rats from dockyard workers and applying for the reward. The order then from the MO was that the rat had to be warm when applying for it…. Finally, the ship was towed across the harbour to the Ammunition Dock for fumigation. All hands were sent on leave. Before leaving we slung our micks, preventing the rats from seeking a place to avoid fumigation. That seemed to solve the problem.[12]

What *Magnificent* may have lacked in shipboard amenities by today's standards, she made up for in character, and characters. An exception to her otherwise humble facilities was a luxurious bathroom located midship aft of the gallery deck mess G-5 and G-6, in the area of cabins inhabited mostly by air crew. It contained a number of tubs lined abreast across the deck. The tubs were typically English, two feet wide and four feet deep. Said bathroom was intended for the exclusive use of the officers on board. One particularly stormy night, a number of enlisted sailors came off the last Dog Watch (1800-2000) and were relaxing in G-5 Mess. A member of the mess, a leading seaman with the moniker "Moose," suddenly appeared in a powder blue bathrobe and headed aft with a towel over his arm. Sullivan explains:

> When asked where he was going, he replied, "For a bath." [He] entered the bathroom, wished his fellow shipmates a good evening, selected a vacant tub and proceeded to draw his bath. Once he had sufficient water in the tub, he removed his robe and placed it on a chair next to the tub. At this point there could have been a problem. [Moose] had a number of tattoos, which could have given him away [to the officers occupying other tubs], but as the Captain,

Commodore Adams, also had a number of tattoos they were not an unusual sight in this location. Moose lathered himself up with soap and was enjoying the luxury of soaking in a nice warm bath when his Divisional Officer entered the bathroom.

[He] and his Divisional Officer were very familiar with each other, having met on more than a few occasions for reasons which are stories in themselves. The German Navy may have developed the snorkel, but at this moment [Moose] perfected it. He had not been nicknamed "Moose" for nothing. His distinctive facial features included a wondrously well-developed nose, which, inspired by self-preservation, he put to good use. He slid down into the tub so that his nose just protruded above the bath water. He remained there until it was safe to leave the sanctuary of the tub, towel off, and return to the so-called lower decks.[13]

One might wonder why Moose would venture into an area clearly designated Out of Bounds, but there was a simple explanation. The bathroom on the gallery deck was much closer than the crew wash space on the main deck. To use the latter, one had to drop through a hatch in the deck of the mess, down to the hanger deck—an exposed weather deck. After that, it was down through another hatch to the main deck, and through a passage, before entering the wash space with its basins and showers. There, one might find the showers turned off to conserve fresh water for the boilers. Everyone else abided the inconvenience of using the after washroom on a sloppy night when the seas were rolling in and through the exposed hanger deck, vice risk disciplinary action if found in "officers' country." Moose did not share this view, and he had the nerve and the equipment to carry off the escapade.[14]

MEDITERRANEAN AND NORTH ATLANTIC CRUISE

Photo 5-7

The Royal Marine detachment aboard the British battleship HMS *Vanguard* stand at attention on the quarterdeck, during "morning colours" (flag-raising ceremony), 12 September 1952. To the rear is the Royal Marine Band. *Vanguard* is about to put to sea with the fleet to begin the NATO exercise Operation Mainbrace.
Naval History and Heritage Command photograph #NH 103680

On 2 June 1952, *Magnificent* left Halifax to take part in exercises with the Royal Navy in the Mediterranean and afterward, NATO exercises in the North Atlantic—taking part in Exercise Mainbrace '52 on the final leg home before returning to Halifax, on 10 October 1952. Ports visited during the deployment were:
- Plymouth and Portsmouth, England (14-17 June, 26-30 June)
- Malta (10-13 July)
- Navarino and Athens, Greece (14-18 July, 19-22 July)
- Istanbul, Turkey (24-27 July)
- Tobruk, Libya (28-31 July 1952)
- Malta (2-11 August, 15-18 August)
- Belfast, Ireland (28 August-3 September)
- Rosyth and Greenock, Scotland (11-26 September, 26 September-1 October)[15]

Exercise MAINBRACE, in which 160 ships took part, was the largest and most ambitious NATO naval exercise since the signing of the North Atlantic Treaty on 4 April 1949. It was conducted to assure the Scandinavian signatories (Norway and Denmark) that their countries would be defended in the event of war. At the start of fleet operations, the following fictitious situation existed: "enemy" armies in play from the east had overrun the plains of western Germany and were pouring into Denmark. The forces of Supreme Allied Commander, Europe, were holding along the German Kiel Canal linking the North Sea to the Baltic Sea, but the "enemy" having invaded Norway, was threatening to send an amphibious landing force around the North Cape in northern Norway.[16]

Over the course of fourteen days of maneuvers, friendly carrier planes struck at Bodo, in northern Norway, to drive the invaders back, and the fleet then moved southward to attack near the Kiel Canal while US Marines were landed in Denmark. At completion of Mainbrace, *Magnificent* proceeded to the Firth of Clyde. She sailed from there at midnight, on 1 October, to rendezvous with the other members of Task Group 155.3—the American carriers USS *Wasp* and *Wright*, and nine U.S. destroyers—to participate in Exercise EMIGRANT during her return voyage to Halifax.[17]

For the purposes of the exercise, the task group was to function as an anti-raider Support Group to assist a convoy liable to be attacked by raiders and submarines. Early in the game, an Avenger from *Magnificent* detected the battleship USS *Wisconsin*, closing at 30 knots, while playing the role of a surface raider. In rapid action, surface combatant ships were sent to attack, and eighty aircraft were launched from *Wasp* and *Wright* to carry out two mock strikes. The exercise continued until 8 October, when "Maggie" and the cruiser HMCS *Quebec* (one of the raiders) were detached to proceed to Halifax, where they were welcomed home by a large gathering of family and friends the following day.[18]

1953 SPITHEAD NAVAL REVIEW

Queen Elizabeth's succession to the throne in February 1952 preceded the Coronation Ceremony, which did not take place until 2 June 1953. Following the ceremony was the imposing spectacle of the Spithead Naval Review on 15 June. In celebration of the Coronation, over 300 vessels assembled in the Solent, a strait of the English Channel adjacent to the major ports of Portsmouth and Southampton. The fleet consisted of major and minor warships representing the UK, Commonwealth, and a number of foreign countries including the

122   Chapter 5

United States and Russia; and numerous merchant vessels, fishing vessels, and private yachts also participated. All these ships and craft were assembled in assigned rows and/or specific areas for review by Her Majesty and Prince Philip from the bridge of the Royal Yacht, HMS *Surprise*.[19]

Photo 5-8

Spithead, England, 1953. The frigate HMS *Surprise* flying the Royal Standard and being used as royal yacht for the occasion, with Her Majesty, Queen Elizabeth II aboard steaming down the lines of ships during the Royal Coronation Naval Review, after Her Majesty's Coronation.
Australian War Memorial photograph 030454

"Maggie" was the flagship of Canada's naval participation in the review, which also included the cruisers HMCS *Ontario* and *Quebec*, destroyer HMCS *Sioux*, and frigates HMCS *Swansea* and *La Hulloise*. On carrier row, she joined probably the greatest gathering ever of Commonwealth aircraft carriers, five fleet ships, and four sister light carriers. The latter included HMS *Theseus* and *Perseus*, and HMAS *Sydney*, which joined *Magnificent* on her return voyage for a visit to Halifax where the Aussie carrier paid a visit followed by a stop in Annapolis, Maryland, before heading to the Panama Canal and home.

NATO EXERCISE MARINER

Later that year, on 23 September, *Magnificent* was part of the "Mariner Miracle" that saw a USN Douglas AD-4B Skyraider from USS *Bennington* land most unexpectedly on her deck in clearing fog. *Maggie*'s presence saved the bomber—a version of the AD-4 designed to carry and deliver nuclear weapons—from ditching. The carriers USS *Wasp*, USS *Bennington*, and HMCS *Magnificent* were conducting Exercise MARINER in the North Atlantic. With forty-two planes aloft, the carriers were completely socked in by fog. Vice Adm. Thomas Selby Combs and Rear Adm. Hugh H. Goodwin ordered all planes to ditch near the submarine USS *Redfin* at 1620. However, the fog suddenly lifted and the aircraft could be recovered safely with only minimum fuel remaining.[20]

On board "Maggie," Canadian sailors painted small red maple leafs on the Skyraider's American stars, that apparently remained despite several subsequent overhauls and repaintings.

Photo 5-9

US Navy Douglas AD-4 Skyraider (similar in appearance to the AD-4B that landed aboard HMCS *Magnificent*) taking off from the USS *Philippine Sea* (CV-47) on a mission to support UN forces in North Korea, 25 November 1950.
National Archives photograph #80-G-439876

MARINER was the largest international naval exercise ever held. It was sponsored jointly by SACLANT (Supreme Allied Commander Atlantic), SACEUR (Supreme Allied Commander Europe), and the Channel Commanders. Allied Command Channel (ACCHAN), established in 1952 to defend the sea areas and allied shipping around the English Channel, included subordinate commanders. Nine countries participated in the exercise lasting nineteen days, which included convoy protection, naval control of shipping, and striking fleet operations in northern waters. The enemy role was taken by surface raiders, submarines, and land-based air elements from NATO forces.[21]

SACLANT Emblem   SACEUR Emblem   ACCHAN Emblem

VISIT TO THE WEST COAST IN 1954

Having sailed from Halifax, on 21 September in company with the cruiser HMCS *Quebec*, "Maggie," in early October 1954, entered the Pacific Ocean via the Panama Canal to visit Canada's west coast. She was the second RCN capital ship to make this passage, being only preceded by HMCS *Warrior* in 1946-1947. This was her first and only visit to Canada's west coast. Joined by the frigate HMCS *Steller* at Panama, she conducted extensive flying training en route. After being welcomed, and well entertained during four-day stays at both San Diego and San Francisco, she arrived at the RCN's west coast base at Esquimalt, on 25 October, where she was similarly welcomed and entertained. (While transiting up America's west coast, "Maggie" had met Canada's then-new ice breaker HMCS *Labrador* at San Francisco. At the time, *Labrador* was homeward bound to Halifax completing a 10,000-mile circumnavigation of North America.)

At the dockyard in Esquimalt, *Magnificent* was open to the public for three days of her five-day visit, while her aircraft enjoyed the runways of the nearby facilities of the Patricia Bay Airfield. A similar five-day visit was made to Vancouver on the mainland, after she voyaged past the Gulf Islands and passed under the Lions Gate Bridge, in company with the destroyer HMCS *Crusader* and frigate HMCS *New Glasgow*, arriving on 1 November. "Maggie" left Vancouver with an expected return date to Halifax by 5 December 1954.

PARTICIPATION IN SUEZ CRISIS PEACEKEEPING

On the night of 7 November 1956, *Magnificent*, while lying at the Tail-of-the-Bank anchorage in the upper Firth of Clyde, received a signal, ordering her to return home immediately at best speed. Upon berthing at Pier 4 in Halifax, on 13 November, a horde of dockyard workmen and naval personnel descended upon "Maggie," to prepare her to serve as a troopship and headquarters vessel in connection with UN action then taking place in the Middle East.[22]

The UN involvement resulted from the "Suez Crisis" precipitated by Egyptian President Gamal Abdel Nasser's decision, in July 1956, to nationalize the Suez Canal, which had been jointly controlled by Great Britain and France. Following military intervention by Israeli, British, and French forces, the UN had passed a resolution calling for a cease-fire, and both the United States and the Soviet Union were pressuring the tripartite forces to withdraw. (Ultimately, British and French troops would depart Egypt, in December 1956, and those of Israel, in March 1957.)[23]

Magnificent's involvement was part of the ten-nation contribution to the first United Nations Emergency Force (UNEF) that was created to allow the withdrawal and to supervise the ceasefire. The first commander of the force was E. L. M. (Eedson Louis Millard) Burns. Canada's foreign minister, later Prime Minister, Lester B. Pearson is credited with the idea of the force. Pearson was later awarded the Nobel Peace Prize for his initiative in resolving the crisis through use of the United Nations, although some of his countrymen accused him of betraying Canada and her ties with the UK.

Modifications made to "Maggie" for Operation RAPID STEP, included removal of guns, ammunition, ready-use lockers, etc., and the installation of berthing and other facilities necessary for an additional 500 men on board. "A" hangar was converted into a dormitory with two-tiered bunks; additional bathrooms were added; and the sonobuoy flat was transformed into a sickbay annex. *Magnificent* moved to Pier 9B to take aboard Army ammunition and 203 vehicles, then returned to Pier 4 to load fourteen heavy vehicles. Except for the impending embarkation of the 950 officers and men of the First Battalion, Queen's Own Rifles, she was ready to go.[24]

Then orders came to revert (lapse) the planned under way time and to be on eight-hours notice to put to sea. Two days later, this was extended to a 24-hours warning. For the rest of November, and eleven days into December, "Maggie" waited orders while UN "top brass" pondered over the requirements of its newly formed Emergency Force. Eventually, it was decided that Canada's military contribution to the UNEF would consist of "housekeeping troops"—whereupon the Queen's Own returned to their base in Calgary.[25]

Preparations for RAPID STEP II involved offloading ammunition and vehicles, and some reorganization on board, as the carrier would be used only for transport duties, and not as a headquarters vessel, as was originally intended. With 406 Canadian troops and their vehicles, along with 4 RCAF de Havilland Canada DHC-3 Otters, and a single HO4S helicopter, "Maggie" slipped her lines on 29 December. Her departure was accompanied by "Auld Lang Syne," played loudly by the bands of HMCS *Stadacona* and the Royal Canadian Artillery, and the pipes and drums of the Royal Highland Regiment of Canada. (Auld Lang Syne was a Scots-language poem written by Robert Burns in 1788, and set to the tune of a traditional folk song.) Landfall was made on Terceira in the Azores, at daybreak on 4 January 1957.[26]

Passing Gibraltar at the entrance to "the Med" and continuing eastward, *Magnificent* arrived at Port Said, Egypt, on 7 January 1957, where the troops and equipment were disembarked. After UN stores were ashore, and an extensive cleaning and painting programme had made "Maggie" shipshape again, Libertymen (120 in each party) went ashore, on 16, 17, and 19 January, for organized trips to Cairo and the Pyramids, as guests of the Egyptian government. Limited liberty was also given in Port Said on the 18th and 19th.[27]

Having fulfilled all her obligations to the UN force, *Magnificent* sailed, on 20 January, for Naples, Italy. Exiting the Mediterranean nine days later, the light fleet carrier steamed up the Irish Sea and entered the Firth of Clyde. After hoisting 59 Sabre jet aircraft on board at King George V dock, Shieldhall, Glasgow, "Maggie" began the Atlantic crossing. The RCAF jets were being returned to Canada after serving as part of Canada's NATO contribution to the defence of Europe. Arriving at Halifax, she entered her home port for the final time. HMCS *Magnificent* sailed from Halifax, on 10 April 1957. Following arrival at Plymouth, England, she was paid off by the RCN and reverted to the Royal Navy, on 14 June 1957.[28]

HMCS *BONAVENTURE*, CANADA'S LAST CARRIER

> *Canada is getting a good value in this ship. Our country is growing and so is the need for naval air power. That is why it is so important that we have made this advance, no matter how modest.*
>
> —Statement to the *Toronto Telegram* by Capt. Harold V. W. Groos, CD RCN, *Bonaventure*'s first commanding officer.[29]

Canada's acquisition and commissioning of HMCS *Bonaventure*, at Belfast on 17 January 1957, an aircraft carrier that could operate in the jet aircraft age, was an occasion of great rejoicing. Completed to Canadian requirements and belonging to the *Majestic*-class, "Bonnie" boasted a strengthened flight deck necessary to operate jet planes; an angled-deck to provide a much longer landing area, a steam catapult to help provide acceleration for planes taking off; and a mirror-landing aid to assist pilots making their final approach to the carrier.[30]

Photo 5-10

HMCS *Bonaventure* (CVL 22) at sea, date and location unknown.
Courtesy of Shearwater Aviation Museum

Following weeks of ship and flying trials, *Bonaventure* left Belfast Lough, on 19 June 1957, bound for Halifax. The pride of the RCN found her homeport enveloped in thick fog but, after groping her way to the jetty, assisted by radar, she was greeted by a large crowd of people. Unlike her predecessors, *Bonaventure* operated McDonnell Douglas F2H-3 Banshee jet fighters, Grumman CS2F Tracker anti-submarine warfare (ASW) aircraft, and Sikorsky HO4S helicopters. Like them, she would enjoy a busy career of flying training and participating in ASW and tactical exercises with ships of other NATO nations.[31]

Photo 5-11

De Havilland Canada (Grumman) CS-2F Tracker in flight over HMCS *Bonaventure*.
RCN photograph

Photo 5-12

McDonnell F2H-3 Banshee (No. 144).
RCN photograph courtesy of the Shearwater Aviation Museum

HMCS *Bonaventure* never saw frontline combat. Her closest brush with this possibility was in late October 1962, during the Cuban missile crisis. "Bonnie" was at Portsmouth, England, having just finished NATO exercises with British, Danish, and Norwegian ships in the North Atlantic, when American President John F. Kennedy ordered a blockade of Cuba. Capt. Frederick C. Frewer, commanding *Bonaventure*, put to sea with all dispatch, and later described his ship's involvement in the crisis:

> Aircraft carriers were spaced about 150 miles apart all the way north of Cuba. One of the *Essex* Class Carriers was just to the south of us, the *LAKE CHAMPLAIN*, I believe it was. We were at the northern end of the picket line, and I think the decision was going to be made within two to three hours as to whether we were going to war. So we were part of the operation, covering the northern flank alert and ready to go with war-loaded aircraft. It was exciting because we knew at the time that there were some submarines accompanying the missile-carrying freighters.[32]

For the next ten days, *Bonaventure* remained at operational readiness, until the crisis eventually abated and she returned to Halifax. Earlier that year, she had lost her Banshee jet fighters, upon disbandment of No. VF 870 Naval Air Squadron, on 7 September 1962.[33]

In 1964, the carrier ferried army equipment and supplies to Cyprus, in late March, in support of the UN Peacekeeping Force. (The reasons for this action are covered in the book's preface.) While the RCAF airlifted the majority of Canada's Peacekeeping forces, "Bonnie" transported the balance of 95 army soldiers, 54 vehicles, and 160 tons of equipment.[34]

In April 1966, *Bonaventure* began a mid-life refit, designed to extend her service into the mid-1970s. The shipyard overhaul was expected to cost $8 million, but ended up being over $11 million. Moreover, it took 16 months to complete, much longer than planned. On 1 February 1968, the Royal Canadian Navy ceased to exist upon unification of it, the Canadian Army, and the Royal Canadian Air Force into one service, the Canadian Forces (CF). These actions probably contributed to the early paying off of HMCS *Bonaventure*.[35]

ELIMINATION OF THE RCN CARRIER PROGRAM

> *The political fallout from the cost overrun of the carrier's [Bonaventure] refit, [Prime Minister] Trudeau's antipathy toward the military and NATO generally, the financial cutbacks, limited personnel to man the new Tribal escorts, a separate unpublicized naval agenda to shift to a helicopter only force, a lack of will to maintain a balanced Canadian Naval Aviation, a muted naval voice with no common objective, [and] a determination of the Air Force to eliminate the sharing of aviation funds with the rival carrier Naval Aviation.*
>
> —Factors cited, all having a degree of credibility, resulting in Canada's decision to scrap HMCS *Bonaventure*. Individually, none of these reasons were dominant; collectively they were overwhelming.[36]

On 20 September 1969, *Bonaventure* and her escort group were engaged in PEACE KEEPER, a NATO exercise in the Eastern Atlantic. Involving over 40 ships and 200 land and carrier-based aircraft from Canada, Germany, the Netherlands, the United Kingdom and the United States, it was designed to test the readiness and effectiveness of the NATO Striking Fleet Atlantic to provide naval support to Alliance nations of the Atlantic community. There was shock aboard "Bonnie" that evening when a CBC (Canadian Broadcasting Corporation, the "Voice of Canada") shortwave news service declared that *Bonaventure* was to be scrapped, and Anti-Submarine Squadron VS-880 was slated for disbandment.[37]

The rationale to scrap the RCN's single carrier, probably resulted from one or more of the factors cited in the quoted material. Whoever engineered the demise of *Bonaventure* probably expected that once she was gone, it would not be long before Canadian Naval Aviation was a non-entity. The absence of a carrier would likely ensure the elimination of the Tracker squadron and supporting fixed-wing training units.[36]

On 1 July 1970, only three years after her mid-life refit, "Bonnie" was paid off, and sold for scrap. Squadron VS-880 survived, albeit with a new mission. With minimal requirements for anti-submarine warfare in the early 1970s, the squadron switched to Maritime Reconnaissance and continued in that role until its operations were halted in 1990.[38]

WISTFUL TALE ABOUT "BONNIE"

Bonaventure was sold for $851,700 to the Vancouver company N. W. Kennedy Ltd., which took possession of her, on 28 October 1970, and had her towed out of Halifax by the tug *Fuji Mary*. As the "Bonnie" proceeded under tow around the Cape of Good Hope and into the Indian Ocean, the basis for a myth was born. When the *Fuji Mary* arrived at Taiwan's Kaohsiung Harbor, on 15 March 1971, a story began to spread in bars in Halifax—thought to be originated by those who served aboard "Bonnie"—that her charge was not the *Bonaventure* at all. It was, instead, the Indian aircraft carrier INS *Vikrant* (ex-HMS *Hercules*) of the same British *Majestic*-class, and outwardly of the same appearance. A switch had been made at sea with the superbly upgraded "Bonnie" joining the Indian Navy and the *Vikrant* going for scrap. The *Bonaventure*, having undergone a highly overrun refit of over $17 million was in far better shape than *Vikrant*.[39]

In a 1997 article for Canada's *Southam Newspapers*, which announced the decommissioning of the *Vikrant*, journalist Jonathan Manthorpe debunked the story indicating that it was a tale of wishful thinking adding much of Bonnie's expensive refit work, even down to her massive bronze propellers, had been stripped from her before leaving Halifax. He conceded, however, that the reason the tale had lived on so long, might have been that "The Bonnie" was perhaps the most loved ship in our navy's history" – indeed, she was a happy ship.

RCN Badge

6

Post-WWII Service of the *Independence*-class CVLs

Photo 6-1

USS *Monterey* (CVL-26) under way in the Gulf of Mexico, 29 January 1953, with her crew spelling out Mardi Gras 1953 on her flight deck. With all of her guns removed, she was then serving as a training carrier, operating out of Pensacola, Florida, a duty undertaken in January 1951 and lasting until June 1955.
Naval History and Heritage Command photograph #NH 97452

The second and third chapters of this book describe the Korean War service of USS *Bataan*, the only one of the Navy's nine *Independence*-class light fleet carriers to serve in that conflict. As mentioned in the book's preface, two additional CVLs (*Saipan*-class ships) were commissioned and put into service after World War II. Their duty—first as carriers, and later, one as a Presidential Command Post, and the other a Major Communications Relay ship—is the subject of Chapters 7 and 8.

Before progressing to the USS *Saipan* and USS *Wright*, it is appropriate to acknowledge the heroic service of their predecessors in World War II, the nine *Independence*-class ships, and the subsequent post-WWII service of three of these ships—*Cabot*, *Bataan*, and *Monterey*.

Although the *Independence* CVLs did not enter service until 1943, relatively late in the war, they collectively garnered two Presidential Unit Citations (PUCs), two Navy Unit Commendations (NUCs), and eighty-seven battle stars. Their story is the subject of Volume I of *Turn in to the Wind*.

Independence-class Light Fleet Aircraft Carriers

Aircraft Carrier	Battle Stars	PUCs	NUCs
Independence (CVL-22)	WWII ★★★★★★★★		
Princeton (CVL-23)	WWII ★★★★★★★★★		
Belleau Wood (CVL-24)	WWII ★★★★★★★★★★★		
Cowpens (CVL-25)	WWII ★★★★★★★★★★★		NUC
Monterey (CVL-26)	WWII ★★★★★★★★★★★		
Langley (CVL-27)	WWII ★★★★★★★★★		NUC
Cabot (CVL-28)	WWII ★★★★★★★★	PUC	
Bataan (CVL-29)	WWII ★★★★★ Korean War ★★★★★★★		
San Jacinto (CVL-30)	WWII ★★★★★★	PUC	
Total Awards	87	2	2

Princeton was scuttled following a Japanese dive-bomber attack, on 24 October 1944, in which she suffered great damage and loss of life. Of the remaining eight CVLs, seven took part in Operation MAGIC CARPET, the transport home of former POWs during the immediate aftermath of the war. *Independence* participated in nuclear tests at Bikini Atoll, was contaminated, and later disposed of. The remaining seven carriers were laid up as part of the post-World War II drawdown. Three—*Bataan*, *Cabot*, and *Monterey*—were returned to service, and ultimately, *Cabot*, *Langley*, and *Belleau Wood* were transferred to Allies. Four CVLs were reclassified as AVTs (Auxiliary Aircraft Transports) while "mothballed" in reserve fleets, but never utilized in this role.

CVL	Magic Carpet	Bikini Atoll Atomic Tests	Foreign Transfer	Korea/Other	AVT
Independence	X	X			
Princeton lost in WWII					
Belleau Wood	X		France		
Cowpens	X				

Monterey	X		X	X
Langley	X	France		
Cabot		Spain	X	X
Bataan	X		X	X
San Jacinto	X			X

Descriptions of these activities follow in the next few pages.

OPERATION MAGIC CARPET

Photo 6-2

Painting *Coming into Golden Gate Bridge* by Franklin Boggs, 1945.
Naval History and Heritage Command Accession #88-159-BR

Following victory in Europe and the surrender of Japan, there remained the enormous task of returning home huge numbers of American and other Allied military personnel scattered across the globe. Operation MAGIC CARPET was the name given to the post-war sealift of military and civilian personnel from Europe, the Pacific, Asia, Alaska, the Caribbean, and South America to the United States.[1]

On 9 September 1945, Rear Adm. Henry S. Kendall, USN (commander, Carrier Division 24), was designated commander, Task Group 16.12 and, as such, was in charge of MAGIC CARPET. During its peak operating period in December 1945, 305 ships, including 222 troopships, 12 hospital ships, 6 battleships, 18 cruisers, and 57 aircraft carriers, on all the oceans of the world, were transporting U.S. servicemen home. So many were being separated from military service that Gen. George C. Marshall told historian Samuel Eliot Morison "...that demobilization had become a rout."[2]

BIKINI ATOLL ATOMIC BOMB TESTS

A destroyer and two transports sank promptly and another destroyer capsized. It later sank, and the Japanese cruiser SAKAWA sank the following day. The superstructure of the submarine SKATE was so badly damaged as to make it unsafe to submerge the vessel. The light carrier INDEPENDENCE was badly wrecked by the explosion, gutted by fire, and further damaged by internal explosions of low order, including those of torpedoes.

—Excerpt from *Bombs at Bikini: The Official Report of Operation Crossroads*, published in 1947.[3]

Photo 6-3

Bikini Atoll A-Bomb Tests. View of the target fleet immediately after the "Able" Day aerial burst, 1 July 1946. USS *Saratoga* (CV-3) is at center-right with USS *Independence* (CVL-22) burning at left-center. Ex-Japanese battleship *Nagato* is between them. National Archives photograph #K-20262

In July 1946, a joint US Army-Navy task force staged two atomic weapons tests at Bikini Atoll in the Marshall Islands, the first atomic explosions since the bombings of Japan in August 1945. The first test, designated Test Able, took place on 1 July. The Navy sought the Bikini tests in order to measure the effects of atomic explosions on warships and other military targets. A fleet of 96 target ships, including the aircraft carriers USS *Saratoga* and USS *Independence*, participated in the tests, under the umbrella codename Operation CROSSROADS.[4]

Test Able, on 1 July, involved an air burst directly above the target ships, created by a plutonium bomb dropped by a B-29 Superfortress. The roughly ninety test vessels were under the command of Rear Adm. Frank G. Fahrion, commander of Task Group 1.2. The aircraft carriers of Task Unit 1.1.2—USS *Saratoga* and USS *Independence*—were under

Capt. Nolan M. Kindell, commanding officer of *Independence*. Capt. Donald S. MacMahan commanded the *Saratoga*.[5]

The bomb drifted off target as it descended, bringing it closer to the *Independence* than planned, leaving the "Mighty-I" tortured and horribly disfigured by the blast, but defiantly afloat. For Test Baker, on 25 July, the bomb was suspended 90 feet beneath the amphibious landing ship *LSM-160* positioned in the lagoon. Sixty-eight target vessels were at their moorings, and twenty-four smaller craft were beached inside the atoll. *Independence* was only 1,390 yards from "Surface Zero," but survived a tidal wave of radioactive spray and steam that rose to smother the fleet." Eight of its members, including *Saratoga*, were sunk, and an additional eight seriously damaged.[6]

After being towed from Bikini, *Independence* was decommissioned at Kwajalein Atoll, on 22 August 1946. Afterward, the ex-*Independence* was towed to San Francisco by the fleet ocean tugs USS *Hitchiti* and USS *Pakana*, arriving at Hunters Point, on 16 June 1947. On 26 January 1951, following extensive study by Naval Radiological Defense Laboratory personnel, and partial decontamination of the remains of CVL-22, explosive charges sent the hulk to the seafloor about thirty miles off Half Moon Bay, California.[7]

Photo 6-4

Battleship USS *Iowa* (BB-61) passes the burned-out hulk of USS *Independence* in San Francisco Bay, July 1947.
Naval History and Heritage Command photograph #NH 70264

LIGHT FLEET CARRIERS LAID UP

The quick building of CVL *Independence*-class ships was an expedient of war, at a time of dire need. But, by the end of the Pacific war, such sufficient numbers of the larger, more capable *Essex*-class had been built by America's amazing wartime production, that the lesser ships would not fit within the needs and constraints of the downsizing peacetime navy budget. In 1947, the surviving light fleet carriers were either placed "out of commission, in reserve," or decommissioned, and laid up in Reserve Fleets.[8]

Ship	Date	Ship	Date
Bataan	11 February 1947	*Langley*	11 February 1947
Belleau Wood	13 January 1947	*Monterey*	11 February 1947
Cabot	11 February 1947	*San Jacinto*	1 March 1947
Cowpens	13 January 1947		

THREE LIGHT CARRIERS PUT BACK INTO SERVICE

Photo 6-5

Grumman AF-2W Guardian submarine hunters of Anti-submarine Squadron VS-24. USS *Cabot* (CVL-28) 1952 Mediterranean cruise book

Cabot was the first CVL to be returned to active service from the Reserve Fleet. She recommissioned, on 27 October 1948, and was assigned to the Naval Air Training Command for duty. In 1950, she underwent overhaul in Philadelphia and returned to the Fleet, in 1951, as the nation's most modern anti-submarine carrier. The light carrier operated out of Pensacola, Florida, then from Naval Air Station Quonset Point, Rhode Island, on cruises to the Caribbean. She had one tour of duty with the Sixth Fleet in the Mediterranean (9 January–26 March 1952).[9]

Photo 6-6

Oran, Algeria, street scene.
USS *Cabot* (CVL-28) 1952 Mediterranean cruise book

Photo 6-7

The Casbah in Tangiers.
USS *Cabot* (CVL-28) 1952 Mediterranean cruise book

Cabot was again taken out of commission and placed in reserve, on 21 January 1955, but was reclassified as an auxiliary aircraft transport (AVT-3), on 15 May 1959. She remained idle, until 30 August 1967, when loaned to the Spanish Navy and renamed *Dedalo*. Spain purchased her, on 1 August 1972, and she continued her service, until August 1989. After being returned by Spain to the United States, attempts to preserve her as a floating museum and a war memorial eventually came to naught, owing to a lack of funding, she was broken-up and scrapped in 2002.[10]

Bataan was the second light fleet carrier to return to service. Heightened tensions between the United States, as a prime member of NATO on the one hand, and the Soviet Union and communist China on the other, led the Truman administration to ask for increased military spending. An expanded Navy budget resulted in *Bataan* being recommissioned at Philadelphia, on 13 May 1950. Her Korean War duty is described in preceding chapters. *Bataan* was decommissioned, on 9 April 1954, and assigned to the Pacific Reserve Fleet at San Francisco. Her name was stricken from the Navy List, on 1 September 1959. She was sold to Nicolai Joffe Corp., Beverly Hills, California, on 19 June 1961, for scrapping.[11]

With the outbreak of hostilities in Korea, on 25 June 1950, *Monterey* was recommissioned, 15 September 1950. She departed Norfolk, 3 January 1951, and proceeded to Pensacola, Florida, where she operated for the next four years, training thousands of naval aviation cadets (civilian and enlisted candidates), commissioned student pilots, and helicopter trainees. Following the war, she rejoined the Atlantic Reserve Fleet, Philadelphia Group. She decommissioned, 16 January 1956, and was sold for scrapping, in May 1971.[12]

LANGLEY AND *BELLEAU WOOD* TRANSFERRED TO FRANCE

Langley and *Belleau Wood* remained in "mothballs" until transferred on a loan basis to France, on 8 January 1951 and 5 September 1953, respectively, under the Mutual Defense Assistance Program. In French service, *Langley* was renamed *Lafayette*. The carrier was returned to the United States, on 20 March 1963, and was sold to the Boston Metals Co., Baltimore, Maryland, for scrapping. *Belleau Wood*, under a similar arrangement, had been returned earlier, in September 1960, after serving as *Bois Belleau* in the French Navy. Boston Metals acquired her, on 21 November 1960, for scrapping.[13]

COWPENS AND *SAN JACINTO* STRUCK

The final two *Independence*-class CVLs remained in the Reserve Fleet until ultimately sold for scrapping. *Cowpens* was struck from the Navy List, on 1 November 1959, and sold for scrap in 1960. *San Jacinto* was struck, on 1 June 1970, and sold for scrapping, on 15 December 1971, to National Metal and Steel Co., Terminal Island, California.[14]

SERVICE REMAINING FOR *SAIPAN* AND *WRIGHT*

The two CVLs of the *Saipan*-class would later be taken from the Reserve Fleet to serve their country, although not as light fleet carriers.

7

National Emergency Command Post USS *Wright* (CC-2)

During our 2-week cruise we would sail to some vacation resort (St. Thomas, St. Croix, Nova Scotia, Bermuda, etc.) and tie up for a week. That was our "cruise." [USS Wright] carried...top brass.... They didn't want to paddle around for 2 weeks at a time, so we always put in at some really nice port along the eastern seaboard. The ship ... was a converted aircraft carrier with a humongous antenna farm on the flight deck. The entire rear section of the ship was a powerful VLF transmitter, with vacuum tubes taller than I am. Each stage of the transmitter was in its own compartment.... They had this helicopter with twin interlocking blades (no tail rotor) that hauled a cable to 10,000 feet for the VLF antenna - the most powerful VLF transmitter in the world at that time (talking about ERP). All the pilot did was take off and land, as it was flown from the ship most of the time it was airborne. Most of the ship was off limits to everyone I knew, and all I did was calibrate & repair electronic test equipment.

—Former crewmember aboard USS *Wright* describing alternating alert duty with USS *Northampton* (CC-1) every two weeks while serving as a potential floating White House/Pentagon.[1]

Photo 7-1

Service as a National Emergency Command Post (CC-2)

11 May 1963 - 27 May 1970

USS *Wright* in June 1963.
Naval History and Heritage Command photograph #NH97621

In the early stages of the Cold War, as a deterrent to a possible nuclear attack by the Soviet Union, the U.S. military kept strategic bombers in the air and ballistic missile submarines at sea armed with nuclear weapons. A Ballistic Missile Early Warning System was developed to provide long-range, immediate warning of a missile attack over the polar region utilizing stations in the northern hemisphere. In conjunction, a Distant Early Warning Line (made up of more than sixty manned-radar installations and extending about 3,000 miles from northwestern Alaska to eastern Baffin Island in northern Canada) served as a warning system for the United States and Canada that could detect and verify the approach of aircraft or intercontinental ballistic missiles (ICBMs) from the Soviet Union.[2]

TOP SECRET DOOMSDAY HIDEOUTS

As each side raced to gain nuclear superiority with ICBMs, the United States government made contingency plans for Continuity of Government in the event of a nuclear attack. Preparations included building underground bunkers and arranging to move high-ranking government officials out of harm's way. The scheme provided the option of subterranean, airborne, and seaborne command posts for use by the president and accompanying top officials. The simplified diagram below depicts possible movement from the White House to the Pentagon, or to an airborne command post, to one of two ships configured as afloat White Houses, or to an underground fortress built for the North American Aerospace Defense Command (NORAD), beneath Cheyenne Mountain in Colorado Springs, Colorado.[3]

Diagram 7-1

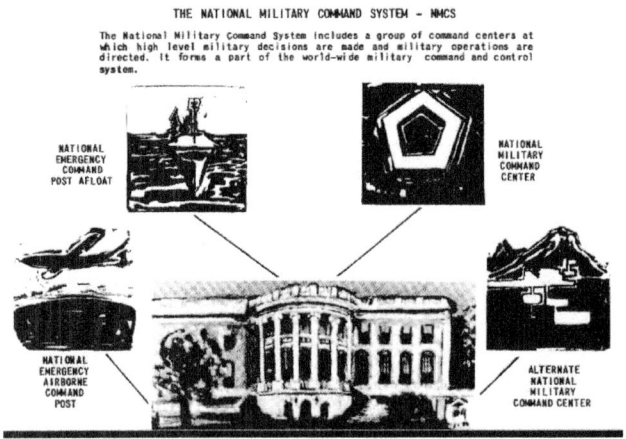

THE NATIONAL MILITARY COMMAND SYSTEM - NMCS

The National Military Command System includes a group of command centers at which high level military decisions are made and military operations are directed. It forms a part of the world-wide military command and control system.

NATIONAL EMERGENCY COMMAND POST AFLOAT

NATIONAL MILITARY COMMAND CENTER

NATIONAL EMERGENCY AIRBORNE COMMAND POST

ALTERNATE NATIONAL MILITARY COMMAND CENTER

USS *Wright* (CC-2) 1967 Welcome Aboard booklet

Two special Navy command ships—the light cruiser USS *Northampton* (CC-1) and light aircraft carrier USS *Wright* (CC-2) —were considered the best options for receiving the evacuation of the president from Washington, D.C., in the event of a nuclear attack. Under the National Emergency Command Post Afloat plan, one of the two "Floating White Houses" was always at sea in the Atlantic; Chesapeake Bay, Virginia; or shadowing the president around the world.[4]

Photo 7-2

Service as a National Emergency Command Post (CC-1)

15 April 1961- 8 April 1970

USS *Northampton* (CC-1) at sea, 26 June 1962.
Naval History and Heritage Command photograph #NH 106503

The two afloat National Emergency Command Posts carried special Joint Chiefs personnel and featured elaborate staterooms with full communications capabilities. When these ships were specially configured and put into service, it was believed that the Soviet Union Navy was so weak, it would be almost impossible for its ships to find them in the grand expanse of the Atlantic. After the introduction of satellite technology made it easy to locate and track ships, it became apparent that it was no longer feasible to hide the president in the Atlantic. The program was dropped in the early 1970s, and both ships were eventually sold for scrap.[5]

PEDIGREE OF COMMAND SHIP USS *WRIGHT* (CC-2)

As previously noted, USS *Wright* (CVL-49) was one of two *Saipan*-class light fleet carriers entering naval service following World War II. The subject of *Saipan* (CVL-48), which would serve as a Major Communications Relay Ship during the Vietnam War, is taken up in the following chapter.

Wright which was built by the New York Shipbuilding Company of Camden, New Jersey, was launched, on 1 September 1945. She was commissioned USS *Wright* (CVL-49) at the Philadelphia Naval Shipyard, on 9 February 1947. During the next eight years and five months, *Wright* served as a carrier in both the Atlantic and Pacific Fleets, where she earned three service medals: Navy Occupation Service Medal, Korean Service Medal, and United Nations Service Medal. (The latter medal was subsequently renamed, United Nations Service Medal for Korea.)[6]

Photo 7-3

Waving the Texas flag from aboard USS *Wright*, 1948.
Naval History and Heritage Command photograph #NH62399

LAID UP IN "MOTH BALLS" IN RESERVE FLEET

As part of the Navy's post-Korean War downsizing, scores of ships were laid up, or disposed of by transfer or sale to Allies or commercial interests. *Wright* was one of these. On 17 October 1955, she arrived at the Puget Sound Naval Shipyard in Bremerton, Washington, for inactivation and preservation. Decommissioned there, on 15 March 1956, she was assigned to the Bremerton Group, U.S. Pacific Reserve Fleet. While idle, on 15 May 1959, *Wright* was reclassified an Auxiliary Aircraft Transport (AVT-7). But as previously indicated, that was not to be her final fate.[7]

Wright entered the Puget Sound Naval Shipyard, on 15 March 1962, for conversion to a command ship. The required work cost $25 million and took more than a year to complete. She was recommissioned, on 11 May 1963. Following several weeks of local operations and sea trials in Puget Sound, *Wright* (CC-2) made passage to Norfolk, arriving there, on 18 December 1963.[8]

Photo 7-4

USS *Wright* (CC-2) arriving at San Diego, California, June 1963.
Naval History and Heritage Command photograph #NH97624

ATLANTIC FLEET DUTY

With her cruiser hull having an overall length of 701 feet, 77-foot beam, 19,265-ton maximum displacement, and a 26-foot draft, *Wright* could make over 30 knots through the water. She was powered by four main turbine engines producing 120,000 total shaft power. Four 40mm guns were her only armament. Ship's complement was 58 officers and 1,190 enlisted men.[9]

Operating from Norfolk, taking up her Atlantic Fleet duty, *Wright* served as an emergency command post, ready to take aboard U.S.

political and military leaders in the event of a threatened nuclear conflict. She also performed communications services, including supporting President Lyndon B. Johnson's attendance at the Latin America Summit in Uruguay, in April 1967.[10]

Wright and *Northampton* alternated the alert duty every two weeks, operating somewhere off the East Coast as a potential floating White House/Pentagon. Just outside of Norfolk, the ships would silently sail past each other as the alert ship was relieved. The relieved ship would then enter port for replenishing, and rest and recreation for the crew.[11]

Both command ships employed a huge dish-like structure used for Troposphere Scatter Communications in conjunction with land-based dish sites located in Massachusetts, North Carolina, and Delaware. The alert ship usually operated within a few hundred miles of one of these dish sites. To decrease radio-direction-finding activities from hostile sources attempting to trace the location of the alert ship, the TROPO system aboard each ship provided a "difficult to zero in on" facility for telephone, teletype, and data circuits. The system's successful operation was a top priority for *Wright* and *Northampton*. The former used the voice radio call sign Zenith, and the latter, Sea Ruler, during communication with other ships, aircraft, and shore stations.[12]

The mission of the two ships was to handle communications and command data for strategic worldwide direction of military operations. *Wright* and *Northampton* were always ready for the president (with special presidential quarters), and both had access to White House Situation Room classified information. In the eventuality of a nuclear war, the alert ship would be third in line behind the Strategic Air Command and the North American Air Defense Command, to maintain Continuity of Government and control of U.S Armed Forces and nuclear weapons.[13]

END OF SERVICE

Wright was decommissioned, on 27 May 1970, and remained inactive until sold for scrapping in July 1980. Six individuals commanded her during her service as an afloat presidential command post.

USS *Wright* (CC-2) Commanding Officers

Capt. John Lindsay Arrington II, USN	11 May 63 – 18 Dec 64
Capt. Francis John Fitzpatrick, USN	18 Dec 64 – 9 Dec 65
Capt. Robert Hastings White, USN	9 Dec 65 – 31 Dec 66
Capt. Frank Maxim Romanick, USN	31 Dec 66 – 10 Aug 68
Capt. Henry Ehrman ("Tim") Thornhill Jr., USN	10 Aug 68 – 24 Sep 69
Capt. Toria Joel Bratten Jr., USN	24 Sep 69 – 27 May 70

8

Saipan (CVL-48) / Later Arlington (AGMR-2)

Photo 8-1

USS *Saipan* (CVL-48) at sea, with eight FH-1 Phantom jet fighters on her flight deck. Naval History and Heritage Command photograph #NH 97612

USS *Arlington* (AGMR-2) was built as the light carrier *Saipan* (CVL-48) by the New York Shipbuilding Corporation, Camden, New Jersey, and was commissioned in the Philadelphia Naval Shipyard, on 14 July 1946. Her initial assignment was to the Naval Air Training Command at Pensacola, Florida, to support carrier training for student aviators. During her eight months in Florida, more than 1,200 landings were made on her flight deck.[1]

148   Chapter 8

She was later reassigned to Norfolk, Virginia, to work with the Operational Development Force. On 18 April 1948, in concert with the assignment of new duties, *Saipan* became the flagship of Rear Adm. Thomas H. Robbins Jr., commander, Carrier Division 17, and left for Quonset Point, Rhode Island. On 3 May 1948, she embarked Fighter Squadron VF-17A and its new McDonnell FH-1 Phantom jet aircraft. Aircraft of the first complete Phantom squadron to operate from an aircraft carrier began launching from *Saipan* that afternoon.[2]

Photo 8-2

The Navy's First Jet Pilots. Pilots of VF-17A pose with a FH-1 Phantom fighter at NAS Quonset Point, Rhode Island, 12 August 1947. (Back row, L-R): Lieutenant D. Payne, Lieutenant Commander W. D. Biggers, Lieutenant C. G. Miller, Lieutenant J. Sullivan, Lieutenant Commander R. A. Mayo, Lieutenant E. A. Buxton; (Front row, L-R): Lieutenant D. E. Runyon, Lieutenant Commander W. W. Brehm, Lieutenant Junior Grade J. Glover, Ensign J. Long, and Lieutenant Junior Grade C. C. Dace. Naval History and Heritage Command #NH 86374

On 24 December 1948, *Saipan* received orders to embark two of the Navy's latest type helicopter, the XHJS-1, and three Marine Corps HRP-1 helicopters, then to proceed north to Greenland to assist in the rescue of eleven airmen downed on the icecap. Departing Norfolk on Christmas day, she arrived off Cape Farewell, on the 28th, and prepared to launch the helicopters as soon as weather allowed. However, on the

29th, a C-47 cargo plane, equipped with jet assisted takeoff (JATO) and skis, landed on the ice; took on the marooned airmen; and safely completed the recovery.[3]

During the second half of May 1949, *Saipan* made a training cruise to Canada, followed three months later by a second cruise to qualify Royal Canadian Navy pilots in carrier landings. On 6 March 1951, she sailed as flagship, Carrier Division 14, for duty with the Sixth Fleet. Deployed for three months, she operated in the western Mediterranean, calling at Gibraltar, Tunis, Golfe Juan, Algiers, and Sicily, then headed for home. Returning to Norfolk, on 8 June, she resumed operations in the western Atlantic from Greenland to the Caribbean.[4]

FAR EAST / AROUND THE WORLD CRUISE

On 28 September 1953, after slipping her last mooring line at Pier 7, Norfolk Naval Base, *Saipan* embarked on an around-the-world cruise. Her first stop was Mayport, Florida, to embark Marine Attack Squadron VMA-324. Passing through the Panama Canal, the CVL joined the Pacific Fleet. Upon reaching Yokosuka Harbor, on 10 November, *Saipan* reported for duty to commander, Naval Forces, Far East. From there, the light carrier proceeded to Sasebo, destined to be her "home away from home" in Japan.[5]

Photo 8-3

USS *Saipan* at Sasebo, Japan, in 1953.
USS *Saipan* (CVL-48) Far East and Around the World 1953-1954 cruise book

Operating from Sasebo, *Saipan* joined Task Force 95, a United Nations Command charged with blockading and escorting along the coast of Korea. Duties included the reconnaissance and surveillance of the west coast of Korea and air inspection of the friendly islands along the 38th Parallel. The Yellow Sea became *Saipan*'s private cruising waters, with patrols lasting about ten days, then back to Sasebo. Three exercises with US Marines at Okinawa, Iwo Jima, and South Korea helped to fill in her time. A visit to Hong Kong offered *Saipan* sailors rest and relaxation, and opportunity to purchase top quality clothing at fantastically low prices. When the CVL left there, on 17 February 1954, over 400 tailor-made civilian suits and sports jackets accompanied her.[6]

Photo 8-4

Hong Kong, British Crown Colony, 1953.
USS *Saipan* (CVL-48) Far East and Around the World 1953-1954 cruise book

A visit to Yokohama was cut short by a worsening war in Indochina between French and Vietnamese forces. Twenty-five AU-1 Corsair attack aircraft were loaded at Yokohama, and Marine pilots of VMA-324 later flew them off the carrier to French forces at Tourane, Indochina (later Da Nang, Vietnam), on 18 April 1954. The French Far East Expeditionary Corps was then embroiled in the Battle of Dien Bien Phu (13 March-7 May 1954) being fought in northwestern Vietnam near the Chinese and Laotian borders.[7]

Leading to a stunning defeat of the French forces, the Vo Nguyen Giap-led Viet Minh occupied the highlands surrounding the battlefield, besieged the French with heavy artillery fire and, after a lengthy siege, overran their garrison and killed or captured most of the forces. Of the French soldiers captured, few survived the ensuing grim death march to Viet Minh prison camps located 300 miles to the east.[8]

Saipan (CVL-48) / Later *Arlington* (AGMR-2) 151

On 25 May 1954, *Saipan* left Sasebo to begin the remainder of her voyage around the world before entering Hampton Roads on her return to Norfolk. Following stops at Singapore, and Columbo, Ceylon (Sri Lanka), the carrier refueled at Aden, on 15 June, allowing several hours of liberty for the crew. Eight months, to the day, after passage through the Panama Canal en route to the Far East, she entered and completed transit of the Suez Canal on the 19th.[9]

Photo 8-5

USS *Saipan* transiting the Suez Canal on 19 June 1954.
USS *Saipan* (CVL-48) Far East and Around the World 1953-1954 cruise book

Saipan's cruise book summarized a series of visits to Mediterranean liberty ports that followed:

> Naples, Italy, welcomed the SAIPAN on 22 June and Ville Franche, Nice and Cannes, France, followed suit on 26 June. The Riviera ... complete with Bikinis, side-walk cafes and cognac ... was all that it was supposed to be ... and liberty was the order of the day. Perfume came aboard in quantity![10]

Photo 8-6

The French Riviera.
USS *Saipan* (CVL-48) Far East and Around the World 1953-1954 cruise book

From Ville Franche, *Saipan* next visited Barcelona, Spain, offering sidewalk cafes and featuring bull fights. After passing out of the Mediterranean, via the Straits of Gibraltar, Lisbon, Portugal, was her final liberty port before beginning the Atlantic crossing. Marine Attack Squadron VMA-324 was offloaded at Mayport, on 18 July 1954. She finally reached Norfolk on the 20th, completing a lengthy cruise lasting nine months and three weeks of absence from home.[11]

In October 1954, *Saipan* sailed south to the Caribbean. She arrived as Hurricane HAZEL hit the Greater Antilles, and razed areas of the island of Hispaniola. The carrier was immediately engaged in relief work delivering food, medical supplies, and personnel to isolated areas of Haiti. After being honored by the Haitian government, she returned to Norfolk.[12]

In June of 1955, *Saipan* was again attached to the aviation training center at Pensacola and, through the summer, conducted pilot qualification exercises. At the end of September, she was ordered to Mexico to assist in hurricane relief work, primarily in the flooded

Tampico area. On 12 October, she returned to Pensacola, where she remained until 1 April 1957, when she sailed for Bayonne, New Jersey, to begin inactivation. Light Fleet Carrier *Saipan* was decommissioned, on 3 October 1957.[13]

DUTY AS USS *ARLINGTON* (AGMR-2)

Photo 8-7

USS *Arlington* (AGMR-2) under way, circa 1967.
Naval History and Heritage Command photograph #NH 97625

Saipan remained in the Atlantic Reserve Fleet until March 1963, when she was taken to Alabama Dry Dock and Shipbuilding Company, Mobile, to begin conversion to a command ship. Briefly designated CC-3 (and intended to join *Northampton* and *Wright* in this role) she was reclassified a Communications Major Relay ship (AGMR-2), on 1 September 1964, while still undergoing conversion. This was a role similar, but different, from that of the command ships previously described. Renamed *Arlington*, she sailed, upon completion of her conversion, to Norfolk, where she was recommissioned, on 27 August 1966. Like *Annapolis* (AGMR-1), her sister ship (a smaller, former escort carrier), her armament consisted of only four 3-inch/50 twin mounts. Ship's manning was also similar to that of *Annapolis*, with 45 officers and 882 enlisted men comprising her crew complement.[14]

Photo 8-8

USS *Arlington*'s crew aboard ship for her commissioning, 27 August 1966.
USS *Arlington* (AGMR-2) 1967 cruise book

Fitting out of the communications ship occupied the remainder of the year. In January 1967, *Arlington* conducted shakedown exercises in the Caribbean and, in February, she sailed for the Bay of Biscay and exercises off northern Europe. At the end of March, she returned to Norfolk, from which she again steamed to the Caribbean in April. On her return to the Hampton Roads area, she prepared for deployment to the western Pacific and the Vietnam War. *Arlington*'s brief duty in the North Atlantic was quite different from her forthcoming duty. It, interspersed with providing support for the Apollo Space Program, would occupy the remainder of her naval service.[15]

Saipan (CVL-48) / Later *Arlington* (AGMR-2) 155

Photo 8-9

Arlington sailors on liberty in Lisbon, Portugal.
USS *Arlington* (AGMR-2) 1967 cruise book

Photo 8-10

Bremerhaven, Germany, situated on the Weser River at its confluence, was the chief port for the embarkation of U.S. troops in Europe.
USS *Arlington* (AGMR-2) 1967 cruise book

Photo 8-11

Oslo, the largest city and capital of Norway, situated at the head of Oslo Fjord against a backdrop of three forest-covered hills.
USS *Arlington* (AGMR-2) 1967 cruise book

Photo 8-12

Arlington sailor makes a close friend in Oslo.
USS *Arlington* (AGMR-2) 1967 cruise book

VIETNAM BOUND

Arlington departed Norfolk, on 7 July 1967, transited the Panama Canal and proceeded on to Pearl Harbor, Yokosuka, and Subic Bay, whence, with *Annapolis*, she began rotations on station off Vietnam. Her first tour of duty began on 22 August 1967, and the last ended 8 July 1969— twelve in total over a nearly two-year period. *Arlington*'s service was mostly spent performing communications relay duties at a location known as Yankee Station in the Tonkin Gulf, but she also provided communications support at a point farther south, for ships involved in coastal surveillance. These efforts were a part of Operation MARKET TIME, established in March 1965 to prevent seaborne infiltration of supplies from North Vietnam into South Vietnam.

Arlington's Vietnam duty was interspersed with support for the Apollo 8, Apollo 10, and Apollo 11 missions, as part of Task Force 130 (Manned Spacecraft Recovery Force, Pacific), in late December 1968, late May 1969, and late July 1969, respectively.

MANNED SPACECRAFT RECOVERY FORCE PACIFIC

> *USS* ARLINGTON *was used during Apollo 11 to provide full support for Presidential communications, and to provide backup communications on recovery day. For Presidential support,* ARLINGTON *established two 6 kHz HF radio trunks with* NAVCOMMSTA HONO *containing three voice and six teletype circuits. Due to the deterioration of* TACSAT *and the poor performance of* ATS, *a third HF trunk was established for* UHF/HF *relay of* CTF 130 C/C *and* NASA PRS COORD *voice circuits.*
>
> —Description of the communications support provided by *Arlington* for President Richard M. Nixon and NASA during recovery of the Apollo 11 command module. Nixon was on scene for the return to Earth of the astronauts involved in the first moon landing.[16]

USS *Arlington*'s first involvement with the Apollo program came on 18 December 1968, when she departed Hawaii with units of Task Force 130. Acting as primary landing area communications relay ship, she participated in the recovery of Apollo 8 and returned to Pearl Harbor twelve days later. Apollo 8 (the second manned spaceflight mission) was the first astronaut-controlled craft to leave low Earth orbit, circle the moon, and return safely to terra firma. Launched on 21 December 1968, with Frank Borman, James Lovell, and William Anders on board, the capsule dropped into the Pacific on 27 December.[17]

The US Navy ships assigned to the Manned Spacecraft Recovery Force, Pacific, for the Apollo 8, 10, and 11 missions are identified in the table. The letters "PRS" denote Primary Recovery Ship.

Apollo 8 21-27 December 1968	Apollo 10 18-26 May 1969	Apollo 11 16-24 July 1969
Yorktown (CVS-10) PRS	*Princeton* (LPH-5) PRS	*Hornet* (CV-12) PRS
Arlington (AGMR-2)	*Arlington* (AGMR-2)	*Arlington* (AGMR-2)
Chipola (AO-63)	*Carpenter* (DD-825)	*Carpenter* (DD-825)
Chuckawan (AO-100)	*Chilton* (LPA-38)	*Goldsborough* (DDG-20)

Cochrane (DDG-21)
Francis Marion (APA-249)
Guadalcanal (LPH-7)
Nicholas (DD-449)
Rankin (AKA-103)
Rupertus (DD-851)
Salinan (ATF-161)
Sandoval (LPA-194)[18]

Ozark (MCS-2)
Rich (DDE-820)
Salinan (ATF-161)

Hassayampa (AO-145)
New (DD-818)
Ozark (MCS-2)
Salinan (ATF-161)

Photo 8-13

USS *Arlington* as viewed by the Apollo 8 astronauts from aboard the recovery ship. USS *Arlington* (AGMR-2) 1968 cruise book

APOLLO 10 MISSION

On 2 May 1969, *Arlington* joined TF 130 in Hawaii, to serve once again as primary landing area communications relay ship. She departed Pearl Harbor, on 11 May, bound for the Apollo 10 recovery area some 2,400 miles south of Hawaii. Splashdown occurred, on the 26th, in calm waters of the South Pacific less than three miles from USS *Princeton*, the vessel tasked with recovering the astronauts and their spacecraft. Navy helicopters carried members of Underwater Demolition Team 11, from *Princeton*'s deck to Apollo 10's command module.[19]

Photo 8-14

Descent of the Apollo 10 space capsule as photographed from USS *Arlington*. USS *Arlington* (AGMR-2) Middle Pacific 1969 cruise book

On 18 May 1969, eight days after departing the Earth for a manned mission to the moon, the command module of Apollo 10 reentered

Earth's atmosphere, travelling at 32 times the speed of sound. Aboard were three astronauts: the mission commander, Col. Thomas P. Stafford, USAF; lunar module pilot, Comdr. Eugene A. Cernan, USN; and command module pilot, John W. Young, USN. Following liftoff, at 1249, and a bumpy escape from the atmosphere, the mission settled into routine, but highly complex, maneuvers that saw the lunar module and the command service module undocked, then docked, undocked, docked, and undocked again, in the course of the journey to and from the moon.[20]

Stafford, Cernan, and Young were the first astronauts to orbit the moon in a spacecraft fully capable of landing a person on the moon. From just 15 kilometers above the moon's surface, Stafford and Cernan were able to identify landing sites for future missions. This information—along with production of lunar maps by robotic probes, and fulfillment of all other primary mission objectives—gave NASA planners the confidence they needed to launch Apollo 11 July of the same year.[21]

At the site of the Apollo 10 recovery, *Arlington* functioned as a communications relay link between Naval Communications Station, Honolulu, 2,500 miles to the northeast, and *Princeton*, a few thousand yards away. Navy and NASA voice circuits were maintained at home-telephone quality for the recovery. After a majestic descent, the command module set down a scant 3.2 miles from *Arlington*. For each manned space mission, the Navy assigned either an aircraft carrier (CVA or CVS) or a helicopter amphibious assault ship (LPH) as the primary recovery ship, because they carried helicopters which were required to lift the recovered astronauts and spacecraft aboard. Navy UDT swimmers were dropped into the water by helicopters to assist with the recovery operations.[22]

Her support of the operation completed, *Arlington* proceeded to Midway Island, to provide communications support for a conference, on 8 June 1969, between Richard M. Nixon and president of South Vietnam, Nguyen Van Thieu.[23]

NIXON-THIEU CONFERENCE AT MIDWAY ISLAND

The war in Vietnam concerns not only Vietnam but the entire Pacific. The people of South Vietnam, however, have the greatest stake. If the peace is inadequate, there will be repercussions all over Asia. There can be no reward for those engaged in aggression. At the same time, self-determination is not only in the Vietnamese interest, but in the American interest as well. It would improve the prospects of peace throughout the Pacific.

—Statement by President Richard M. Nixon to South Vietnamese president Nguyen Van Thieu, at the Midway Island conference, on 8 June 1969, while emphasizing the importance of ending the Vietnam War honorably.[24]

Although Midway had adequate naval communications for ordinary message traffic, the Pacific Fleet headquarters sent *Arlington* to the isolated island (located more than 1,000 miles to the northwest of Hawaii) to provide additional circuits for the influx of correspondents covering the conference. This was accomplished by establishing 10 two-way circuits for relay, via her powerful transmitters and sensitive receivers, that were channeled at Honolulu into regular commercial circuits to the continental United States.[25]

Photo 8-15

U.S. Naval Air Station, Midway.
USS *Arlington* (AGMR-2) Middle Pacific 1969 cruise book

Photo 8-16

President Richard M. Nixon and entourage debarking from Airforce One.
USS *Arlington* (AGMR-2) Middle Pacific 1969 cruise book

At the meeting, on 8 June, Nixon and Thieu discussed the withdrawal of U.S. troops from Vietnam and U.S. negotiating strategy with the North Vietnamese at the Paris Peace Talks. Following the meeting, Nixon announced the impending scheduled withdrawal of 25,000 American troops. This action was in concert with the administration's Vietnamization policy, enacted soon after President Nixon took office, in January 1969. The plan was to train, equip and expand South Vietnamese forces so that they could take over more military responsibilities for their own defense against the North Vietnamese Communists. It was believed this action would allow the U.S., at the same time, to gradually withdraw its combat troops from South Vietnam, which were then at 475,200 personnel.[26]

Photo 8-17

President Nixon and President Thieu shaking hands.
USS *Arlington* (AGMR-2) Middle Pacific 1969 cruise book

When Nixon took office in 1969, U.S. combat troops had already been fighting in Vietnam since 1965. In nearly four years, some 31,000 American lives had been lost. In spite of these losses, and additional military support and commitment, little progress in defeating North Vietnamese troops and the Viet Cong had been made. Under continuing fierce and intense protests at home, Nixon and his advisers sought a way to disengage and withdraw U.S. combat forces without appearing to abandon South Vietnam in the war against the Communists. The strategy to do so was called Vietnamization.[27]

A battalion of the U.S. 9th Infantry Division left, on 7 July 1969, in the initial withdrawal of U.S. troops. The 814 soldiers were the first of 25,000 troops withdrawn in the initial stage of the U.S. disengagement. There would be fourteen more increments in the withdrawal, with the last U.S. troops leaving after the Paris Peace Accords signings, in January 1973.[28]

APOLLO 11

Photo 8-18

A Navy helicopter from Helicopter Anti-submarine Squadron HS-4 picking up the astronauts from the Apollo 11 command module, on 24 July 1969. Naval History and Heritage Command photograph

The month following the Midway conference, Apollo 11 was launched, on 16 July 1969, from the Kennedy Space Center in Florida, atop a massive Saturn V rocket. Neil Armstrong was the mission commander, Edwin "Buzz" Aldrin, the "Eagle" lunar excursion module pilot, and Michael Collins, the "Columbia" command module pilot. Armstrong was a naval officer, while Aldrin and Collins were both US Air Force officers. Armstrong piloted the lunar module to the moon's surface, on 20 July, with Aldrin aboard. Collins remained aboard the command module.[29]

Armstrong exited the lunar module, at 1056, and exclaimed, "That's one small step for [a] man, one giant leap for mankind," as he made his famous first step on the moon. Armstrong and Aldrin then collected samples, conducted experiments, and took photographs, including ones of their own footprints, before blasting up to join Collins. Returning to Earth on 24 July, the Apollo 11 craft came down in the Pacific, west of Hawaii. The crew and the craft were picked up by the *Hornet*, and the three astronauts were put into quarantine for three weeks.[30]

Photo 8-19

Armstrong, Aldrin, and Collins enter the Mobile Quarantine Facility aboard USS *Hornet* (CVS-12), following the recovery of Apollo 11, on 24 July 1969. Naval History and Heritage Command photograph

Prior to the landing, *Arlington* had arrived in the recovery area (about 1,100 miles southwest of Oahu), on 21 July, tested her equipment and, the following day, moved to Johnston Atoll, where she embarked President Nixon for an overnight visit, on the 23rd. Nixon, and an entourage that included Secretary of State William P. Rogers and

National Security Advisor Henry Kissinger, had flown on Air Force One to the atoll, and then transferred on Marine One to the *Arlington*. On the 24th, the party took the helicopter to *Hornet*, and were greeted by Adm. John S. McCain, Jr., the commander in chief, Pacific Command.[31]

With crew and capsule successfully recovered, and the astronauts ensconced in the mobile quarantine facility aboard *Hornet*, they were welcomed back by President Nixon through its window. Mission accomplished, *Arlington* then headed for Hawaii. From there, she proceeded to Long Beach, California, arriving on 21 August. Four days later, she moved south to San Diego to begin inactivation. She was decommissioned, on 14 January 1970, and joined the Inactive Fleet at San Diego.[32]

Photo 8-20

Banner depicting *Arlington*'s unofficial nickname "The Roadrunner" and the English translation of her ship's motto, UBI ACTIO EST (Latin), meaning "Where there is Action" or "Where the Action is."
USS *Arlington* (AGMR-2) Pacific 1968 cruise book

Annapolis, her sister ship, had been decommissioned earlier, on 20 December 1969, at Naval Station Norfolk; transferred to the Atlantic Reserve Fleet; and towed to the Philadelphia Naval Shipyard, where she was "placed in mothballs" (laid up).[33]

LAURELS FOR THE COMMUNICATIONS SHIPS

USS *Arlington* earned three Meritorious Unit Commendations (MUCs) for her support of the Apollo 8, Apollo 10, and Apollo 11 missions, respectively. The associated eligibility periods were 11-29 December 1968, 4-31 May 1969, and 20-25 July 1969.

9

The Australian Aircraft Carrier Program
By Commodore Hector Donohue AM RAN (Rtd)

THE BEGINNING

The gestation of the decision to introduce naval air power into the Royal Australian Navy (RAN) began in 1944. Government had directed Defence in January to commence planning for the size and shape of the post-war defence force, also to review the war effort in the light of the present situation, and distinguish what was needed to meet operational requirements in the South West Pacific area.

Discussions had taken place with the Admiralty (the government department that managed British naval affairs as well as functioning as the operational authority for the Royal Navy) about the RAN acquiring an aircraft carrier and one or two cruisers to contribute to the allied naval build up in the Pacific to conclude the war against Japan. The concept suited both nations, as Britain had too many ships in the water or under construction for the pool of manpower available, and the RAN had suffered a decline in the number and quality of its fighting strength. The RAN considered a carrier task group to be the logical way ahead.

The response was favourable with various proposals placed on the table including the offer of the *Colossus*-class light fleet carrier, HMS *Ocean*. But despite this optimism the RAN did not have the capacity to man an aircraft carrier and two cruisers. There was also the question of payment. Initially the First Sea Lord had advised the ships would be a free transfer and, although Prime Minister Winston Churchill was also inclined to give them free, his War Cabinet took a harder view. With the War concluding, the gift of ships could adversely impact British shipyard's potential post-war sales.

Meanwhile in Australia, apart from the manpower issue, defence funding priorities and the question as to whether a naval Fleet Air Arm (FAA) should be independent of the air force remained unresolved. All of which caused the Government to delay any carrier decision until World War II hostilities had ceased.[1]

APPROVAL FOR A FLEET AIR ARM

The value of the aircraft carrier had been amply demonstrated during the war in the Pacific, and a fleet based around the carrier was seen as appropriate for the RAN. Lieutenant Commander VAT Smith (later Admiral Sir Victor Smith) went to the UK in late 1945 and with Admiralty assistance began to work on the details for the establishment of a RAN FAA.[2]

Photo 9-1

A young Lieutenant Victor Smith wearing the ribbon of the DSC awarded for outstanding zeal while serving with the Royal Navy during World War II. (RAN)

Smith attained his wings as an observer in 1937 after which he served in HMS *Glorious*, *Ark Royal*, *Shropshire* and, in 1943 transferred to aircraft carrier *Tracker* during her deployment as escort for Atlantic and Russian convoys. When stationed at Royal Naval Air Station Sparrowhawk, Smith was responsible for an attack on the German battleship *Scharnhorst* for which he was awarded the Distinguished Service Cross (DSC). After surviving the sinking of cruiser HMAS *Canberra* during the battle of Savo Island, Smith went on to serve as the Air Planning Officer for the Normandy invasion in 1944.

Smith's distinguished career included service in the Korean War as HMAS *Sydney*'s Executive Officer. This highly respected RAN officer is known as the 'Father of the FAA' as his contribution to the formation of the Fleet Air Arm was instrumental.

In April 1946 the RAN received prime ministerial permission to investigate the establishment of a naval FAA along British lines. Navy established a RAN FAA Planning Office and, with a small team of RAN and three on loan RN officers, developed a detailed plan for the acquisition of two aircraft carriers, together with air groups and the establishment of a naval air station – the Naval Plan.

It had been accepted within the Australian defence establishment that a balanced naval task force should include aircraft carriers and that these should be included in the RAN's force structure. The issue remained, as the Chief of Air Staff stated, whether the Royal Navy had the ability to establish naval air in Australia or whether the Royal Australian Air Force (RAAF) should perform the task. He was strongly of the opinion that the establishment of Australian air power should be from a unified and fully coordinated Air Force. He was concerned the Naval Plan implied complete independence on air matters and reliance on the UK for equipment and personnel.

The Defence Committee (the senior committee that advised the Minister), in May 1947, finally recorded that navy and army supported the Naval Plan which embodied British and Canadian practice. It was considered highly desirable that Australia adopted the form of organisation most compatible with its allies. Air force dissented remaining of the opinion that the RAAF Plan should be adopted.

The Council of Defence considered the Naval Plan 'Status of the Naval Aviation Branch' on 3 July 1947. The debate centred on the RAN and RAAF Plans, the latter insisting that RAAF control both land-based and ship-borne aircraft and their personnel. The meeting generated considerable debate and Prime Minister Chifley, at the time also Acting Minister for Defence, finally interjected and exclaimed that '...this debate could last for 20 years.' He was impressed that the great navies had decided to give their naval air to their navies, and came to the conclusion that the Naval Plan should be supported. The Council concluded that 'The status and control of the Naval Aviation Branch should be in accordance with the principles and proposals of the Naval Plan.' The Minister for Air dissented. Chifley gave Governmental approval to the Council's recommendations immediately after the meeting and Cabinet endorsed his decision on 15 August 1947.

The concept of acquiring carriers had been made easier by a generous offer from the British Government. There were no fewer than ten Light Fleet Carriers in various stages of construction in the UK, and the British were aware they could never be operated in peacetime by a manpower-strapped Royal Navy. They would, however, be immensely useful in Commonwealth hands and a generous arrangement to get them there was far preferable to the cost of completion, or even maintaining them in suspended RN reserve. In September 1946 the Admiralty had informed the RAN that they were happy to bear half of the cost of the carriers transferred to Australia.

Despite the generosity of the offer the Australian Government hesitated, mainly due to the revelation that additional ongoing modification costs would be incurred. Options other than the purchase of two *Majestic*-class carriers were investigated, but after much debate it was decided that the offer would be accepted provided no modernisation program would be commenced within five years.

The concern of modernisation was relevant, as the cost of refits and their propensity to blow-out was an unpalatable thought. The Admiralty, on the other hand, was keen to see at least one of the two carriers modernised during construction to ensure a truly front-line ship was delivered. This could be done for £500,000 – a figure much cheaper than a stand-alone refit – and options were examined to see if this additional cost could be deferred. In the event, Australia agreed to cover the additional burden without deferring it, but the program would only apply to the second carrier.

The first, HMAS *Sydney*, therefore had no provision for modernisation. Without it, she would not be able to operate jet aircraft and there was therefore no obvious growth path for her. It was a compromise the RAN was prepared to accept.

During the latter part of 1947 the Navy moved quickly to bring about the Government's decision. This included ordering the two *Majestic*-class carriers, the purchase of aircraft and associated equipment, securing two air bases and the recruitment and training of aircrew and maintainers. The first pilot's course commenced on 7 December 1947, and the first group of RAN sailors training for the Fleet Air Arm departed for the UK on 1 January 1948.[3]

In early 1951 the Admiralty advised that *Melbourne* would not be completed until March 1954. This represented a two-year delay to the agreed delivery date on which the naval aviation plan was based. Concerned on the impact this would have on its plan, the RAN sought to acquire a carrier on loan from the Admiralty. The British Government responded positively and offered the *Colossus*-class carrier HMS *Vengeance* at no cost from late 1952 until 1955.[4]

HMAS *SYDNEY*

The RAN's first 'flat-top' carrier, HMAS *Sydney* was commissioned on 16 December 1948. She was the former HMS *Terrible*, one of six *Majestic*-class light-fleet carriers in British dockyards upon which work had been suspended in the closing stages of WWII. Although the light-fleet carriers did not carry the armour or guns of the larger fleet carriers, experience gained in the Pacific War meant several improvements could be incorporated when dockyard work resumed. The catapult, arrestor cables, and aircraft lifts were upgraded to handle faster and heavier aircraft, while the flight deck was reinforced. Improved weapons and radars were fitted, and replenishment at sea equipment was installed.

The carrier acquisition had attracted significant public interest and The *Sydney Morning Herald* ran a piece in December 1947 speculating that the carriers would be named after Australian statesmen. The follow up story suggested that this had occurred as Navy had advised the first one was called *Terrible*.

The aircraft chosen for the RAN FAA's 20th and 21st Carrier Air Groups (CAG) were both well tested by the RN at sea. They were the Hawker Sea Fury FB.11, a single seat fighter-bomber with an impressive performance, and the Fairey Firefly Mk 5 two-seat armed reconnaissance/strike and anti-submarine aircraft. The Sea Fury had a top speed of around 390 knots and a radius of action of about 350 nautical miles at 250 knots. The Firefly was slower, with a top speed of around 300 knots and a radius of action of about 300 nautical miles at 200 knots. The 20th Carrier Air Group had been formed at Royal Naval Air Station Eglinton (near Londonderry, Northern Ireland) in August 1948 and comprised 805 Squadron (Sea Furies) and 816 Squadron (Fireflies), both of which undertook significant training with the Royal Navy before embarking on HMAS *Sydney* for her maiden voyage to Australia.

Sydney sailed from Devonport on 12 February 1949 to undertake a work-up and departed UK on 11 April with the 20th CAG embarked. She disembarked her aircraft to the Royal Australian Naval Air Station (RANAS) Nowra before arriving in her namesake city on 28 May 1949.[5]

RANAS NOWRA-HMAS ALBATROSS

The air station at Nowra, on the South Coast of NSW some 100 miles south of Sydney and 12 miles inland from Jervis Bay, is the home of the RAN FAA. The airfield was originally occupied by the RAAF during WWII as a torpedo-bomber base, then by US Forces, and between 1945 and 1946 by the British Pacific Fleet.

The air station was transferred to the RAN on 15 December 1947, and after renovation work it was commissioned as HMAS Albatross (RANAS Nowra) on 31 August 1948. Albatross became the shore base for the CAG squadrons when not at sea, and was also the training base for the second-line squadrons 723, 724, 725; and later 850 and 851 front line squadrons.

In the early 1950s, RANAS Nowra was a hive of activity with pilot and observer training, the building of hangars and workshops, and maintainer training. With the commissioning of Albatross and the arrival of the CAGs, the RAN FAA was on a firm footing. The generous assistance of the Royal Navy in the formation of the squadrons, aircrew and maintainer training, both in the UK and at Nowra, was a significant factor in the successful establishment of the RAN FAA.

Photo 9-2

HMAS Albatross, RANAS Nowra, NSW, June 1950. Maintenance work being carried out on the engine of a Sea Fury FB.11 fighter. Australian War Memorial (AWM)

In July 1951, the plan for the second Naval Air Station at Schofields, west of Sydney, began taking shape. It had initially been built for the RAAF in 1941 as a satellite airfield, but was taken over by the British Pacific Fleet in early 1945. It was returned to the RAAF in 1946 but with the establishment of a FAA, it was designated as an aircraft storage area and maintenance yard; a technical training school; and a second airfield for one of the Carrier Air Groups. Initially known as HMAS Albatross II, RAN Aircraft Repair Yard, it was commissioned as HMAS Nirimba in April 1953.[6]

HMAS *SYDNEY*'S INITIAL OPERATIONAL PERIOD

Photo 9-3

Two Hawker Sea Fury FB.11 fighter aircraft taxiing on the deck of HMAS *Sydney*, circa 1951. (AWM)

Following a leave period and maintenance, *Sydney* embarked on months of exercises as her crew settled in to the business of effectively conducting flying operations. Daylight operations, night time operations, as well as launching and recovering aircraft in varying sea states and weather conditions, were a necessary part of ensuring that the RAN's new carrier was prepared for future operations. This pattern of exercises continued throughout the remainder of 1949 and into 1950.

In July 1950 *Sydney* returned to the UK to collect the 21st CAG consisting of 808 Squadron (Sea Furies) and 817 Squadron (Fireflies). This Air Group had been intended for Australia's second carrier, to be named HMAS *Melbourne*, but her delivery to the RAN had been delayed.

Consequently, HMAS *Sydney* had returned to UK and embarked the 21st Carrier Air Group in October, arriving back in Australia in November 1950.

The delivery of the 21st CAG brought the RAN Fleet Air Arm to full strength, with its four Squadrons being front-line. They operated from *Sydney* at sea or from RANAS Nowra. Other Squadrons were commissioned for training aircrew.[7]

THE KOREAN WAR

Photo 9-4

HMAS *Sydney* in Korean waters, circa 1951. (AWM)

In May 1951 the Australian Government announced that the aircraft carrier HMAS *Sydney* would relieve the Royal Navy's HMS *Glory* in the Korean War for a period of about three months from October 1951. By then the war on the ground had reached a stalemate, with both sides gridlocked roughly around the 38th Parallel. *Sydney* was given about three months to work up the Air Group and arrive in theatre. *Sydney*'s Air Group of two Sea Fury Squadrons (805 and 808) comprising 24 aircraft and one Firefly Squadron (817) comprising 14 aircraft, was embarked and she commenced work-up.

Sydney began operations in Korea on 5 October 1951 under the command of Capt. David H. Harries, RAN. During her deployments, she undertook extensive operations in support of Operation STRANGLE – a strategy designed to deprive the North Koreans of transport, supply and infrastructure.

Photo 9-5

Captain Harries conferring with Commander (Air), Commander Launcelot John Kiggell DSC RN onboard HMAS *Sydney* during her time in Korea. (RAN)

Sydney spent 64 days in the operational area (not including passage from Sasebo or Kure) mainly as the British Commonwealth carrier of the west coast patrol. Of these days 9.5 were taken up by replenishment or passage between the west and east coasts. Bad weather accounted for 11.7 flying days, leaving a total of 2,366 sorties flown. The average daily sortie rate was 55.2 per full flying day. Ammunition expenditure during the course of *Sydney*'s seven patrols totaled 269,249 x 20mm rounds; 6,359 rocket projectiles; and 902 bombs of 1000-lb and 500-lb weight.

On 29 January 1952 *Sydney* left Korean waters. She had been 118 days in the area of operations during which time she had completed seven separate patrols. Ten of her aircraft had been shot down and numerous others damaged by flak. Her casualties included one killed, two missing and six wounded. A number of her crew were decorated and all received the Imperial Korea Medal and United Nations medal (bar KOREA) in recognition of their involvement.

Captain Harries was later made a Commander of the British Empire for:

> Devotion to duty while in command of HMAS *Sydney*, operating off the west coast of Korea for four months, during which time this most efficient carrier created a sortie record and consistently kept up a very high rate of sorties, which could only have been achieved by high efficiency of all hands from hard training under the supervision of Captain Harries. He displayed excellent qualities of command and leadership under conditions of great strain and bad weather, all tasks asked for were accurately carried out.[8]

A more complete description of the contribution made by *Sydney* and her Air Group are covered in Chapter 2 and 3.

SYDNEY POST-KOREA

Sydney arrived in Fremantle on 22 February 1952 in the middle of industrial unrest on the waterfront. Union action meant that no tugs arrived to pull *Sydney* out of the harbour on her departure date three days later. In response, the ship initiated an action known as "Operation Pinwheel" whereby the Sea Furies of 805 and 808 Squadrons started the engines of the aircraft sitting on *Sydney*'s flight deck and used their thrust to pull the carrier clear.

That October, *Sydney* participated in Operation HURRICANE the name given to the British nuclear tests in the Monte Bello Islands off the North West coast of Western Australia. *Sydney*'s aircraft were involved in enforcing the prohibited area around the tests and the detonation, which took place on 3 October 1952, the 'mushroom' cloud being visible from the carrier some 97 kilometres distant.

The tests successfully-concluded, *Sydney* returned to NAS Nowra that November before sailing for Queen Elizabeth II's Coronation Fleet Review in England in March 1953 with 817 Squadron embarked. Flying opportunities were limited on the trip, though the Squadron did participate in exercises with the Mediterranean Fleet and with Canadian warships in the Atlantic Ocean on the voyage back to Australia. The Coronation Review featured some 229 ships from around the world and the flypast, which included the Fireflies of 817 Squadron, was made up of over 300 aircraft from 37 squadrons. *Sydney* returned to Australia in

August and visited Canada, the United States, the West Indies, Panama, and New Zealand on her voyage home.

Photo 9-6

Monte Bello Islands, October 1952.
Australian War Memorial photograph P00131.002

Photo 9-7

Portsmouth, England. 1953. His Royal Highness, The Duke of Gloucester KG, KT, KP, GCB, GCMG, GCVO (right), and Capt. Herbert James Buchanan DSO, ADC RAN (left), salute the Quarter Deck as His Royal Highness arrives aboard the aircraft carrier HMAS *Sydney*, to inspect members of the Australian and New Zealand Coronation Contingent on their arrival in England for the coronation of Her Majesty, Queen Elizabeth II.
Australian War Memorial photograph 030429

After her arrival back in Australia, a maintenance and leave period was followed by exercises in Queensland waters before *Sydney* again deployed for Korean waters during the post-armistice period.

HMAS *SYDNEY*'S SECOND KOREAN DEPLOYMENT

The Korean Armistice was signed on 27 July 1953 and shortly afterwards HMAS *Sydney* was deployed there for peace-keeping operations. In September, 850 and 805 Squadrons (Sea Furies) and 816 Squadron (Fireflies) embarked for work-up exercises.

On 19 October 1953 she sailed from Sydney, Australia, for Hong Kong where she relieved HMS *Ocean*, embarking two 'Dragonfly' helicopters from that ship for SAR (Search and Rescue) work. She departed Hong Kong on 12 November arriving at Sasebo, Japan, on 16 November, where repair work was carried out on her aircraft catapult. Kure was reached on 20 November, and from there *Sydney* began her Korean operational patrols on 26 November 1953.

The Korean Peninsula patrols worked to a schedule, with Sea Fury and Firefly aircraft conducting flights along the cease-fire line and coast, interspersed with resupply calls at Kure and Sasebo. *Sydney* also visited several other Japanese ports and Hong Kong. This second tour was generally quiet, but marred by the death of two pilots from accidents, and the serious injury of an aircraft handler.

At the end of March 1954 *Sydney* completed her patrol duties and on 1 May collected 26 RN aircraft at Iwakuni for shipment to Singapore, calling via Hong Kong on the way. She arrived at Singapore on 18 May where the RN aircraft were off-loaded, and six RAN Fireflies were collected. Arriving off Jervis Bay on 10 June to disembark the squadrons to RANAS Nowra, *Sydney* then berthed at Garden Island, Sydney, Australia, on 11 June 1954.

Following her return from Korea in June 1954, *Sydney* was taken into refit in Captain Cook Graving Dock, Garden Island. Emerging from it in August 1954 the ship was soon back at sea undertaking exercises off the eastern seaboard. This pattern of exercises continued for the remainder of the year.[9]

IMPACT OF GOVERNMENT BUDGET REDUCTIONS

In 1953, with the Korean War drawing to a close, Government determined that there should be a reduction in defence spending to a level which was sustainable within the Australian economic situation. The decision on what the impact would be on force structure was determined by 1954. From the navy perspective, the major change was to retain only one carrier with a front-line aircraft establishment reduced

The Australian Aircraft Carrier Program   179

from 48 to 40. After much discussion it was agreed that HMAS *Vengeance* would be used as a training ship to be replaced by *Sydney* when *Vengeance* returned to UK. She was employed in the training ship role from July to September 1954 and from February to April 1955, when *Sydney* was designated the fleet training ship. The second Air Station, HMAS Nirimba at Schofields, was to be closed but the base remained in RAN hands, and in 1955 became the RAN Apprentice Training Establishment.

Photo 9-8

1953, HMAS *Vengeance* (foreground) and HMAS *Sydney* exercising off the Queensland coast. (AWM)

It was considered that the provision of carriers in the Pacific should be left to the US Navy and the Australian carrier would focus on anti-submarine warfare in support of the deployment of Australian Expeditionary Forces.[10]

While the cuts were a disappointment, the ongoing delays and mounting cost of modernising *Melbourne* was adversely impacting on navy's budget. On the positive side, *Melbourne* was being fitted with larger lifts, an angled flight deck, a mirror-aided landing device, steam catapult and improved arrester wire system, making her 'state of the art.' Further, her forthcoming DH Sea Venom and Fairey Gannet aircraft would significantly improve the CAG (Carrier Air Group) capability. Meanwhile, on 18 June 1954, the RAN's first DH Vampire T22 jet trainer arrived at Nowra. The new concept of anti-submarine warfare (ASW) helicopters with dipping sonar was also under consideration.

HMAS *VENGEANCE*

Because *Melbourne*'s delivery date was delayed as a result of the modernisation program, HMS *Vengeance*, was lent by the Admiralty and commissioned into the RAN as HMAS *Vengeance*, on 13 November 1952. She was a *Colossus*-class carrier that had served with the British Pacific Fleet in 1945, then with the Home Fleet, and as an aircraft ferry and training ship.

Sailing from England in January 1953, under the command of Capt. Henry M. Burrell, RAN, *Vengeance* arrived in Sydney on 11 March 1953. Following a three-month refit in Sydney, she commenced seagoing service with the Australian fleet in June 1953, working up in preparation for a deployment to Korea. While the work-up proceeded well, it revealed several defects which made *Vengeance* unsuitable for front-line service in Korea – the most prominent being problems with the hydraulic catapult. In July 1953 it was announced that *Sydney* would do the second Korean deployment instead.

Vengeance remained in Australian waters and between February and April 1954, she was one of several Australian warships tasked with Royal Escort duty during the first visit to Australia of Her Majesty Queen Elizabeth II and Prince Phillip. *Vengeance* and her aircraft provided the escort and ceremonial fly pasts to SS *Gothic* with the Royal party embarked, to the Cocos Islands, in company with HMA Ships *Anzac* and *Bataan*, handing over escort duties to HM Ships *Colombo* and *Newfoundland* in April 1954.

In July 1954 *Vengeance* was reclassified as a training ship for National Service and General Service trainees. In October 1954 she sailed from Sydney for Japan to embark aircraft, men and equipment of No. 77

Squadron, Royal Australian Air Force, and return them to Australia. *Vengeance* sailed from Yokosuka mid-November 1954 and arrived in Sydney on 3 December.

Photo 9-9

Indian Ocean 1954, Royal Yacht *Gothic* being escorted by HMAS *Vengeance* with three RAN destroyers, HMAS *Anzac* and *Bataan* together with the cruiser, HMS *Ceylon*. (AWM)

Following a three-month refit which was completed in February 1955, *Vengeance* resumed training duties which occupied her until late April. On 16 June 1955 she sailed from Sydney to commence the long passage to England and reversion to the Royal Navy, with almost 1,000 officers and sailors who were to commission HMAS *Melbourne*.

She called in at Singapore and Malta to collect RN aircraft for the UK, and arrived in Devonport on 5 August, at which time administrative control was assumed by the Senior Officer Reserve Fleet, Plymouth. *Vengeance* decommissioned on 25 October 1955 and reverted to the Royal Navy. HMAS *Melbourne* was commissioned three days later on 28 October 1955.

Vengeance remained in the Reserve Fleet until 14 December 1956 when she was sold to Brazil. Following extensive reconstruction and modernisation in Rotterdam, *Vengeance* was renamed and commissioned by the Brazilian Navy as *Minas Gerais* on 6 December 1960. The ship was further modernised in the late 1970s and early 1990s and finally decommissioned in 2001, after over 40-years' service in the Brazilian Navy.[11]

NEW ROLES FOR HMAS *SYDNEY*

Photo 9-10

Crew members form up 1RAR on the flight deck of HMAS *Sydney*, en route to Vietnam. Courtesy of Sea Power Centre – Australia

On 22 April 1955, 805, 816 and 817 Squadrons disembarked from *Sydney* to the Naval Air Station at Nowra, HMAS Albatross, heralding the impending change of the ship's role from an aircraft carrier to a training ship.

As the fleet training ship, *Sydney* was host to numerous drafts of Royal Australian Naval Reserve National Servicemen who joined the carrier to complete the seagoing component of their training. Groups of engineering sailors were also embarked and training cruises saw *Sydney* visit a variety of Australian, New Zealand and South East Asian ports between April 1955 and December 1957. *Sydney* remained in commission until 30 May 1958 at which time she was paid off into Special Reserve in Sydney, Australia, after steaming 315,958 miles since commissioning.

Sydney recommissioned as a fast troop transport in early 1962, with her first operational deployment in mid-1964, deploying Australian Army units to Malaysia as part of Australia's initial contribution to the Indonesian Confrontation. *Sydney* began her first voyage to Vietnam in May 1965, transporting 1st Battalion Royal Australian Regiment (1RAR) from Sydney, Australia, to Vung Tau.

By 1966 with Australian ground forces well established in Vietnam, *Sydney* began a regular pattern of disembarking one battalion at Vung Tau and back loading another for the return passage to Australia. In the early days *Sydney*'s turnaround in Vung Tau took two days, but this was gradually reduced until, by 1967, the unloading and back loading of men and equipment generally took only half a day. She was quickly known and remembered fondly by those involved as the "Vung Tau Ferry."

Australia's combat role in South Vietnam ceased in March 1972 when *Sydney* brought home the last combat elements. *Sydney* returned to Vung Tau for one final visit in November 1972, when she delivered a cargo of defence aid for Vietnam and Cambodia. Between 1965 and 1972 *Sydney* undertook 24 voyages to Vietnam, transporting 16,094 troops some 6,000 tonnes of cargo and 2,375 vehicles during this period.

On 20 July 1973 the ship's company was informed that it had been decided to pay off *Sydney* instead of proceeding with a planned refit. On 12 November 1973 the ship decommissioned, by which time she had steamed 395,591 miles as a fast troop transport. Since first commissioning in 1948 she had steamed 711,549 miles.

Stripped of all useful fittings, *Sydney* returned to Athol Bight in Sydney Harbour where she languished until sold for scrap to the Dongkuk Steel Mill Company, Limited of Seoul, South Korea, on 28 October 1975. The former aircraft carrier and fast troop transport left Sydney under tow on 23 December 1975.[12]

HMAS *MELBOURNE*

HMAS *Melbourne* was a *Majestic*-class light aircraft carrier and operated in the RAN from 1955 until 1982. The ship was laid down for the Royal Navy as the lead ship of the *Majestic*-class in April 1943, and was launched as HMS *Majestic* in February 1945. At the end of World War II, work on the ship was suspended until she was purchased by the Australian Government in 1947.

At the time of purchase, it was decided to incorporate new aircraft carrier technologies into the design, making *Melbourne* the third ship to be constructed with an angled flight deck. Delays in construction and integrating the enhancements meant that the carrier was not commissioned until 1955.

Photo 9-11

Melbourne undergoing trials off Barrow-in-Furness, England, 1956. (RAN)

Work resumed on *Melbourne* in 1949 at which time it was decided to increase the size of the flight deck lifts to accommodate the larger aircraft coming into service. In 1952, a modified angled flight deck of 5½ degrees was added as was a steam catapult and mirror deck-landing system.

On 28 October 1955 HMAS *Melbourne* was commissioned into the RAN at Barrow-in-Furness in Cumbria, North-West England, under the command of Capt. Galfrey Gatacre, DSO DSC RAN. She then began five months of acceptance trials in British waters before loading the cocooned Sea Venom and Gannet aircraft at Glasgow over the period 8-11 March 1956. The following day she sailed for Australia. The final leg of her voyage 'home' was via Jervis Bay where the 64 aircraft that *Melbourne* had brought from the UK were transferred ashore via lighter for road transport to the Naval Air Station at Nowra. Finally, on 9 May she arrived in Sydney for the first time. Thousands of people turned out to watch her arrive in the harbour and three days later she replaced HMAS *Sydney* as the flagship of the RAN.

The Sea Venom is a descendant of the DH100 Vampire and was an all-weather, radar equipped, interceptor/strike aircraft, capable of day and night operations with a speed of 575 mph and range of 705 miles. The pilot and observer were seated side-by-side, with the latter positioned slightly aft to accommodate the radar viewer.

The Fairey Gannet was a rugged aircraft, with two contra-rotating propellers on a single hub; thus, giving it a single-engine profile with two-engine performance. With a top speed of 300 mph and range of some 660 miles and a munitions load of up to 2,850 lbs, the Gannet AS-1 was well equipped for operating over a large area, in adverse weather conditions for either day or night anti-submarine patrols.

Following a brief refit and docking, *Melbourne* sailed for Jervis Bay in July 1956 to embark her aircraft squadrons and commence work-up. She then sailed for Brisbane and the Hervey Bay area to conduct flying training. That September *Melbourne* sailed for what was to be the first of many deployments to South East Asia. The Australian Government had by this time committed naval forces to what became known as the Far East Strategic Reserve, a joint agreement between Australia, New Zealand and Britain. The Reserve's primary role was to deter communist aggression in Southeast Asia, and to respond swiftly if deterrence failed. As a secondary role, the forces committed to the Reserve were to participate in actions against the communist guerrillas in Malaya (today Malaysia). This provided for an annual visit from an aircraft carrier as part of the RAN's contribution. *Melbourne* maintained this commitment with the Strategic Reserve and later with ANZUK forces, participating in many exercises conducted under the auspices of the South East Asia Treaty Organisation (SEATO) through to the late 1960s.

There was a moment of levity during the exercises in 1959 when *Melbourne* refueled from the fleet oiler USS *Ponchatoula* and the American replenishment vessel demonstrated its method of passing the first line with a baseball and bat. The Australians got one up on their American counterparts, however, when Sub Lieutenant Charlie Morris, RAN, was piped up to the flight deck 'with hammer.' Morris was an Australian record holder in the hammer throw and had represented Australia at the 1956 Olympic Games and the 1958 Commonwealth Games. He would later finish fourth at the 1962 Commonwealth Games. Charlie Morris was larger than life and he recounts how these skills were put to good effect at sea:

> I was sitting in my cabin when there was a pipe over the ships broadcast. 'Sub-Lieutenant Morris, flight deck with hammer.' I rushed up top where John Goble, our Commander (Air) said 'If you can't get a line over to that ship you're on stoppage of leave until we get back to Australia!' There was the USS *Pontachula*'s deck officer hitting a baseball to which was attached a line from their deck over to our replenishment station. I wound up, did two turns and my hammer struck the *Pontachula*'s smoke stack.[13]

Photo 9-12

USS *Ponchatoula* replenishing HMAS *Melbourne* at sea.
Courtesy of Sea Power Centre - Australia

Charlie Morris was born in the UK on 07 Jun 1926 and served through World War II in the Royal Navy as an Electrical Rating. He joined the RAN in September 1948 as an Able Seaman Electrician and retired in 1980 as a Commander (Weapons Electrical). During

Melbourne's 1960 deployment Charlie's physical prowess came to the fore during a rescue as recounted by Lt. Peter Frank McNay, RAN, who was landing a Gannet aircraft:

> I came into land with everything going smoothly. As I approached the stern of the ship, my port engine failed and, with the resultant loss of power, I sank rapidly, hitting the 'round down', bouncing onto the deck and rolling on to my port side. This manoeuvre tore off the port wing and I slid down the deck on my side towards the edge. Finally, I caught a wire, or should I say a wire caught me, wrapping itself around my cockpit, bringing me to a halt. After turning everything off to avert a possible fire, I attempted to open my canopy, which was hydraulically operated. Nothing happened as the arrester wire, which was under tons of pressure, kept it from opening. The next thing I saw was an axe trying to break through the canopy. All I could think of was the darned thing coming straight through and collecting my skull! However, my saviour arrived in the form of Charlie Morris, our Squadron Electrical Officer and former Olympic hammer thrower. He literally grabbed the poor young Naval Airman, who was only trying to do the job he was trained for and threw him off the fuselage. He then grabbed the wire and, with an enormous heave, lifted it just sufficiently to enable the canopy to slide open under its own momentum, having already been activated.[14]

On 10 February 1964, *Melbourne* was involved in a collision with the *Daring*-class destroyer HMAS *Voyager* some 30 miles south east of Jervis Bay. *Melbourne* was engaged in night flying exercises and *Voyager* was plane guard. At approximately 2100 *Melbourne* struck *Voyager* at the after end of her bridge, heeling her over to an angle of about 50 degrees. The impact pushed *Voyager* through the water laterally for a few seconds, and then she broke in two. Her forward section passed down *Melbourne*'s port side, and the stern section down the starboard side. The forward section sank soon afterwards and the after section about three hours later. The disaster resulted in the loss of 82 lives - 14 officers, including the Commanding Officer, Captain Duncan Stevens, 67 sailors and one civilian dockyard employee. There were 232 survivors. *Melbourne* was damaged but sustained no casualties and following search and rescue operations she returned to Sydney on 12 February.

Repair work kept *Melbourne* alongside in Sydney for three months. She returned to sea in May 1964 and following work-up exercises she sailed from Sydney for her South East Asian deployment on 22 June. During the deployment *Melbourne* undertook flight trials with A-4

Skyhawks and Grumman S-2 Trackers during a visit to US Naval Base, Subic Bay in the Philippines.[15]

Photo 9-13

View from the cockpit of a Tracker landing on HMAS *Melbourne*. (RAN)

Photo 9-14

Tracker landing on *Melbourne*'s flight deck. (RAN)

In late 1964 the RAN sought the Government's approval to upgrade *Melbourne* and purchase a force of 18 Skyhawks and 16 Trackers. The Skyhawks were intended to be used to provide air defence for the fleet as well as to attack warships and targets on land. Following a search for suitable aircraft, two US Navy aircraft were selected: the McDonnell Douglas A-4 Skyhawk fighter-bomber and the S-2E Grumman Tracker. Government approval to the proposal to modernise the carrier and acquire Trackers was received in November 1964 and for the Skyhawks in early 1965.

Photo 9-15

Commander Ken Douglas, Commander (Air), and Lieutenant Commander Graham Rohrsheim in Flight Control, watch a Skyhawk land. (RAN)

Budgetary constraints from the late 1950s had placed some doubt over the future of naval aviation given the large financial outlay required to operate aircraft carriers and their associated aircraft. On 26 November 1959, the Minister for Defence, the Hon. Athol Townley MP, announced that fixed-wing naval aviation would be disbanded in 1963 when *Melbourne* became due for a major refit. The Minister for the Navy, Senator John Gorton, however, argued for *Melbourne*'s retention in an anti-submarine capacity and 27 Westland Wessex anti-submarine helicopters were subsequently ordered, the first coming into service in November 1962. The service life of the Sea Venoms and the Gannets, meanwhile, was extended past 1963.[15]

The RAN Skyhawk A4G was a single seat delta-wing aircraft with single engine, capable of 586 Knots (Mach 0.88) at sea level. It had a combat radius of 625 nm with external tanks, and a service ceiling of 40,000 feet. The A4G had considerable striking power for attack and defence, with five hard points, two under each wing and one centred, capable of carrying a wide variety of munitions. The eight fighter-aircraft were allotted to 805 Squadron whose primary roles included air defence, maritime strike, and support to the Army when configured in land attack role.

The Grumman Tracker S-2E/G was well suited to their ASW role, serving on the carrier and at RANAS Nowra. Other duties included coastal surveillance and fishery patrols from 1975 to December 1980. The Tracker was a high-wing monoplane, powered by two, air-cooled, radial piston engines fitted with 3-blade variable pitch propellers. This provided the airframe with a top speed of 280 miles per hour and a cruise speed of 150 miles per hour. Range was out to 1,350 miles with a service ceiling maxing at 22,000 feet. The aircraft was also fitted with a range of electronic sensors to assist in its surveillance and ASW roles.

Photo 9-16

Skyhawks front and centre on the deck of HMAS *Melbourne* with Trackers and Wessex helicopters in the background. A Royal Navy frigate is stationed on *Melbourne's* starboard quarter and HMAS *Brisbane* on her port quarter. (RAN)

In 1967, *Melbourne* sailed to the United States, taking on board new Douglas Skyhawk and Grumman Tracker aircraft before returning to Australia for a major refit which kept her in dock for most of 1968.

Melbourne left for the Far East in May 1969 equipped with Skyhawks of 805 Squadron, Trackers of 816 Squadron, and the Wessex of 817 Squadron.

In the early hours of 3 June 1969, the destroyer USS *Frank E. Evans* crossed *Melbourne's* bow while attempting to move in the plane guard position, and was cut in two. The forward section of *Evans* sank quickly while her stern section was secured to *Melbourne*'s starboard side enabling that part of the ship to be searched for survivors. Seventy-four of *Evans*' crew lost their lives, and *Melbourne* sustained extensive damage to her bow section. Search and rescue operations began immediately and 199 men were saved, many of them embarking and receiving treatment in the Australian carrier before transferring to the American carrier, USS *Kearsarge*. Temporary repairs were affected at sea before *Melbourne* proceeded to Singapore that afternoon. She steamed into Singapore on 6 June with flags flying at half-mast.

Following temporary repairs at Singapore, *Melbourne* sailed on 27 June bound for Australia, arriving in Sydney on 9 July where repairs were carried out. She returned to sea on 11 October to commence work-up exercises and shortly thereafter resumed a regular program of exercises, training and maintenance.

Melbourne continued to exercise in Far Eastern waters, until a major refit which lasted for most of 1971. She embarked on board 805, 816 and 817 Squadrons in September, and participated in joint exercises near Hawaii in November. She took part in a series of exercises over the next few years, underwent a further refit in 1973, and visited California in 1974. When Darwin, Northern Territory, was devastated by Cyclone Tracey on Christmas Day 1974, *Melbourne* sailed from Sydney the next day to assist with a large cargo of urgently-needed supplies.

When Australia took delivery of the Westland Sea King helicopter in 1975, they were allocated to 817 Squadron aboard *Melbourne*, as well as being assigned to the land base at Nowra. After another refit in 1975-76, *Melbourne* was involved in further exercises. Exercise Kangaroo II, in October 1976, saw *Melbourne* operating with the carrier USS *Enterprise*.

Early in 1977, *Melbourne* collected 16 Grumman Trackers from the US, to replace ten of the aircraft lost in a hangar fire at Nowra the previous December. In May 1977, she sailed with the guided missile destroyer HMAS *Brisbane*, bound for England to take part in the celebration of the Queen's Silver Jubilee.

Later she remained in Australian waters, with two more periods in dock, one including a substantial refit. *Melbourne* continued to take part in exercises and occasional rescue tasks until 1981, when she put in to Sydney for maintenance. During this period a decision was made to decommission her, and this occurred on 30 June 1982.

Melbourne spent her last days moored at Athol Bight in Sydney Harbour, awaiting a decision on disposal. The ship was initially sold in June 1984 to an Australian company for A$1.7 million, however the sale fell through. In February 1985 the former Flagship was sold to the China

United Shipbuilding Co Ltd for A$1.4 million to be broken up for scrap metal in the port of Dalian, China.[16]

But even then, the old lady continued to surprise. She departed Sydney on 27 April 1985, under tow for Guangzhou, China. The journey was delayed when the towing line began to part, requiring the carrier and tug to shelter in Moreton Bay, Queensland, on 30 April. The towing gear broke a day later, requiring a second tug to secure the carrier whilst repairs were made. Three days later, *Melbourne* ran aground while still in Moreton Bay. She finally arrived in China on 13 June 1985. The Australian government reportedly received a Telex on this day, reading:

> Please be advised that HMAS *Melbourne* arrived at Port Huangpu [Guangzhou], intact and safely afloat, proud and majestic. She has been innocent, never once bowed to the natural or human force, in spite of the heavy storm and the talked about jinx.[17]

Carrier design and pilot training in China received a major boost with the arrival of *Melbourne* from Australia. At that time the Australian government did not oppose the sale, because China was seen as an important strategic counterweight to perceived Soviet expansionism in Asia. The purchase helped the PLAN's R&D program in two ways. (The People's Liberation Army Navy, also known as the PLA Navy or PLAN, is the naval warfare branch of the People's Liberation Army.) First, as the carrier was being dismantled for scrap, Chinese naval architects and engineers were able to see at firsthand how it had been designed and built; using this information naval architects were able to prepare drawings for a light carrier. Second, the flight deck of the *Melbourne* was kept intact and used for pilot training in carrier takeoffs and landings (though a static flight deck would, of course, have been of limited utility, since it could not replicate the pitch and roll of an aircraft carrier at sea). China's carrier R&D program remained top secret. In 1987 Colonel General Xu Xing denied that China wanted to acquire an aircraft carrier capability, citing the country's 'defensive' military doctrine.[18]

HMAS *MELBOURNE*'S LEGACY

Throughout her long life, *Melbourne* was a great asset to Australia and served her nation well. For much of her life she formed part of the Far East Strategic Reserve and took part in a number of big exercises with other Commonwealth warships. *Melbourne* was a frequent participant in exercises with other Pacific nations which brought the RAN into close contact with regional navies as well as the RN and USN. For many participants in the annual RIMPAC (Rim of the Pacific countries) exercises, *Melbourne* was the epitome of the Navy's ability to project power forward in a variety of different ways. Although she never went into combat, *Melbourne* escorted her sister ship *Sydney*, by then converted into a fast troop transport, on three voyages that carried Australian military personnel to Vietnam.

Melbourne carried out over thirty-five overseas deployments and visited more than twenty-two countries. She was probably seen by more people outside than inside Australia and her sailors were invariably good ambassadors on whom the standards of the nation were judged. She continued to show the latent power that her air group gave the RAN until the end of her life and in April 1980, she led the largest task force assembled by the RAN since the Second World War into the Indian Ocean for exercises and visits. She had spent 62,036 hours underway and steamed 868,893 nautical miles.

REPLACEMENT PLANS

The RAN sought a replacement carrier with increasing urgency as *Melbourne* grew older. The favoured solution was a USN *Iwo Jima*-class amphibious helicopter design, modified to suit RAN requirements but in 1981 the British Government offered the new light carrier *Invincible* for sale at a bargain price of £175 million. She had only been completed in 1980 and was not even fully operational yet. This surprising offer 'out of the blue' followed the Review of the RN carried out by British Defence Secretary John Nott who wanted to eliminate much of the surface fleet and concentrate on nuclear submarines based in the North Atlantic. In February, 1982, the Australian Government announced that it had agreed to buy *Invincible* that she was to be re-named Australia and operated, initially, as a helicopter carrier. A decision on whether to buy Sea Harriers for her was to be taken at a later date, but since the RAN already had pilots flying them in the UK, it was confidently expected that this logical next step would happen.

The purchase of the Royal Navy carrier *Invincible* was subsequently cancelled when the British Government decided it was necessary to retain the aircraft carrier following lessons learned during the Falklands War. In March 1983 the incoming Australian Labor Government announced that it would implement its election commitment not to replace *Melbourne* and as a result of these two decisions the RAN ceased to have a carrier in its force structure.

10

Some Australian Fleet Air Arm Personalities

By Commodore Hector Donohue AM RAN (Rtd)

NEW CAPABILITY, NEW EXPERIENCES

With the introduction of a Fleet Air Arm into the RAN in 1948 and participation in the Korean War some four years later, the RAN drew from a range of backgrounds to consolidate this new capability. The pilots were from three sources: Second World War veterans (ex RN, ex RNZN and RAN officers); loan RN officers, many with war experience; and newly trained RAN junior officers. This chapter highlights the contribution made by officers from these backgrounds and experience, as well as others in the early days of Australia's Fleet Air Arm. Some of the quoted material is comprised of excerpts from original articles, and presented in quoted material format to more easily convey that it is derived from first-hand accounts.

JEFFREY GLEDHILL – THE WORLD WAR II VETERAN

Photo 10-1

Captain Jeffrey Gledhill DSC RAN. (RAN)

Captain Jeffrey Allan Gledhill was a WWII veteran who had dive bombed the German battleship *Tirpitz*. He was a sub-lieutenant when, on 3 April 1944, he took off from the carrier HMS *Victorious* in his Fairey Barracuda dive-bomber as part of an attack on the *Tirpitz*. On his final approach to the Norwegian fjords, where the ship was hiding, he climbed over mountains to 2,500 feet, then began a 45-degree dive and released his 1,600lb armour-piercing bomb (post-war analysis showed that it struck one of *Tirpitz*'s two 15-inch guns). The battleship was badly crippled by this and other direct hits. After further operations that April, Gledhill was awarded a Distinguished Service Cross.

Jeffrey Allan Gledhill was born on 11 November 1921 in Wellington, New Zealand, and joined the RNZVR in 1941. On his sea voyage to UK his ship *Tamaroa* almost blundered into the battle between the *Bismark* and HMS *Hood*. As he recounted the incident:

> World War II broke out while I was a teenager, and in 1940 I joined up to serve in the Navy as a Fleet Air Arm pilot. A party of us were entered at the then [cruiser] HMS *Philomel* in Auckland and, in early 1941, we departed in a lightly armed merchant ship with a cruiser escort for two days. Crossing the Pacific, through the Panama Canal, then north to Greenland, we entered a thick sea fog, which remained for days despite a strong wind, but as we had no escort the fog probably saved us from attack. Somewhere south of the Denmark Strait, we emerged from the fog and were directed to look for gun flashes, for we were not far distant from the battle between HMS *Hood*, *Prince of Wales* and the German battleship, *Bismark* and the *Prince Eugen*. *Hood* blew up and only three of her complement of 1419 was picked up. It was as well we were not sighted by enemy ships, submarines or aircraft.
>
> We reached Glasgow unscathed. Our train to Portsmouth had stops for air raids and on our first night in naval barracks the area was heavily bombed. With knots and splices, seamanship, navigation and gunnery all essential to urgently needed naval aviators, we were split up. With others, I went to the RAF at Birmingham and then to RAF Netheravon on the frequently snowbound Salisbury Plain – so cold my fingers could not press an engine starter. Then it was back to the Navy and some intensive torpedo, bombing and deck-landing training on Swordfish biplanes with open cockpits and Albacore biplanes with closed cockpits. These old aircraft were slow, but highly manoeuvrable and most effective at night.

Gledhill saw service in the aircraft carriers HM Ships *Furious* and *Victorious*, in the North Atlantic and Norwegian waters. After the war he returned to New Zealand but in 1947, moved to Australia to join the RAN, where he served in the cruiser HMAS *Australia* and later, the destroyer, HMAS *Bataan*. In 1948, he was posted to the UK to the 21st Carrier Air Group in 817 Squadron as a Firefly pilot. During this period, says Gledhill, 'a controller was letting me down from about 6000 feet, in thick cloud, to a naval air station in Somerset. Suddenly, whilst still in cloud, I glimpsed a hedge, which I was skimming in hills south of the airfield. Still on instruments, I pulled up hard and missed the high ground. The controller bought me a beer, needless to say!'

The squadron joined the aircraft carrier HMAS *Sydney* for work around the UK coast and returned to Sydney in early 1951. But its stay in the ship's home town was short-lived as, within months, the carrier was sent off to the Korean War. Operating in the Yellow Sea, the ship's aircraft attacked targets in North Korea, such as bridges, rail lines and troop concentrations.

> Bombs would ricochet off the icy ground and shoot back into the air (recalls Gledhill of the severe conditions faced by those in the air and on the ground). At first, the weather was reasonable, but by the end of the year heavy snow fell and at one stage cloaked the flight deck and aircraft, preventing flying. We had to wear rubber immersion suits with survival vests on top and then webbing belts with revolver and ammunition – a cumbersome outfit.

In 1952 Gledhill was promoted to Lieutenant Commander and was posted to the Naval Air Base Nowra. He was commanding officer of 817 Squadron which recommissioned at RNAS *Culdrose*, UK with Fairey Gannets in August 1955 and joined HMAS *Melbourne* shortly after commissioning. Following *Melbourne*'s fist deployment to south-east Asia, he was promoted to Acting Commander to head air operations at NAS Nowra. He was confirmed as a commander in 1957 and promoted to Captain in 1963. He retired in 1975 after his final appointment as Director of Naval Intelligence.[1]

ROBERT BLUETT AND PETER MCNAY – FEARLESS RN LOAN OFFICERS

Lieutenant John Robert (Bob) Tenison Bluett and Lieutenant Peter Frank McNay were Royal Navy loan (exchange) officers serving in 805 Squadron in 1955 when they were unexpectedly called to action. Bluett was the Squadron's senior pilot and had seen service in the Korean War

198   Chapter 10

in HMS *Glory*. McNay had only been in Australia eight months after completing his training in England. On the morning of 30 August 1955, they were involved in one of the oddest 'shoot downs' in the history of military aviation, when 805 Squadron was called upon to fire on an unusual 'enemy' in the skies over Sydney!

Photo 10-2

Royal Australian Navy Auster J/4 Archer aircraft. (RAN)

For more than three hours on a fine, calm August morning in 1955, the eyes of Sydney's suburbia were fixed skyward, anxiously watching the flight of a pilotless Auster J/4 Archer aircraft as it circled above and headed from Bankstown to the City. It was school holiday time, the alert had gone out over the radio, and the mothers had herded in their children, police patrolled areas by car, cycle and foot, firemen stood by their tenders, ambulance men remained on the alert and fire tugs stood in readiness in the harbour . . . all eyes still looked up . . . no one knew when or where the plane might suddenly come hurtling down.

The end came - thankfully five miles off the coast - when two Navy Sea Furies opened fire on the Auster, which levelled out pouring smoke, then started down in a slow spiral. The two Navy pilots followed it down, firing two or three more short bursts on the way and with a splash, the errant aircraft, still in one piece, hit the water at 1142 and disappeared. It was all over! The media had a field day . . . with such newspaper headings as 'Possible disaster in flight,' and 'Thousands watch air drama of flyaway plane,' reaching the overseas press. Politicians asked embarrassing questions and criticism of the Services followed as did a Department of Civil Aviation enquiry - but how, when and why did it happen?

On the morning of August 30, 1955, Mr. Anthony Thrower, aged 30, of Granville, Sydney, rented an Auster from Kingsford Smith Aviation School. He had completed only one circuit of his planned one-hour practice when the engine failed ten feet above the ground. Landing the plane in the middle of the strip he climbed out swung the propeller by hand (there was no self-starter) and the engine immediately roared into life. In a million-to-one chance the brake failed to hold and although pilot Thrower grabbed a wing strut to check the plane, he was quickly forced to jump clear, just avoiding the tail. Aided by a favourable south-east wind with well-trimmed controls, the pilotless plane sped across the strip and became airborne.

It then narrowly missed the control tower, which was subsequently evacuated, and other airport buildings, then slowly circled the aerodrome at low altitude. After continuing right hand circuits of Bankstown for a further 15 minutes the Auster steadily gained height and began drifting towards the City. Bankstown Aerodrome officials alerted control personnel at Mascot which broadcast a general alarm to all aircraft as well as the police and other Government organisations. One report stated that a schoolboy might be at the controls. The police radio station at Bourke Street broadcast at almost one-minute intervals the plane's last known whereabouts.

Meanwhile, Commander John R. W. Groves RN, another loan officer, was returning from Nowra to Schofields airfield from exercises, with three other personnel onboard a Navy Auster. At 0850 he was alerted by Mascot of the runaway plane. Nearing Bankstown they saw it at 1,500 feet and climbing in tight circles. Approaching to within 50 yards it was noted to be unoccupied and that the controls were fixed in the one position. Groves, offered to trail the runaway Auster, then heading across town to the Sydney Central Business District.

By 0953 the Auster was over Vaucluse in east Sydney at 5,000 feet. An Air Force CAC Wirraway (training and general-purpose aircraft) departed Richmond at 1010 to despatch the runaway aircraft. The rear canopy and fairing were removed to allow a hand-held Bren gun to be used to shoot at the Auster. The target was contacted at 1020, two and a half miles offshore and now at an altitude of 7,000 feet. Instructions were then received that they were not to open fire until the Auster was five miles offshore and there were no fishing or coastal boats below. The Auster continued climbing in tight orbit to 10,300 feet and at 1045 reached a point estimated at five miles from the coast. Two firing passes were then made with the Bren gun from the rear cockpit without any noticeable effect. Squadron Leader James who was manning the gun was so cold - it was minus five degrees Celsius – that he was unable to change the magazine and his hands were sticking to the gun.

Meanwhile a RAAF Meteor jet fighter had arrived from RAAF Base Williamtown near Newcastle and after directing it to the target the

Wirraway broke off the attack and returned to Richmond. The Navy Auster, which had now been airborne some 3¼ hours, headed for its base at Schofields at about the same time.

But luck was not with the RAAF that day. Firstly, Meteor *A77-80* had been delayed some 13 minutes on departure when a Sabre preceding his departure, had burst a tyre on landing and obstructed the runway. Then after arriving in the target area, and in the Meteor's initial firing pass from the rear, both cannons jammed after only a few rounds had been fired. Some strikes were observed on the starboard side of the Auster. The pilot of the Meteor then requested that two more Meteors be sent and the reply was received that they were on the way in addition to two Sea Furies from the Naval Air Station Nowra.

While awaiting their arrival, *A77-80* made four passes directly below the runaway Auster and pulled up sharply in an attempt to dislodge it from its flight path and into a dive. However, the jet wash was not sufficient and the plane continued in the same determined fashion.

Sea Furies from 805 Squadron Nowra appeared on the scene at 1135, piloted by Lieutenants Bob Bluett and Peter McNay. As a precaution, to ensure the Auster was empty, McNay lowered his flaps and undercarriage, slowing his prop-driven Sea Fury - to check the cabin – as a report had been received that a schoolboy might be onboard. Ensuring it was empty; McNay repositioned his Sea Fury behind the Auster, now flying at about 10,000 feet and some distance out to sea.

McNay fired a short burst from his 20mm cannons - hitting the Auster and knocking it out of balance. Bluett, in the other Sea Fury, then fired from a beam-on position, causing the Auster's cockpit to burst into flames. Badly damaged, the Auster nosed-down in a slow spiral. McNay followed with another burst from his cannons, sending the Auster crashing into the sea. From the first strikes on the Auster until the time it hit the sea was 1½ minutes.

At 1145 a police broadcast announced 'The Auster has been shot down. It's all over.' The barrage of calls from anxious enquirers gradually subsided at the police, newspaper and radio station switchboards throughout Sydney. When the Navy Sea Furies returned to Nowra, enthusiastic ground staff quickly painted a small yellow silhouette representing an Auster on the fuselage of Bluett's plane, being awarded the 'kill.'

The remarkable thing is the runaway Auster was airborne for so long and fortunately not involved in a major accident. Deeply embarrassed, the RAAF later explained that its fighter squadrons at Williamtown were stood down when the incident happened.[2]

Bob Bluett returned to UK in 1956 on completion of his two-year loan service in Australia. Peter McNay transferred to the RAN on a short service commission serving mainly as a pilot. He was promoted to Lieutenant Commander in 1962 and left the RAN in June 1969.

Photo 10-3

Lieutenants Bob Bluett (left) and Peter McNay reliving their successful action against a pilotless Auster in 1955. (RAN)

NORMAN LEE – JUNIOR FIREFLY PILOT IN KOREA

Norman Ernest Lee enlisted in the RAN in May 1948 as a recruit rating pilot. Following initial naval training at HMAS Cerberus (Flinders Naval Depot), he commenced pilot training with the RAAF at the Point Cook base. Graduating as a probationary pilot, he travelled to the United Kingdom aboard SS *Strathmore* for deck landing training with the Royal Navy. On return to Australia he was promoted to Sub Lieutenant and undertook further naval training prior to joining No. 817 Squadron at the Naval Air Station, HMAS Albatross.

Lee saw service in the Korean War aboard HMAS *Sydney* in September 1951, when the *Sydney* relieved HMS *Glory* as the carrier

Chapter 10

representative of the British naval forces in the Korean theatre. Norman remembers that as *Sydney* berthed on the other side of the pontoon, *Glory*'s band played, *If I'd known you were coming, I'd have baked a cake*, a popular tune at the time.

Photo 10-4

Commodore Norman Lee standing in front of a Firefly, circa 1980. (FAA Association)

Following the war, Norman remained in the navy and rose to the rank of Commodore. During his thirty-three years of service Norman flew twenty-five different types of military aircraft. He commanded HMA Ships *Queenborough* and *Vampire*, No. 724 Naval Air Squadron, and shore establishments HMAS Kuttabul and HMAS Albatross. Norman retired in 1981.

Norman Lee gave a presentation on his experiences in Korea at a Naval History Seminar at the Australian War Memorial in 1989. An edited version follows:

> I was a newly qualified pilot with 817 Squadron which, together with 805 and 808, formed *Sydney*'s Carrier Air Group. We were equipped with 12 Mark 6 Fireflies. The Firefly was an anti-submarine aircraft and therefore had no cannon. When we were detailed to go to Korea we swapped our aircraft for those of 816 Squadron which had Mark 5 Fireflies which carried four 20mm cannon. It was decided that the Sea Furies would rocket and we would bomb and our normal load was two 500-pound bombs and 120 rounds of 20mm ammunition. We naturally required a work-up before we left.

We did our work-up on that site well known to the RAN, Beecroft Head at Jervis Bay. We also did a deck landing work-up which was a bit disastrous as a lot of aircraft were crashed or lost over the side. We arrived in Korea in September 1951 to relieve HMS *Glory*.

We were originally planned to dive bomb, in fact we started off dive bombing. Our tactical profile was from 8,000 feet to 3,000 feet in a 55-degree dive and, in the old Firefly, if you didn't get full right rudder on at the top of the dive, it went down sideways. As with the Sea Furies, the Fireflies found that we could put bombs on either side of a bridge – literally straddle it – and do absolutely no damage at all. You must hit a bridge to damage it.

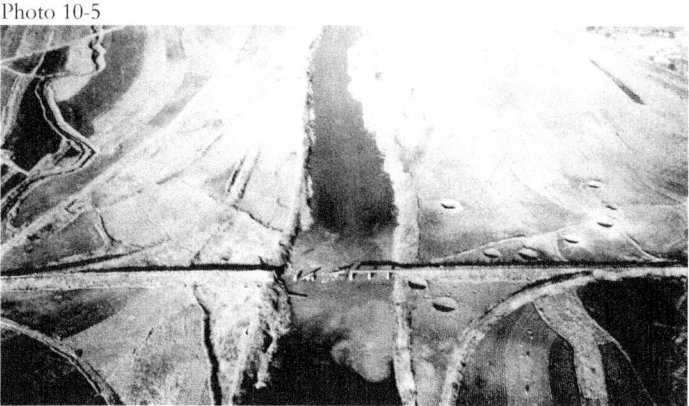

Photo 10-5

An aerial view of a bridge between Haeju and Yonan on 27 November 1951. (817 Squadron Record)

No. 817 Squadron subsequently took up low level bombing, which required some changes in tactics:

> We also established that, contrary to what we thought, the opposition was not that great. There was small-arms fire with the odd small cannon, but the threat was not that bad, so a bold decision was made to go to low level bombing. To achieve this we modified our anti-submarine depth charge attack to descend to 100 feet in a 20-degree dive using delay fuses set to 37 seconds. We were operating in flights of four aircraft, so if you were 'Tail-End Charlie' – as we poor sub-lieutenants always were – you had to get in within less than 37 seconds from when your leader dropped the first bomb, otherwise you wore it. I don't think that anybody got blown up, but it is marvellous how it sharpens the wit when you know you can be blown out of the sky.

Our tactical profile proved to be very successful. We were taking out bridges with monotonous regularity and eventually reduced down to one aircraft attacking instead of four – on one occasion we knocked out a bridge with a single bomb. You had to be careful that the bomb did not bounce in cold weather, the ground being frozen solid. This meant a steeper dive was necessary because the bomb would either break up and there would be just a white puff, or it would bounce. There was one reported incident where precisely this happened and the bomb hit an ammunition dump. To everyone's great surprise, this blew up some distance away from our intended attack.

After we had dropped our bombs we would carry out an armed reconnaissance at about 2,000 feet. Analysis after the war determined this to be the perfect height not to fly at because the aircraft was going at just about the right height and speed for small-arms fire. The North Koreans were rather clever chaps, they had rifle sections with a leader with a whistle. They would all aim towards the approaching aircraft, pointing the rifles at different angles and, on the sound of the whistle; they would fire as one. In this way they would straddle the aircraft. This tactic was reasonably successful because a number of aircraft were hit.

Pilot adherence to the authorized Rules of Engagement required changes in one's perspective regarding targets:

We learned our rules of engagement, what might be a genuine target and what must not be attacked. Ox carts, we were told, were legitimate targets. This was difficult for some of us until one ox cart blew up during a strafing attack, proving it was loaded with ammunition. Lighthouses were sacrosanct, including the one on the south shore of the Chinnampo Estuary from where an amazingly accurate machine-gunner plied his lethal trade. We avoided civilian targets, such as villages, unless briefed to attack a specific structure. In one railway bridge attack, Sub Lieutenant Neil MacMillan, saw his Firefly's bomb ricochet from a frozen embankment 500 meters or more away directly into a nearby peaceful-looking village. The pilot watched in horror as the delay fuse set off the bomb, only to see it followed by a huge explosion and many secondaries. The 'village' burned for days. It was a huge ammunition dump.

We used a gridding plot on our maps, so we could readily indicate positions to other types of aircraft, which was really quite successful. It was just an arbitrary grid which we determined ourselves.

Commodore Lee's presentation then moved on to discussion of improvements made in "trapping" (landing aboard the carrier) following missions; how he acquired a souvenir piece of shrapnel taken from his aircraft; and launching from the carrier with and without the assistance of the catapult:

> On completion of the sortie, we would return to the *Sydney* via a rendezvous point. At that stage, the Firefly had something of a reputation for hook bounce. The hook only came down to a limited angle and, in consequence, a modification had been introduced (the Mod 12.11 from memory) which was a much heavier damper and it really put the hook down. When formed up the routine was to drop your hook to make certain you had not suffered any damage to it. If you didn't have the modification it was very sobering to see the other fellows with their hooks right down knowing full well that yours was only a little one from a deck landing point of view. Anyhow, our deck landing accident rate reduced practically to zero which is indicative of a good work-up, however fraught.
>
> On one occasion we bombed a village which was known to be a North Korean supply point and we were a bit casual in our attack profile. Instead of doing a dive bombing attack, we used instantaneous fuses and did a sort of semi-dive bombing low-level attack. As I pulled out I saw a dint in the left wing. As everyone else had suffered battle damage at this point, I thought: 'At last, I'm a hero!' We landed on and, sure enough, there was a hole about the size of a two shilling piece in the wing. The maintenance crews recovered the piece of shrapnel which caused the hole and I kept it as a souvenir. When we returned to Australia, my father, who was an engineer officer in the RAAF, asked, 'How did it go, son?' and I said, 'Rough, Dad, look at this bit I got hit with.' And he looked at it and said, 'Looks like a bit of bomb to me, son.' He was dead right.
>
> Prior to Korea we had mostly carried out free take offs from the ship. It is marvellous how things customarily happen. Free take offs were the thing, so we did free take offs. We sub-lieutenants used to be at the front end of the deck park and you had to be pretty sharp about it to make certain that you got airborne in the available deck length. Because we had three squadrons on board for Korea, it was decided that we should try the alternatives, which were Rocket Assisted Take Off Gear (RATOG), which meant individual rockets strapped to the side of the aircraft, and the ship's catapult. I have the dubious honour of having carried out the last-rocket assisted take-off in the RAN from a carrier because the chap behind me unfortunately torque stalled, causing the aircraft to revolve out of control, and he was killed.
>
> I mentioned the hydraulic catapult. The very nature of the thing meant that you got maximum thrust almost instantaneously and it

was almost like being kicked up the backside by an elephant. The catapult was a very effective way of getting airborne and from there on in we rarely went back to free take-offs. The other advantage of catapult operations was that they made moving the aircraft about the deck and striking them up from the hangar much simpler.

Photo 10-6

Firefly landing on HMAS *Sydney* during Korean War. (AWM)

Pilot duties also involved some shipboard work, and support of combatant ships carrying out shore bombardment of enemy targets:

> During patrol we would have a break in the middle for a replenishment day. It was indicative of the thinking, shall we say, of those old days that we sub-lieutenants were sent back to school where we did seamanship and the duties of second officer of the watch. Then the next day was on with our flying suits and back to the war. It always struck me as a little odd. We generally flew one to two sorties a day of an hour and a half. As I noted, we operated as a patrol of four aircraft. This occasionally went up to five which was a very unwieldy combination. I was busily following my section leader chasing after an ox cart on one occasion and thinking, 'he's not flying like he normally flies – he's a fairly sedate fellow.' Nevertheless, we were having fun and when we formed up it turned out that I'd latched on to the other number two and the pair of us, a couple of sub-lieutenants, were fighting our own private war over Korea.
>
> I was tasked to carry out a shoot with a destroyer, HMAS *Tobruk*, which was one of the Australian Battle class. My section leader was to spot for HMS *Belfast*. Away we went and I was busily correcting the fall of shot when *Tobruk* came up and said that she would have to come closer to the coast to effect the last correction I had given. Anyway, my sub-lieutenant's computer went "whirr whirr,"

something is wrong, I can see *Tobruk* and she is quite close in. The penny dropped. I replied, 'Are you using Willie Peter?' This was white phosphorous ranging shot. The reply was negative. I was ranging *Tobruk* on *Belfast*'s fall of shot. We then tried to find *Tobruk*'s shot but in the early morning high explosive shells are very difficult to see. She ended up firing broadsides until finally I saw her shot and gave her a correction which measured thousands of yards. She got into the target area, fired for effect and called it a day. I slunk off back to the ship very embarrassed. Sometime later, I was in the frigate HMAS *Murchison* doing my watchkeeping time when I met a certain gunnery officer in the Wardroom who said: 'Oh, you're an aviator. I met the biggest idiot aviator up in Korea.' I let him go on and then said, 'Yes, that was me!'

Photo 10-7

HMAS *Tobruk* in Korean waters, 1951. (AWM)

Photo 10-8

RAN Firefly from HMAS *Sydney* in Korean waters, 1951. (AWM)

The very informative and colourful presentation ended with revisiting combat operations, and humour associated with *Sydney*'s encounter with a typhoon:

> During the time on the east coast we attacked a railway tunnel with 1,000 pound bombs. We had to reduce our loads of fuel and ammunition to bring the aircraft in to its maximum permissible all-up weight with this weapon. We hit the thing with 10,000 pounds of bombs and some weeks later were credited with a train which they used to hide in the tunnels.
>
> You may have heard mention of the dinghy drop to a downed B29 crew member. I was sent off on a hasty mission to drop a special type dinghy and I well recall on my way north very carefully testing my cannon in case we came across any MiG fighters. Fortunately, we did not. I reckon that I could have outflown them at low-level but how long we would have survived I don't know.
>
> Typhoon Ruth caused its share of excitement. We were in Sasebo, as I recall, and we sailed as soon as we could. It was a pretty rough night. As I remember it, the ship rolled 35 degrees, we had electrical fires all over the place as salt water got into areas it normally did not. Paint was stripped off the ship's side, a Firefly went over the side, damaging other aircraft with it, and we lost a tractor and a small boat from the flight deck. There were, however, a couple of amusing incidents. There was a pipe on the main broadcast right in the middle of this howling typhoon, 'Fuel danger, No smoking on the flight or weather decks.' You couldn't even stand on the flight or weather decks. The other one I recall was, 'Fire! Fire! Fire! Fire in the bomb room.' We sub-lieutenants, those who were off watch and not monitoring the aircraft in the hangar, were up forward, naughty, playing pontoon and we looked at each other because we were sitting right on top of the bomb room. And the question might be asked, what did we do? The answer was simple: another hand was dealt – there was nothing we could do. As you can imagine, the fire didn't come to anything.
>
> But if we thought it was rough, it was a lot rougher for flight deck and maintenance crews to be up there the whole time. Their performance was extraordinary and the *Sydney* Carrier Air Group's impressive operational performance was in large measure due to their efforts.[3]

TOM HENRY - CHOCKMAN THE BRAVE

Thomas (Tom) Frederick Henry joined the RAN in 1949 and qualified as an Aircraft Handler. He subsequently served in HMA Ships *Sydney, Vengeance* and *Melbourne,* rising to the rank of Chief Petty Officer before leaving the Navy in 1972. Whilst a young Able Seaman serving in *Sydney* during the Korean War, he was involved in an incident when a Sea Fury undertook a power run and which he has never forgotten. His account of this unusual flight deck accident, which was published in the Fleet Air Arm Association Journal *Slipstream*, follows:

> It was late 1951 aboard HMAS *Sydney* off the north coast of Korea, the sea was very rough and the weather very cold. During a break in flying operations, the Flight Deck Officer (Lieutenant Commander Richard Graham How RN, a loan officer) called out, 'Tom Henry, slip down the after lift, there is another chockman required for a Fury coming up from Charlie hangar for a power run.' As I made my way down to the after lift, I thought to myself how unlucky I was. This aircraft had most probably had an engine change and I was likely to be stuck on the chocks for up to half an hour. The Fury was eventually parked on the Port quarter with the after fuselage aligned over one of the flight deck ring bolts. The mechanics soon had lashing around the after fuselage and secured to the ring bolt.

Photo 10-9

Aircraft handlers about to remove chocks from a Sea Fury onboard HMAS *Sydney*, 1951. These, in conjunction with chains, secure aircraft in place. (AWM)

> Prior to that, the young pilot had manned the cockpit. I checked the lashings on my chock, and then got into position on the deck with my feet around the after chock and my arms and body wrapped around the wheel and the front of the chock. Needless to say it was a very uncomfortable position and I was grateful for the special

issue fur lined helmet and gloves that gave some protection from the frigid weather conditions we were unaccustomed to.

As the powerful Bristol Centaurus engine burst into life, I noticed that the yellow coated Director and the Fireman had moved away, probably to get out of the cold. I remember thinking that under these conditions lying on a hard deck was a stupid place to be, the noise and the huge five-bladed prop blowing bitterly cold air over me added to my discomfort. My thoughts drifted to my home town in northern New South Wales where it would be warm and everyone thinking about Christmas and the holidays.

My dreaming came to a sudden halt as I realised that the pilot was increasing the power considerably! At the same time I noticed that the deck movement was becoming more pronounced, maybe getting rougher or the ship was changing course. The aircraft was approaching full power when my fellow chockman caught my eye by frantically pointing to the rear of the aircraft. I checked to see what was grabbing his attention – the fuselage lashing was starting to fray!

Henry, finding himself in a potential life-ending situation (his own), fortunately came through it unscathed:

> From my cramped position I anxiously looked around for someone to get the attention of the pilot - there was no one in sight! My mind started working overtime. What will happen if the lashing parts? Will the aircraft ground loop and go over the side? Or what if.... The possibilities were endless, or so it seemed. It was now freezing cold, the Fury was really roaring, the deck was now heaving from the rough seas and I could sense that something was about to happen. I buried my face between my arm and the aircraft tyre. There was a deafening noise and I was suddenly sprayed with debris, then all was quiet. I looked up to see the Fury precariously balanced on its nose atop a badly bent propeller.
>
> The Flight Deck Officer and others were soon on the scene and the Fury was restored to its original position. 'Good lad Henry, sticking with your chocks! You may have helped save the aircraft' said the Flight Deck Officer. At this point one of my Aircraft Handler mates tapped me on the shoulder and whispered 'you silly bastard, you should have shot through, you could have been killed.' Little did they know that because of the severe cold and 'Fury Fear' I was more or less frozen to the spot with fright.
>
> I was thankfully noting that the debris which had struck me was only several layers of deck paint, when the Flight Deck Officer said 'You can go below for a stand easy Henry.' Then added with a grin: 'You may need to change your underpants.'[4]

IAN WEBSTER – DITCHING A SEA FURY

On 11 September 1951, as HMAS *Sydney* was on passage to Korea, a Sea Fury from 805 Squadron was having engine trouble and called for an emergency landing, but it crashed on the sea about 1,000 metres from *Sydney*. The pilot, Sub Lieutenant Ian Webster RN, made a successful ditching in his Sea Fury – believed to be a world first. Until then, there were fears about the heavy engine nosing-down and flipping as the aircraft hit the water. Therefore, the advice to pilots was, where possible, to bale-out and avoid ditching.

After experiencing an oil pressure failure, Webster tried to return to the ship for an emergency landing but the engine suddenly failed when he was downwind. With his undercarriage and flaps down, the aircraft dropped like a stone. There was not time even to retract the undercarriage. The Sea Fury certainly nosed over when it hit the water, but although the cockpit went under water and stayed under, the aircraft sank slowly enough for Webster to get clear and inflate his dinghy.

The accompanying rescue destroyer, HMAS *Tobruk*, saw the crash and headed for it at high speed, but overshot the floundering pilot and tipped him out of his dinghy. Before the destroyer could turn around for another attempt, *Sydney*'s seaboat came to his aid. However, by the time it had reached him, Webster had reboarded his dinghy, opened the rescue pack, devoured all the food (except for an iron-hard block of chocolate) and even deployed his fishing line. (Squadron aircrew learned initiative along with survival skills.) This incident showed that even in the hot and humid conditions of the tropics, the chocolate was so hard that aircrew resolved to use it as a throwing weapon, rather than a form of sustenance, should anyone be shot down.

The accident demonstrated not only that the Sea Fury could ditch successfully, but it could even ditch safely with wheels down. This was the forerunner of a number of successful RAN and RN Sea Fury ditching after enemy action in Korea.[5]

BRIAN DUTCH AND SANDY SANDBERG – TRAINING ACCIDENT

In June 1960, Sub Lieutenant Brian Aubrey Dutch RAN (Pilot) and Lieutenant Edward Donald (Sandy) Sandberg RAN (Observer) successfully ejected at night from a Sea Venom FAW 53 jet aircraft at HMAS Albatross. This was the first ejection in the RAN and the first night ejection from a Sea Venom in the world. Sandy Sandberg had joined the RAN in 1950 as a recruit naval airman and qualified as an observer in 1952. By 1960 he had served in HMA Ships *Sydney*, *Vengeance* and *Melbourne* and was serving in 724 Training Squadron. Brian

Dutch had joined the RAN as a recruit naval airman in 1957 and qualified as a pilot in 1959, receiving his commission as a Sub Lieutenant that year. He had served in *Melbourne* and was serving in 724 Training Squadron completing an All Weather Fighter Course at the time of the incident. Both these men qualified for the award of a Bremont MB watch which is uniquely reserved for those whose lives have been saved by a Martin-Baker (MB) ejection seat.

Diagram 10-1

Cartoon from the cover of *Slipstream*, No 39, July 1960. (The poem reads: A certain young pilot named Dutch, Scrapped a Venom which rattled too much; Bits flew far and wide, So its hard to decide – Did Dutch ditch it, or did it ditch Dutch?)

The following is an edited version of a letter sent to *Slipstream* magazine and published in June 2017 by Brian Dutch, the pilot of the aircraft, which begins with some explanatory material:

> 724 Training Squadron at RANAS Nowra NSW was under considerable pressure to complete an All Weather Fighter Course on the Sea Venom (FAW 53) Aircraft to provide replacement pilots for 805 Squadron, which was the Front Line Squadron. 805 Squadron was due to commence a work up for embarkation on HMAS *Melbourne* for the Short Cruise of 1960.
>
> The air intercept exercises consisted of a Sea Venom 'target', simulating a bomber type of aircraft by limiting its speed and turn rates to those of a bomber aircraft. They would also turn off their navigation lights once radar contact was established in night sorties.
>
> The Observer was responsible for the Navigation and Radar control. He could detect the target on radar and by a variety of orders position the Pilot into a gun firing position at about 200ft below the target and 200 yards astern. The Pilot then had to pull up and fire the 20mm cannons. This could be done in all weathers and at night. I often wondered just what would happen in a real attack should one manage to hit the target. It would be challenging to avoid the debris!

During the night exercises I had had problems in trusting the Radar System in the final stages of an intercept at night when I could not see the target and felt that the closing speed was too fast or there was insufficient height separation. In the correct firing position the Pilot could look up and see the jet pipe of the target. On my final night exercise I failed to sight a 'Jet Pipe' and it was necessary to repeat the exercise by flying another sortie.

While I do not think that fatigue was a factor in the accident, I had already flown two day sorties and due to the failed night exercise, my Observer for the trip, Lieutenant Edward (Sandy) Sandberg and I manned aircraft for a second night sortie. As we settled into the climb for the exercise Sandy found that the radar was not working correctly so we had to land again and find a serviceable aircraft for the fifth sortie of the day.

Photo 10-10

Sea Venom onboard HMAS *Melbourne*. (RAN)

Dutch then provides details about his setup for and problems encountered whilst coming in for a landing at the Naval Air Station:

> An important point at this stage was that during the evening the wind strength had been strongly increasing from the North West.
>
> I put all my effort into passing the final test and was rewarded by spotting a glowing jet pipe which I must say looked dangerously close but worth the effort. I then descended for a landing.
>
> In 1960 the tactical thinking was that, to avoid giving away the position of the aircraft carrier to enemy radar we flew the day circuit for landing at 200 feet above sea level. At night the circuit was flown

at 400 feet. It was also normal practice at the airfield to fly the circuits at similar heights above the airfield datum height.

The 26/08 runway dipped slightly lower in the centre than the thresholds of the runway. The 26 runway threshold was on the edge of a gully which in some wind condition could cause a dangerous down draft of the air mass, causing aircraft to undershoot the runway with some fatalities. I also found that at the approximate position where aircraft would turn for the downwind leg of the landing circuit and the pilot lowered the undercarriage that the ground was slightly higher than the runway datum with trees adding to the height. This therefore reduced the height available for the low circuit.

I joined the upwind leg at 400 feet above the runway datum and was advised by the Control Tower that the wind had now strengthened and was 22 knots gusting to 58 knots and varying from 280 degrees to 320 degrees in the gusts. This meant that during a gust the wind could exceed the cross wind limits of the aircraft undercarriage for landing. The Tower advised that they would report the wind conditions on my final approach.

I was at 240 knots to join the landing circuit and commenced the turn for the downwind leg in a tightly banked turn to wash off speed before I could lower the undercarriage at 220 knots. This was the limiting speed for having the undercarriage down.

I saw that my Observer, Sandy was stowing his navigation gear and I was satisfied that I was established in a level turn.

Dutch's belief that everything was going as planned as he made his approach, disappeared as rapid and unexpected, violent actions by the aircraft developed:

> When I selected the undercarriage down at 220 knots the aircraft rolled rapidly to port and slightly over the vertical so I had to apply full aileron to the right and then full right rudder to try to arrest the roll. The Sea Venom with its high twin tail boom and tail plane design did not roll directly around the longitudinal axis of the aircraft and it tended to 'dish' or 'barrel' in the rolling plane. By the time the aircraft was responding to my control movements and just as I had got it back to about 10 to 15 degrees of bank there was a violent crashing.
>
> The windscreen went opaque and the aircraft was yawing violently so I applied full power to gain height. I realised that the radar dome was probably damaged and as the undercarriage lights were not showing locked, there was more than likely damage to the wheel system. The aircraft was juddering violently so I decided that it was therefore not possible to fly or land the aircraft safely.

Photographs later showed that the aircraft had mowed the top off a tree.

Owing to considerable damage to the jet aircraft, and loss of his control of it, Dutch knew:

> Our only option was to eject. I knew that I had to gain as much height as possible and applied full power in a steep climb as the Martin Baker Mark 4B ejection seat required 200 knots of forward speed and 200 feet of height above ground level to ensure the safe operation of the seat.
>
> The canopy of the aircraft had a solid beam down its centre axis for strength so it was not possible to eject through it. As the ejection seats were sloped slightly towards one another it was necessary for the Observer to eject first. The procedure for ejection was that the Pilot gave the order 'Eject, eject' and the Observer had to pull the canopy ejection handle to blast off the canopy.
>
> I called, 'Eject, Eject!' but there was no re-action from Sandy. It was obvious that we had also lost our inter communications system so I had to change hands on the controls so that I could eject the canopy with my right hand. This made Sandy realise that he would have to eject. I recall the widening of Sandy's eyes as he realised he had to go and he immediately ejected. The air speed was slowing rapidly in the climb. I stayed with the aircraft to just under 120 knots and before the stalling speed, I ejected.
>
> During my parachute descent I had heard Sandy shouting and felt that he might be injured. When I got to him he was trying to light a cigarette due to the wind and his reaction to the accident. He had seen my parachute drift and was shouting to warn me of the danger of the fire. We sat in the darkness and waited while a rescue helicopter approached. It was a notable flight by the Sycamore helicopter pilot as the Sycamore did not have the instrumentation for night hovering but the pilot managed to safely winch down Dr Tommy Thompson, an aviation specialist to check us out.
>
> After a night in the Sick Bay for observation by the Doctors, Sandy and I were granted a week of Survivors Leave. At the end of the week I re-joined the squadron to continue the workup and joined 805 Squadron for the embarkation on HMAS *Melbourne*.

Brian Aubrey Dutch closed out his letter by noting that he was in agreement with the findings of the investigation of the accident, and grateful for his career in the Royal Australian Navy:

It is of particular note that by the time I got back from my Survivors Leave the circuit height had been raised to 1000 feet above ground level and trees were being cleared around the airfield.

Some years ago Sandy contributed an article to the Fleet Air Arm Association of Australia magazine, *Slipstream*, which reflected his consideration of the accident. It included much of the Board of Inquiry text. As it was the first time I had seen the Board Report I was satisfied with my interpretation of the accident and I did not feel that it was appropriate for me to respond.

I am simply grateful that I was able to enjoy a wonderful career in the RAN as an Aviator in the Fleet Air Arm and as a Seaman Officer in ships. I always remained confident in the knowledge that in a 'life and death' situation, I would not freeze and die, but that I would take action to save my life.

The bottom line is that Sandy and I survived, thanks to the successful operation of the Martin Baker Mark 4B Ejection seat, even well below the safe limits for operation of the seat.[6]

Photo 10-11

Burnt out Sea Venom after crash. (RAN)

Postscript

Commander Guy Alexander Beange DSC RAN
By Commodore Hector Donohue AM RAN (Rtd)

Commander Guy Alexander Beange, DSC RAN served with the Royal New Zealand Navy Volunteer Reserve during the Second World War and trained as a Fleet Air Arm pilot in the UK and USA. He served on loan to the Royal Navy in HMS *Glory* before demobilising in late 1945. He joined the Royal Australian Navy (RAN) in 1948 as a pilot, and served in HMAS *Sydney* during the Korean War for which he was awarded the Distinguished Service Cross in 1952. Thereafter, Beange served in the RAN with his career closely paralleled to that of the RAN carrier program. Following a range of appointments, he retired in 1979 and died in 2004. The material for this summary of his career came from naval records and Guy Beange's Private Collection held in the Australian War Memorial.

Photo Postscript-1

Lieutenant Commander Guy Beange at Government House in Sydney having just received the DSC from Her Majesty Queen Elizabeth II, 6 February 1954. (G.J. Beange)

EARLY DAYS

Photo Postscript-2

Guy Beange as a soldier of the New Zealand Army, Waiouru Training Camp, 1941. (G. J. Beange)

Guy Alexander Beange was born on 5 November 1922 at Hamilton, in the Waikato region of New Zealand's North Island. In October 1940, aged 18, he joined the Waikato Mounted Rifles, a Territorial Force (Army Reserve), which had its headquarters in Hamilton.

At the outbreak of war, rather than mobilising its Territorial Force, the New Zealand Government decided to raise a separate force to send overseas to fight – the Second New Zealand Expeditionary Force (2 NZEF). The Territorial Force was kept intact within New Zealand and prepared for home defence.

Following initial training at Waiouru Training Camp, Beange was posted in April 1941 to Hopuhopu Military Camp at Ngaruawahia, some 12 miles north of Hamilton. The Camp had been established for Territorial Force training but had developed into a mobilization camp for volunteers of the 2 NZEF.

In November 1941, it was decided that the mounted rifles regiments were to be reconstituted as armoured units. Waikato Mounted Rifles thus became the 4th Light Armoured Fighting Vehicle regiment, based at Hopuhopu Camp. With the entry of the Japanese into the war in December 1941, home-defence measures were intensified, and the Territorials were mobilised for war.

Beange left the Army in January 1942, intending to join the New Zealand Air Force, but responded to a recruiting drive by the Royal New Zealand Naval Volunteer Reserve (RNZNVR) which was seeking men to train as carrier pilots for loan to the Royal Navy. While waiting for his request to be processed, he served as a seaman on board the SS *Empire Grace*, a fast refrigerated-cargo liner operated by the British Ministry of War Transport

ROYAL NEW ZEALAND NAVAL VOLUNTEER RESERVE

The rapid increase in the number of aircraft carriers in the Royal Navy during the Second World War created a requirement for more aircrew. A series of secondment schemes greatly expanded the New Zealand presence in the Royal Navy and, in 1942, New Zealand was invited to recruit personnel to serve in the Fleet Air Arm, under what was called 'Scheme F.' Under this plan, candidates would be entered as Naval Airman, 2nd class, and go to the UK for initial training. They would then be promoted to acting Leading Airman and undergo training as a pilot or observer and, on qualifying, would be granted a commission.

Some 1,066 recruits left New Zealand under this scheme of whom a total of some 600 served as frontline pilots or observers. They formed a significant proportion of the Fleet Air Arm and saw action in many operations.

Beange joined the RNZNVR at HMNZS Philomel, on 13 January 1943, as a Naval Airman and was sent to the UK in June. He initially joined the Royal Naval Air Station Lee-on-Solent, HMS Daedalus, one of the primary shore airfields of the Fleet Air Arm, four miles west of Portsmouth, Hampshire. He was promoted Acting Leading Airman in September and posted to HMS Saker at Lewiston, Maine, USA, the Royal Navy's administrative base for its personnel undertaking courses in America.

220　Postscript

In October 1943, he was sent to Pensacola, Florida, in the United States, to begin training as a carrier pilot. Beange graduated on 30 June 1944 and was promoted to Provisional Temporary Sub Lieutenant (Acting) RNZNVR. He remained in the US for further training in Vought F4U Corsair fighter aircraft before returning to England for advanced instrument training in March 1945. He was now a Temporary Sub Lieutenant (Acting), with seniority of 26 October 1944.

Following instrument training, he was posted to No 1831 Naval Air Squadron, which joined the *Colossus*-class light carrier HMS *Glory* in April shortly after she commissioned. *Glory* embarked two Naval Air Squadrons: No. 837 (flying Barracuda aircraft) and No. 1831 (flying Corsair aircraft).

Photo Postscript-3

Corsair of 1831 Squadron landing aboard HMS *Glory* under the control of the Deck Landing Officer, June 1945. (HMS *Glory* Association)

The Admiralty had decided that, due to the threat of U-Boat attack in the traditional training areas in the Irish Sea, the new *Colossus*-class Light Fleet Carriers would work-up in the Mediterranean. *Glory* sailed from UK waters in late May, completed work-up by late June, and sailed for Sydney to join the British Pacific Fleet (BPF). The ship was off the coast of Australia when the news of the Japanese surrender was announced on 15 August 1945. Beange had arrived too late to see active service, but the ship did conduct an extensive flying program on passage to Australia.

On 25 August, the Australian government requested Admiral Sir Bruce Fraser, commander in chief BPF, to provide a major warship to accept the surrender of the Japanese forces in New Guinea, New

Britain, New Ireland, Bougainville, and adjacent islands. *Glory* was chosen for this operation and she sailed on 1 September. On 6 September, General Hitoshi Imamura, commander in chief of the Japanese Imperial Southeastern Army, and Vice Admiral Jinichi Kusaka, commander, South East Area Fleet, surrendered all Japanese army and naval forces under their command to Lieutenant General Vernon Sturdee, general officer commanding 1st Australian Army, on the flight deck of HMS *Glory* anchored off Rabaul. Beange was in the flight of Corsairs which circled overhead to provide air cover. All onboard were subsequently given a photograph of the surrender ceremony.

Photo Postscript-4

Surrender ceremony onboard HMS *Glory*, 6 September 1945. (HMS *Glory* Association)

On her return to Australia on 11 September, *Glory* disembarked her air squadrons to Royal Navy Air Station, Jervis Bay in New South Wales. The ship was then employed on repatriation duties, sailing from Sydney, on 26 September, for Manila, to collect former Canadian POWs for passage home to Vancouver. In November, she sailed for Manila and other ports on the return leg to Sydney, arriving back, mid-December, carrying former Australian POWs.

Ashore in Australia, flying training continued at Jervis Bay but Beange, now a Sub Lieutenant (Acting) RNZNVR, left the squadron on 13 October. His squadron commanding officer, Lieutenant Commander Robert W. M. Walsh, RN, gave his assessment of Beange in his flying log as 'Above average.' Beange returned to New Zealand on 16 October, to join HMNZS Cook, a naval depot in Wellington, and was demobilised on 25 October 1945. Later, he moved to Australia, living at Mount Compass, a small town in the Mount Lofty Ranges, south of Adelaide, South Australia.

ROYAL AUSTRALIAN NAVY

On 3 February 1948, Beange joined the RAN in Adelaide as a Lieutenant (Pilot) (Acting) (on Probation), in the Permanent Naval Force, with seniority of 5 May 1945. He was posted to the Training Establishment HMAS Cerberus at Flinders Naval Depot for introductory courses and joined HMAS *Warramunga*, in July, for seaman officer training when he ceased being 'on probation.' He was awarded his Watchkeeping Certificate, in February 1949, and confirmed in the rank of Lieutenant. His commanding officer, Capt. Wilfred H. Harrington, DSO RAN, wrote in his officer's report '...a reliable young officer who can be trusted to take charge.'

In May 1949, Beange went to the UK for flying courses initially joining Royal Naval Air Station Yeovilton, HMS Heron, in Somerset, which included carrier experience in HMS *Illustrious*. He was trained to fly Sea Fury aircraft at Royal Naval Air Station Anthorn, HMS Nuthatch, in Cumbria, North West England, before undertaking a Naval Air Warfare course at Royal Naval Air Station St Merryn, HMS Vulture, in Cornwall. In mid-April 1950, he joined the RAN's 808 Squadron on its formation at Vulture.

Photo Postscript-5

HMAS *Sydney* with Fireflies and Sea Fury aircraft flying overhead in 1950. (AWM)

The second Australian carrier air group (21st Carrier Air Group), comprising 808 (Hawker Sea Fury) and 817 (Fairey Firefly) Squadrons, commissioned at Vulture on 25 April 1950. The Sea Fury was a single seater, high-performance, piston-engine fighter aircraft. It had a top speed of around 390 knots, and a radius of action of about 350 nautical miles at 250 knots. The Firefly was a slow, two-seater reconnaissance, strike and anti-submarine warfare aircraft. It had a top speed of around 300 knots, and a radius of action of about 300 nautical miles at 200 knots.

This Air Group had been intended for Australia's second carrier, to be named HMAS *Melbourne*, but her delivery to the RAN had been delayed. Consequently, HMAS *Sydney* (Australia's first carrier) returned to the UK, and embarked the 21st Carrier Air Group in October, arriving back in Australia in November 1950.

KOREAN WAR

In May 1951, the Australian Government announced that the aircraft carrier HMAS *Sydney* would relieve the Royal Navy's HMS *Glory* in the Korean War for a period of about three months, from October 1951. By then, the war on the ground had reached a stalemate, with both sides gridlocked roughly around the 38th Parallel. *Sydney* was given about three months to work-up the Air Group and arrive in theatre. *Sydney*'s Air Group of two Sea Fury Squadrons (805 and 808) comprising 24 aircraft, and one Firefly Squadron (817) comprising 14 aircraft, were embarked and she commenced work-up.

In addition to *Sydney*, the RAN deployed a further eight ships as part of the British Commonwealth naval contribution to the Korean War. These comprised the destroyers *Bataan*, *Warramunga*, *Anzac* and *Tobruk*, and the *River*-class frigates *Murchison*, *Shoalhaven*, *Condamine* and *Culgoa*.

Sydney began operations in Korea, on 5 October 1951, under the command of Capt. David H. Harries, RAN. On 11 October, during operations against troop concentrations and suspected store dumps on the east coast, she flew a record 89 sorties, an effort bringing praise from American and British authorities.

On 25 and 26 October, three aircraft were lost, the last involving a dangerous pickup of shot-down aircrew by the ship's helicopter. Enemy infantry attempting to capture the aircrew were suppressed by fire from other *Sydney* aircraft.

Normal daily operations were aimed at 54 sorties. This however, was often difficult to achieve on an axial deck carrier, requiring a constant movement of aircraft around the deck, often in foul weather and especially as a freezing winter set in. The principal role of the Air Group was to disrupt the enemy's supply chain by attacking all means of transport, but other tasks such as close army support, naval gunfire spotting, targeting guerrillas, anti-shipping strikes, and armed reconnaissance were not infrequent. Aerial photography was mainly undertaken by Sea Furies, using fixed vertical and oblique cameras. This helped in both the selection of targets and for subsequent damage assessment. There was also a daily reconnaissance flight known as the 'Milk Run' which consisted of a flight of aircraft flying low along the coast scouring the beaches, inlets, and islands for signs of enemy junks which were the main form of enemy transportation.

On 14 October, Typhoon RUTH caused damage to the carrier and the loss of aircraft. *Sydney* sailed from Sasebo Harbour in order to minimise possible damage from the typhoon. She lost overboard one of the eighteen aircraft stored on deck, with major damage occurring to several others, including Guy Beange's aircraft. Two full days were required to repair all the damage received and repairable within the capacity of the ship, with three days elapsing before she was returned to full operational readiness.

Photo Postscript-6

HMAS *Sydney*'s flight deck whilst at sea during Typhoon Ruth. (AWM)

While no match for Chinese jets, *Sydney*'s piston-engine aircraft were invaluable for ground attack duties. Normally, the Fireflies carried bombs and the Sea Furies rockets. Both aircraft mounted four 20mm cannon. Targets attacked included troops, gun positions, and transport infrastructure. *Sydney*'s aircraft were credited with causing 3,000 communist casualties, as well as the destruction of 66 bridges, seven tunnels, 38 railway sections, seven sidings, five water towers, three locomotives, 59 wagons, 2,060 houses, 495 junks and sampans, and 15 guns. They also carried out target spotting and reconnaissance, for which the two-seat Firefly was particularly well-suited, as well as combat air and anti-submarine patrols around the carrier and her escorts.

Photo Postscript-7

A Hawker Sea Fury aircraft from 808 Squadron landing on the flight deck of HMAS *Sydney* during the Korean War. (AWM)

Enemy anti-aircraft fire was the main danger. *Sydney* had 99 aircraft hit and nine were shot down. Casualties were: three aircrew killed and six wounded.

After seven intense nine-day operational periods, *Sydney* departed for Australia, on 29 January 1952.

For his 'distinguished and devoted service aboard HMAS *Sydney* in Korean waters,' Beange was awarded the Distinguished Service Cross, on 28 October 1952, one of only three RAN pilots to receive the award in this war. His squadron commander, Lieutenant Commander John L. Appleby, RN, described him as '...an excellent operational pilot.'

Beange remained in 808 Squadron after *Sydney* returned from Korea, rotating between the carrier and the RAN Naval Air Station Nowra, HMAS Albatross, around 100 miles south of Sydney. In December 1952 he was appointed as senior pilot to 805 Squadron, stationed in Albatross.

SQUADRON COMMAND

In May 1953 Beange was promoted to lieutenant commander and was appointed in command of 808 Squadron, which in September, embarked in HMAS *Vengeance*, a *Colossus*-class carrier on loan from the

Royal Navy and commissioned into the RAN in the UK, in November 1952, arriving in Sydney in March 1953. Between February and April 1954, *Vengeance* was one of several Australian warships tasked with royal escort duty during the first visit to Australia of Her Majesty Queen Elizabeth II and Prince Phillip. She escorted the SS *Gothic* with the Royal party embarked, to the Cocos Islands, in company with HMA Ships *Anzac* and *Bataan*, handing over escort duties to HM Ships *Colombo* and *Newfoundland*, in April 1954. On leaving *Vengeance*, his commanding officer, Captain Otto H. Becher, DSO DSC* RAN, wrote in his officer's report '...an officer of promise whose leadership is worthy of praise. I am sorry to lose him.'

Beange was posted to the Navy Office in July on the staff of the Director of Naval Air Warfare Organisation and Training. He spent two years in the Fleet Air Arm's Policy Directorate before joining HMAS *Junee* in command, in October 1956. He was reported by the director, Captain V A T Smith (later Admiral Smith) as '... an officer who provides a great practical knowledge of all aspects of naval aviation. Shows good initiative and produces excellent results.'

COMMAND OF HMAS *JUNEE*

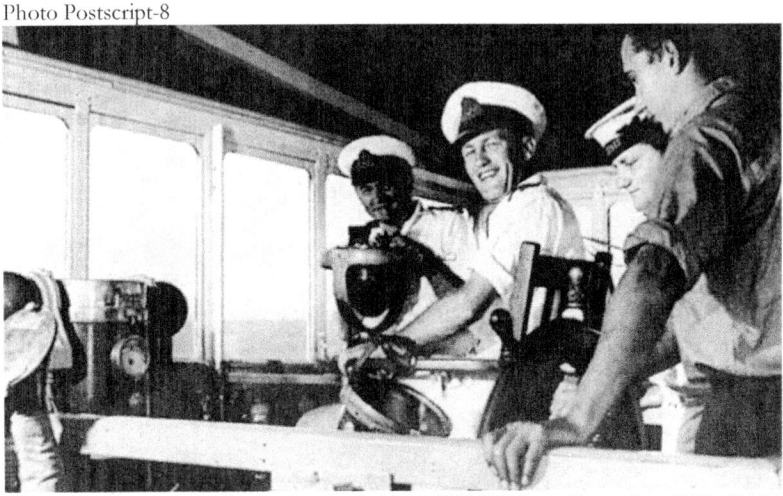

Photo Postscript-8

Lieutenant Commander Beange on the bridge of HMAS *Junee*, December 1956. (RAN)

HMAS *Junee*, named after the town of Junee in the Riverina region of New South Wales, was one of sixty Australian Minesweepers (commonly known as corvettes) built during World War II. She was decommissioned in 1946, but recommissioned as a training ship in Melbourne, on February 1953.

Junee operated in eastern Australian waters until August 1953, when she sailed from Melbourne for Fremantle. She was subsequently engaged, mainly on training duties in western and north western Australian waters, until 1957. The main function of these ships was to give sea training to National Servicemen and to officers and men of the RAN Reserve. The ships were manned with sufficient permanent personnel in all departments to maintain them and to provide the necessary instruction and supervision, as required, of the National Servicemen and the Reserves. Beange remained in command until August 1957, when *Junee* was decommissioned and sold.

RETURN TO FLYING

Beange returned to flying duties, undertaking a number of courses including jet refresher and night fighter courses, at Albatross, before taking command of 805 Squadron, on 17 March 1958. 805 Squadron (Sea Fury's) was decommissioned at NAS Nowra on 26 March, and recommissioned just one week later, on 31 March 1958, now equipped with de Havilland Sea Venom all-weather jet fighters. The Squadron embarked in HMAS *Melbourne*, in October. The carrier had commissioned in the UK, in October 1955, and arrived in Sydney, in May 1956. *Melbourne* maintained a regular program of exercises, training and maintenance over the next few years, including annual deployments to the Asia-Pacific region.

Photo Postscript-9

Sea Venoms flying in formation. (RAN)

At the end of January 1959, *Melbourne* returned to her namesake city for the unique experience of filming scenes for the movie *On the Beach*. She once again departed for her South East Asian deployment from Fremantle, with a fleet of warships. On return to Australia at the end of June, 805 Squadron disembarked to *Albatross*. On leaving the Naval Air Station in July, his commanding officer, Captain VAT Smith wrote '…a thoroughly dependable and loyal officer with marked initiative and drive.'

In August Beange was posted to the UK for the Royal Navy Staff Course at Greenwich, London. He was promoted to commander, on 31 December 1959, and on completion of the staff course, in March 1960, was posted to *Melbourne* as Commander (Air) and Fleet Aviation Officer.

Melbourne continued a busy program, taking part in the convoy defence exercise PASAD, in the Tasman Sea, in March 1960, before departing for the annual South East Asian deployment, from Darwin, in April. She participated in Exercise SEALION, which was the largest SEATO exercise, to date, involving more than 60 ships from Australia, New Zealand, the US, the UK, France, India, the Philippines, Thailand, and Pakistan.

Melbourne's South East Asian deployment began slightly earlier, in 1961, as the ship departed from Fremantle, on 20 February, in order to participate in Exercise JET 61, in the Indian Ocean off Sri Lanka. This was the eleventh JET exercise, the third to include Australia, and involved some 41 naval units from six countries. *Melbourne* then took part in the year's SEATO exercise PONY EXPRESS, before returning home in June.

After a busy two years in *Melbourne*, Beange was selected for diplomatic duty as Australian Service Attaché, Manila, joining, in November 1961, and serving in that post until April 1964. On return to Australia, he was posted to HMAS Leeuwin at Fremantle, as executive officer. Leeuwin was the Junior Recruit Training Establishment, where young men of 15 to 16 years would undergo a year of secondary education, together with basic naval training, before being sent to other establishments for specialist naval training.

In July 1965, Beange was appointed as commanding officer HMAS Waterhen in Sydney, and as commander Mine Countermeasures on the staff of the Fleet Commander. Waterhen was the parent establishment for Australia's Mine Countermeasures Force, Clearance Diving Team One, and a variety of Support Craft and is located in Waverton, on Sydney's lower north shore.

In June 1966 he was appointed to the Flag Officer in Charge East Australia Area (FOICEA) staff, as the Command Aviation officer, responsible for policy matters relating to the Squadrons at the RAN Naval Air Station Nowra. In August 1968, Beange was moved to HMAS Lonsdale, in Melbourne, Victoria, as commanding officer of the depot and as Deputy Naval Officer in Charge, Victoria. In March 1971 he returned as Command Aviation Officer to the retitled Flag Officer Commanding East Australia. He moved to the Retired List in 1973, but returned as a Reserve List Officer in 1977, and spent two years within the Defence Headquarters before finally retiring in 1979.

REFLECTION

Guy Beange had a distinguished and eventful career encompassing all appointments a Fleet Air Arm pilot could aspire to. He was in the vanguard of naval aviation in Australia, embarking in *Sydney* in 1950, just one year after she became operational in the RAN. He remained onboard *Sydney* during the Korean War 1951-52, becoming one of three RAN pilots to be awarded the DSC. He served as a Squadron Commander onboard *Vengeance*, in 1953, shortly after she joined the RAN, and again was Squadron Commander for the first jet fighters onboard *Melbourne* in 1958, some two years after she arrived in Australia. He served as Commander (Air) and Fleet Aviation Officer onboard *Melbourne*, as well as Command Aviation Officer with the Flag Officer in Charge East Australia Area. He was held in high regard in aviation circles and contributed to the excellent naval air skills honed in the RAN's three aircraft carriers. All New Zealanders living in Australia, who are successful, are regarded as true Australians – Guy was one of those!

Photo Postscript-10

Medals of Commander Guy Alexander Beange, DSC RAN (Retired). (AWM REL37352.007)

Bibliography/Chapter Notes

Boose Jr., Donald W. *Over the Beach US Army Amphibious Operations in the Korean War.* Leavenworth, KS: Combat Studies Institute Press US Army Combined Arms Center Fort Leavenworth, 2008.

Bruhn, David D. *Wooden Ships and Iron Men, The U.S. Navy's Coastal and Inshore Minesweepers, and the Minecraft That Served in Vietnam, 1953-1976.* Westminster, MD: Heritage Books, 2011.

—*Wooden Ships and Iron Men: The U.S. Navy's Coastal and Motor Minesweepers, 1941-1953.* Westminster, MD: Heritage Books, 2009.

—*Wooden Ships and Iron Men: The U.S. Navy's Ocean Minesweepers, 1953-1994.* Westminster, MD: Heritage Books, 2006.

Bruhn, David D., Rob Hoole. *Enemy Waters: Royal Navy, Royal Canadian Navy, Royal Norwegian Navy, U.S. Navy, and Other Allied Mine Forces Battling the Germans and Italians in World War II.* Berwyn Heights, MD: Heritage Books, 2019.

—*Home Waters: Royal Navy, Royal Canadian Navy, and U.S. Navy Mine Forces Battling U-Boats in World War I.* Berwyn Heights, MD: Heritage Books, 2018.

Donohue, Hector. *From Empire Defence to the Long Haul, Post war defence policy and its impact on naval force structure planning, 1945-55.* Canberra, Australia: Maritime Studies Program, 1996.

Dorr, Robert F., Jon Lake, Warrant Thompson. *Korean War Aces, Volume 4. Aircraft of the Aces # 4.* Oxford, UK: Osprey Publishing, 1995.

Frame, T. R., J. V. P. Goldrick, P. D. Jones, Ed. *Reflections on the Royal Australian Navy.* Sydney: Kangaroo Press, 1991.

Haas, Michael E. *Apollo's Warriors US Air Force Special Operations during the Cold War.* Maxwell, AL: Air University Press Maxwell Air Force Base, Alabama, 1997.

Haas, Michael E., Dale K. Robinson. *Air Commando! 1950-1975 Twenty-five years at the Tip of the Spear.* Mary Esther, FL: Air Force Special Operations Command, 1994.

Herzog, Bodo. *Deutsche U-Boote, 1906-1966.* Herrsching: Pawlak Verlag, 1990.

Hobbs, David. *British Aircraft Carriers: Design, Development & Service Histories.* Barnsley, UK: Seaforth, 2013.

Kealy, J. D., E. C. Russell. *A History of Canadian Naval Aviation, 1918-1962.* Ottawa: The Naval Historical Section Canadian Forces

Headquarters Department of National Defence Ottawa, 1965.
Meid, Pat, James M. Yingling. *U.S. Marine Operations in Korea 1950-1953 Vol. V. Operations in West Korea*. Washington, DC: Historical Division, Headquarters U.S. Marine Corps, 1972.
McCart, Neil. *The Illustrious & Implacable Classes of Aircraft Carrier 1940-1969*. Cheltenham, UK: Fan Publications, 2000.
Miller Jr., John, Owen J. Curroll, Margaret E. Tackley. *KOREA 1951-1953*. Washington, DC: Center of Military History, Department of the Army, 1997.
Naval Staff History B.R. 1736(54). *British Commonwealth Naval Operations, Korea, 1950-53*. Portsmouth, UK: Ministry of Defence Historical Branch (Naval), 1967.
Perkins, J. W. *Battle Stars and Naval Awards*. Seminole, FL: Self-published, 2004.
Ravenstein, Charles A. *Air Force Combat Wings, Lineage & Honors Histories 1947-1977*. Washington, DC: Office of Air Force History, 1984.
Roskill, S. W. *The War at Sea 1939-1945. Volume III: The Offensive Part II*. London: Her Majesty's Stationery Office, 1961.
Rössler, Eberhard. *Die Torpedos der deutschen U-Boote*. Bonn and Berlin: Mittler Verlag, 2007.
Rottman, Gordon L. *Korean War Order of Battle: United States, United Nations, and Commonwealth Ground, Naval, and Air Forces, 1950-1953*. Westport, CT: Praeger, 2002.
Sambito, William J. *A History of Marine Fighter Attack Squadron 312*. Washington, DC: USMC, History and Museums Division, Headquarters, U.S. Marine Corps, 1978.
Schnabel, James F., Robert J. Watson. *The Joint Chiefs of Staff and National Policy, Volume III 1951-1953, The Korean War Part Two*. Washington, DC: Office of the Chairman of the Joint Chiefs of Staff, 1998.
Shurcliff, W. A. *Bombs at Bikini: The Official Report of Operation Crossroads*. New York: Wm. H. Wise & Co., 1947.
Stevens, David, ed. *The Royal Australian Navy: The Australian Centenary History of Defence, Vol. III*. Melbourne: Oxford University Press, 2001.
Thorgrimsson, Thor, E. C. Russell. *Canadian Naval Operations in Korean Waters 1950-1955*. Ottawa: The Naval Historical Section Canadian Forces Headquarters Department of National Defence, 1965.
Tracy, Nicolas. *A Two-Edged Sword: The Navy as an Instrument of Canadian Foreign Policy*. Montreal: McGill-Queen's University Press, 2012.
Turner, Mike, Hector Donohue. *Australian Minesweepers at War*.

Canberra: Sea Power Centre – Australia, 2018.

Wood, Herbert Fairlie. *Strange Battleground: The Operations in Korea and their Effects on the Defence Policy of Canada*. Ottawa: The Minister of National Defence, 1966.

PREFACE NOTES:

[1] "Flight of Angels" by Bill Babbitt, *Warrior*, Summer 2010, 49.

[2] "From Fleet Exercise to Fast Carrier Task Force: The Development of Multicarrier Formations" by Will Edwards (http://www.ijnhonline.org/2016/05/26/from-fleet-exercise-to-fast-carrier-task-force-the-development-of-multicarrier-formations/: accessed 9 March 2020).

[3] "The U.S. Navy's Essex Class Aircraft Carrier: The Best Ever to Sail? Or not?" by Sebastien Roblin (https://nationalinterest.org/blog/buzz/us-navys-essex-class-aircraft-carrier-best-ever-sail-52527: accessed 11 March 2020).

[4] J. W. Perkins, *Battle Stars and Naval Awards*; "Essex Class Aircraft Carrier Data" (http://www.steelnavy.com/essex_data.htm: accessed 9 March 2020).

[5] "Independence Class, U.S. Light Carriers" (http://pwencycl.kgbudge.com/I/n/Independence_class.htm: accessed 9 March 2020).

[6] Ibid.

[7] "World Aircraft Carriers List: US Light Fleet Carriers, WWII Era" (https://www.hazegray.org/navhist/carriers/us_light.htm: accessed 10 March 2020).

[8] Ibid.

[9] Ibid.

[10] Ibid.

[11] "*Colossus* class Aircraft Carrier" (http://www.seaforces.org/marint/Royal-Navy/Aircraft-Carrier/Colossus-class.htm: accessed 2 March 2020).

[12] "World Aircraft Carriers List: US Light Fleet Carriers, WWII Era."

[13] Rear Adm. Allan du Toit, RAN (Retired) correspondence of 6 May 2020.

[14] "*Majestic* class Aircraft Carrier" (http://www.seaforces.org/marint/Royal-Navy/Aircraft-Carrier/Majestic-class.htm: accessed 12 March 2020).

[15] "HMCS *Warrior* Colossus Class Aircraft Carrier" (http://www.forposterityssake.ca/Navy/HMCS_WARRIOR_31.htm: accessed 13 March 2020).

[16] "HMCS *Warrior*" (http://www.forposterityssake.ca/Navy/HMCS_MAGNIFICENT_CVL21.htm); "HMCS *Warrior* Colossus Class Aircraft Carrier"; "HMCS *Magnificent* (21)" (http://www.readyayeready.com/ships/shipview.php?id=1239&ship=MAGNIFICENT): both accessed 13 March 2020.

[17] "HMCS *Bonaventure*" (https://www.canada.ca/en/navy/services/history/ships-histories/bonaventure.html: accessed 13 March 2020).
[18] "HMCS *Bonaventure*"
[19] "Inside the Government's Top-Secret Doomsday Hideouts" by Christopher Klein (https://www.history.com/news/inside-the-governments-top-secret-doomsday-hideouts: accessed 20 April 2020).
[20] Ibid.
[21] "40 Commando RM - The Assault on Port Said - 6 November 1956" (https://www.royalmarines.uk/threads/40-commando-rm-the-assault-on-port-said-6-november-1956.73825/: 13 March 2020).
[22] Ibid.
[23] Ibid.
[24] "Maggie delivers peacekeepers to the Suez Canal" (https://legionmagazine.com/en/2019/01/maggie-delivers-peacekeepers-to-the-suez-canal/: accessed 20 March 2020).
[25] Ibid.
[26] "Cyprus (1960-present)" (https://uca.edu/politicalscience/dadm-project/europerussiacentral-asia-region/cyprus-1960-present/); Fact Sheet 12 HMCS *Bonaventur* (https://www.friends-amis.org/index.php/en/document-repository/english/fact-sheets/45-hmcs-bonaventure/file); "The Canadian Armed Forces in Cyprus" (https://www.veterans.gc.ca/eng/remembrance/classroom/cyprus: all accessed 13 March 2020).
[27] Ut supra.
[28] "Indonesian Confrontation, 1963-66" (https://www.awm.gov.au/articles/event/indonesian-confrontation: accessed 3 May 2020).
[29] Ibid.
[30] "HMAS *Sydney* (III)" (https://www.navy.gov.au/hmas-sydney-iii: accessed 14 March 2020).
[31] Ibid.
[32] Ibid.
[33] Ibid.
[34] Ibid.
[35] Ibid.
[36] "HMAS *Vengeance*" (https://www.navy.gov.au/hmas-vengeance: accessed 14 March 2020).
[37] Ibid.
[38] Ibid.
[39] Ibid.
[40] "HMAS *Melbourne* (II)" (https://www.navy.gov.au/hmas-melbourne-ii: accessed 14 March 2020).
[41] Ibid.
[42] Ibid.
[43] Ibid.

[44] Ibid.
[45] Ibid.
[46] Ibid.

CHAPTER 1 NOTES:
[1] "The 581st's Helicopters at K-16" by Robert F. Sullivan (http://usafhpa.org/581stARCS/581starcs.html: accessed 27 March 2020).
[2] Commanding Officer and Commander Task Unit 95.1.1, Action Report 15 February through 26 February 1953 (https://www.history.navy.mil/content/history/nhhc/research/archives/digitized-collections/action-reports/korean-war-carrier-combat/bataan-cvl29.html: accessed 14 April 2020).
[3] Ibid.
[4] "Korean Air War," *Naval Aviation News*, June 1953.
[5] Commanding Officer and Commander Task Unit 95.1.1, Action Report 15 February through 26 February 1953; "Korean Air War," *Naval Aviation News*, June 1953.
[6] Ut supra.
[7] Commanding Officer and Commander Task Unit 95.1.1, Action Report 15 February through 26 February 1953; Michael E. Haas, Dale K. Robinson, *Air Commando! 1950-1975 Twenty-five years at the Tip of the Spear*, 24.
[8] Ut supra.
[9] Charles A. Ravenstein, *Air Force Combat Wings, Lineage & Honors Histories 1947–1977*, 289.
[10] Haas, *Air Commando! 1950-1975*, 16.
[11] Haas, *Air Commando! 1950-1975*, 18; "2157th Air Rescue Squadron" (http://usafunithistory.com/PDF/2000/2157%20AIR%20RESCUE%20SQ.pdf: accessed 14 April 2020).
[12] "2157th Air Rescue Squadron" (http://usafhpa.org/2157ARS/2157th.html: accessed 14 April 2020).
[13] Haas, *Air Commando! 1950-1975*, 22-23; "2157th Air Rescue Squadron."
[14] "The 581st's Helicopters at K-16" by Robert F. Sullivan.
[15] Commanding Officer and Commander Task Unit 95.1.1, Action Report 15 February through 26 February 1953; Haas, *Air Commando! 1950-1975*, 24.
[16] Haas, *Air Commando! 1950-1975*, 24-25; HQ Far East Air Forces General Order #246; Michael E. Haas, *Apollo's Warriors US Air Force Special Operations during the Cold War*, 88-89.

CHAPTER 2 NOTES:
[1] David D. Bruhn, *Wooden Ships and Iron Men: The U.S. Navy's Coastal and Motor Minesweepers, 1941-1953*, 127.
[2] Ibid, 128.
[3] Ibid, 129.
[4] Ibid, 129-130.
[5] History of US Naval Operations: Korea, Chapter 3: War Begins (https://www.history.navy.mil/research/library/online-reading-room/title-

list-alphabetically/h/history-us-naval-operations-korea/chapter3-war-begins.html: accessed 2 March 2020).
[6] Ibid.
[7] Ibid.
[8] Ibid.
[9] Ibid.
[10] Ibid.
[11] Ibid.
[12] Ibid.
[13] Ibid.
[14] History of US Naval Operations: Korea, Chapter 4: Help on the Way (https://www.history.navy.mil/research/library/online-reading-room/title-list-alphabetically/h/history-us-naval-operations-korea/chapter4-help-way.html); "Korean War" (https://www.veterans.gc.ca/eng/remembrance/people-and-stories/royal-canadian-navy/korean_war: both accessed 5 March 2020).
[15] "Korean War"; Thor Thorgrimsson and E. C. Russell, *Canadian Naval Operations in Korean Waters 1950-1955*.
[16] History of US Naval Operations: Korea, Chapter 5: Into the Perimeter (https://www.history.navy.mil/research/library/online-reading-room/title-list-alphabetically/h/history-us-naval-operations-korea/chapter5-into-perimeter.html: accessed 6 March 2020).
[17] Ibid.
[18] Ibid.
[19] History of US Naval Operations: Korea, Chapter 5: Into the Perimeter; Thorgrimsson and Russell, *Canadian Naval Operations in Korean Waters 1950-1955*, 7.
[20] Thorgrimsson and Russell, *Canadian Naval Operations in Korean Waters 1950-1955*, 7.
[21] History of US Naval Operations: Korea, Chapter 5: Into the Perimeter.
[22] Bruhn, *Wooden Ships and Iron Men: The U.S. Navy's Coastal and Motor Minesweepers, 1941-1953*, 138.
[23] Ibid, 138-139.
[24] History of US Naval Operations: Korea, Chapter 7: Back to the Parallel (https://www.history.navy.mil/research/library/online-reading-room/title-list-alphabetically/h/history-us-naval-operations-korea/chapter7-back-parallel.html: accessed 5 March 2020).
[25] Thorgrimsson and Russell, *Canadian Naval Operations in Korean Waters 1950-1955*, 13-14.
[26] History of US Naval Operations: Korea, Chapter 7: Back to the Parallel.
[27] Donald W. Boose Jr., *Over the Beach US Army Amphibious Operations in the Korean War*, 163.
[28] Thorgrimsson and Russell, *Canadian Naval Operations in Korean Waters 1950-1955*, 13-14.
[29] Bruhn, *Wooden Ships and Iron Men: The U.S. Navy's Coastal and Motor Minesweepers, 1941-1953*, 139-140; "Inchon"

(https://www.history.navy.mil/content/history/nhhc/our-collections/art/exhibits/conflicts-and-operations/remembering-the-forgotten-war-korea-1950-1953/inchon.html: accessed 6 March 2020).
[30] "HMS *Triumph* - Colossus-class Light Fleet Aircraft Carrier" (https://www.naval-history.net/xGM-Chrono-04CV-Triumph%20%28ii%29.htm); "Operations in Korea" (http://www.hmstheseus.co.uk/Operations.htm): both accessed 2 March 2020).
[31] "Operations in Korea."
[32] History of US Naval Operations: Korea, Chapter 7: Back to the Parallel; "Operations in Korea."
[33] "Operations in Korea"; "History of US Naval Operations: Korea, Chapter 10" (https://www.history.navy.mil/content/history/nhhc/research/library/online-reading-room/title-list-alphabetically/h/history-us-naval-operations-korea/chapter10-second-six-months.html: accessed 3 March 2020).
[34] "Spanish Navy (Spain) Aircraft Carrying Ships" (http://www.navypedia.org/ships/spain/sp_cv_dedalo2.htm: accessed 7 March 2020).
[35] Bruhn, *Wooden Ships and Iron Men: The U.S. Navy's Coastal and Motor Minesweepers, 1941-1953*, 140, 142.
[36] Ibid, 142-143.
[37] Ibid, 143.
[38] Ibid, 167.
[39] Ibid.
[40] Georgi Lobov, "Black Spots of History: In the Skies of North Korea," *Joint Publication Research Service Report*, (JPRS), JPRS-UAC-91-003, 28 June 1991, 30; Sebastian Rablin, "Russia vs. America: How U.S. Jets and Soviet MiG's Secretly Battled During the Korean War, *The National Interest*, 2 November 2018, 32; Steven J. Zaloga, "The Russians in MiG Alley," *Air Force Magazine*, 5 September 2008; Zhang Xiaoming, "China, the Soviet Union, and the Korean War: From an Abortive Air War Plan to a Wartime Relationship," *Journal of Conflict Studies*, (Spring 2002), Gregg Centre for the Study of War and Society, 22.
[41] Ut supra.
[42] Ut supra.
[43] Ut supra.
[44] "Operations in Korea."
[45] "Operations in Korea"; History of US Naval Operations: Korea, Chapter 9: Retreat South (https://www.history.navy.mil/research/library/online-reading-room/title-list-alphabetically/h/history-us-naval-operations-korea/chapter9-retreat-south.html: accessed 7 March 2020).
[46] Ibid.
[47] "Operations in Korea"; Commanding Officer, USS *Bataan*, Action Report; period 15 January 1951-7 April 1951; submission of, 17 April 1951.

[48] "World Aircraft Carriers List: US Light Fleet Carriers, WWII Era" (https://www.hazegray.org/navhist/carriers/us_light.htm: accessed 7 March 2020).
[49] "Operations in Korea."
[50] "Operations in Korea."
[51] Commanding Officer, USS *Bataan*, Action Report; period 15 January 1951-7 April 1951.
[52] Ibid.
[53] Ibid.
[55] Ibid.
[55] Ibid.
[56] Ibid.
[57] Commanding Officer, USS *Bataan*, Action Report; period 15 January 1951-7 April 1951; "USS *St Paul* (CA-73) (originally *Rochester*)" (http://www.historyofwar.org/articles/weapons_USS_St_Paul_CA73.html: accessed 15 March 2020).
[58] Commanding Officer, USS *Bataan*, Action Report; period 15 January 1951-7 April 1951.
[59] Ibid.
[60] Ibid.
[61] Ibid.
[62] Ibid.
[63] Commanding Officer, USS *Bataan*, Action Report; period 8 April 1951-11 May 1951; submission of, 12 June 1951.
[64] Ibid.
[65] Commanding Officer, USS *Bataan*, Action Report; period 8 April 1951-11 May 1951; *Manchester*, *DANFS*.
[66] Commanding Officer, USS *Bataan*, Action Report; period 8 April 1951-11 May 1951.
[67] Ibid.
[68] Ibid.
[69] Ibid.
[70] Ibid.
[71] Ibid.
[72] Ibid.
[73] Ibid.
[74] "HMS *Glory* (1945) CVL (5th)" (http://www.britainsnavy.co.uk/Ships/HMS%20Glory/HMS%20Glory%20(1945)%20CVL%205.htm: accessed 3 March 2020).
[75] Ibid.
[76] "HMAS *Sydney* R17" (http://www.nepeannaval.org.au/Museum/Aircraft-Carriers/HMAS-Sydney-R17.html: accessed 8 March 2020).
[77] "HMAS *Sydney* R17."
[78] Ibid.
[79] Ibid.

[80] "HMAS *Sydney*" by Alan Zammit (http://www.koreanwaronline.com/history/oz/kr/chapter28.htm: accessed 8 March 2020).
[81] Ibid.
[82] Ibid.
[83] Ibid.
[84] "HMAS *Sydney* R17"; "HMAS *Sydney*" by Alan Zammit.
[85] Ibid.
[86] Ibid.
[87] "HMAS *Sydney* R17"; "817 Squadron History" (https://www.navy.gov.au/history/squadron-histories/817-squadron-history); "The FAA In Korea" (https://www.faaaa.asn.au/heritage-sea-fury-korea/); "805 Squadron History" (https://www.navy.gov.au/history/squadron-histories/805-squadron-history: all accessed 9 March 2020).
[88] "HMAS *Sydney* R17"; "The FAA In Korea."
[89] "Seabirds over Korea" by Hank Caruso, *Naval Aviation News*, March-April 2006.
[90] "HMAS *Sydney* R17"; "The FAA In Korea."
[91] Ut supra.
[92] "HMAS *Sydney* R17."
[93] "HMAS *Sydney* R17"; "Lieutenant Keith Elwood Clarkson" (https://www.awm.gov.au/collection/P10319096: accessed 9 March 2020).
[94] "The FAA In Korea."
[95] "HMAS Sydney R17"; "The FAA In Korea."
[96] "HMAS *Sydney* R17"; "Korean War: Chronology of U.S. Pacific Fleet Operations, July–December 1951" (https://www.history.navy.mil/content/history/nhhc/research/library/online-reading-room/title-list-alphabetically/k/korean-war-chronology/july-december-1951.html: accessed 8 March 2020).
[97] "HMAS *Sydney* R17."
[98] "HMAS *Sydney* R17"; "805 Squadron History."
[99] Ut supra.
[100] "HMAS *Sydney* R17."
[101] Ibid.
[102] "The FAA In Korea."
[103] Ibid.
[104] "HMAS *Sydney* R17."
[105] "HMAS *Sydney* R17"; "The FAA In Korea."
[106] "HMAS *Sydney* R17"; "805 Squadron History."
[107] "HMAS *Sydney* R17"; "The FAA In Korea"; "Knitted scarf: Lieutenant P Goldrick, 808 Squadron, HMAS *Sydney*" (https://www.awm.gov.au/collection/C1224883: accessed 8 March 2020).
[108] "HMAS *Sydney* R17"; "The FAA In Korea"; "HMAS Sydney (III)" (https://www.navy.gov.au/hmas-sydney-iii: accessed 28 March 2020).
[109] "The FAA In Korea."

[110] *London Gazette*, Tuesday, 28 October 1952, p. 5679.

CHAPTER 3 NOTES:
[1] William J. Sambito, *A History of Marine Fighter Attack Squadron 312*, 12.
[2] Gordon L. Rottman, *Korean War Order of Battle: United States, United Nations, and Commonwealth Ground, Naval, and Air Forces, 1950-1953*, 145.
[3] "British Commonwealth Carrier Operations in the Korean War" by David Hobbs, *Air & Space Journal* Winter 2004), 66; Kev Darling, *Hawker Sea Fury* (Big Bird Aviation Publication, 2009), 83.
[4] John Miller Jr., Owen J. Curroll, Margaret E. Tackley, *KOREA 1951–1953*, 205.
[5] "1st Commonwealth Division" (https://www.canadiansoldiers.com/organization/fieldforces/commonwealthdivision.htm); "Korean War – The Commonwealth Division" (https://nzhistory.govt.nz/war/korean-war/the-commonwealth-division): both accessed 23 March 2020).
[6] "Battle for Maryang San" (https://www.awm.gov.au/articles/encyclopedia/korea/maryang_san: accessed 24 March 2020).
[7] "Out in the Cold: Australia's involvement in the Korean War" (https://www.awm.gov.au/visit/exhibitions/korea/operations/maryang_san/: accessed 24 March 2020).
[8] "Out in the Cold: Australia's involvement in the Korean War"; "Battle of Kapyong" (https://www.britannica.com/event/Battle-of-Kapyong: accessed 3 April 2020).
[9] Ibid.
[10] Ibid.
[11] Ibid.
[12] Ibid.
[13] "Battle for Maryang San."
[14] "3rd Battalion, The Royal Australian Regimen" (https://www.awm.gov.au/collection/U52113: accessed 24 March 2020).
[15] Darling, *Hawker Sea Fury*, 83.
[16] Ibid, 83-84.
[17] "The FAA in Korea."
[18] Darling, *Hawker Sea Fury*, 84.
[19] Ibid, 84-85;
[20] "1945-2008 - Casualty Lists of the Royal Navy" (https://www.naval-history.net/xDKCas1952.htm: accessed 29 March 2020).
[21] Darling, *Hawker Sea Fury*, 85.
[22] Ibid, 86.
[23] Ibid.
[24] Ibid, 87.
[25] Ibid.
[26] Commanding Officer and Commander Task Element 95.11, Action Report 29 April through 11 May 1952, 1 June 1952; *Bataan, DANFS*.

[27] Commanding Officer and Commander Task Element 95.11, Action Report 29 April through 11 May 1952, 1 June 1952; Thorgrimsson and Russell, *Canadian Naval Operations in Korean Waters 1950-1955*, 88.
[28] Thorgrimsson and Russell, *Canadian Naval Operations in Korean Waters 1950-1955*, 88.
[29] Commanding Officer and Commander Task Element 95.11, Action Report 29 April through 11 May 1952, 1 June 1952.
[30] Ibid.
[31] "HMS *Ocean* in the Korean War" by Russ Mallace (http://branches.britishlegion.org.uk/branches/byfield-district-branch-in-rural-sw-northants-uk/stories/hms-ocean-in-the-korean-war: both accessed 8 March 2020).
[32] Ibid.
[33] Ibid.
[34] Ibid.
[35] Ibid.
[36] Ibid.
[37] Ibid.
[38] Commanding Officer and Commander Task Element 95.11, Action Report 18 May through 30 May 1952, 28 June 1952.
[39] Ibid.
[40] Commanding Officer and Commander Task Element 95.11, Action Report 18 May through 30 May 1952; *Bataan, DANFS*.
[41] Commanding Officer and Commander Task Element 95.11, Action Report 5 June through 16 June 1952, 10 July 1952.
[42] Ibid.
[43] Ibid.
[44] Commanding Officer and Commander Task Element 95.11, Action Report 23 June through 4 July 1952, 27 July 1952.
[45] Ibid.
[46] Ibid.
[47] Commanding Officer and Commander Task Element 95.11, Action Report 12 July through 23 July 1952, 4 August 1952.
[48] MacFarlane, John M. (2016) Some Notes on HMCS *Iroquois* In the Korean War. *Nauticapedia.ca* 2016 (http://nauticapedia.ca/Articles/Iroquois_in_Korea.php: accessed 8 March 2020).
[49] Commanding Officer and Commander Task Element 95.11, Action Report 12 July through 23 July 1952.
[50] "The Army's Guerrilla Command in Korea Part II: The Rest of the Story" by Michael E. Krivdo (https://arsof-history.org/articles/v9n1_guerrilla_comm_page_1.html: accessed 26 March 2020).
[51] Commanding Officer and Commander Task Element 95.11, Action Report 12 July through 23 July 1952.

[52] Pat Meid, James M. Yingling, U.S. Marine Operations in Korea 1950-1953 Vol. V. Operations in West Korea, 53; "The Army's Guerrilla Command in Korea Part II: The Rest of the Story" by Michael E. Krivdo.
[53] "The Army's Guerrilla Command in Korea Part II: The Rest of the Story" by Michael E. Krivdo.
[54] Ibid.
[55] "The Army's Guerrilla Command in Korea Part II: The Rest of the Story" by Michael E. Krivdo; "Korean War: Chronology of U.S. Pacific Fleet Operations, January–April 1952" (https://www.history.navy.mil/content/history/nhhc/research/library/online-reading-room/title-list-alphabetically/k/korean-war-chronology/january-april-1952.html: accessed 26 March 2020).
[56] "Korean War: Chronology of U.S. Pacific Fleet Operations, May–August 1952" (http://overlord-wot.blogspot.com/2017_10_15_archive.html: accessed 26 July 2020).
[57] Commanding Officer and Commander Task Element 95.11, Action Report 12 July through 23 July 1952.
[58] "Korean War: Chronology of U.S. Pacific Fleet Operations, May–August 1952."
[59] Commanding Officer and Commander Task Element 95.11, Action Report 12 July through 23 July 1952.
[60] Robert F. Dorr, Jon Lake, Warrant Thompson, *Korean War Aces, Volume 4. Aircraft of the Aces # 4.*, 96; "British Sea Furies and MiGs in Korea" by Ian D'Costa (https://tacairnet.com/2015/02/23/british-sea-furies-and-migs-in-korea: accessed 30 March 2020).
[61] "British Sea Furies and MiGs in Korea"; "Sea Fury vs MiG-15 - the true story" by Paul Beaver (https://www.aerosociety.com/news/sea-fury-vs-mig-15-the-true-story/); "No.802 Sqn FAA" (https://www.worldnavalships.com/directory/squadronprofile.php?SquadronID=17) both accessed 29 March 2020).
[62] Ut supra.
[63] Ut supra.
[64] Ut supra.
[65] "British Commonwealth Carrier Operations in the Korean War" by David Hobbs, *Air & Space Power Journal*, Winter 2004; "1945-2008 - Casualty Lists of the Royal Navy" (http://www.naval-history.net/xDKCas1952.htm, and http://www.naval-history.net/xDKCas1953.htm): both accessed 29 March 2020.
[66] Darling, *Hawker Sea Fury*, 95.
[67] "MiG Alley" by John T. Correll (https://www.airforcemag.com/article/0410alley/: accessed 30 March 2020); Darling, *Hawker Sea Fury*, 96.
[68] Dwight Messimer correspondence of 4 April 2020.
[69] Darling, *Hawker Sea Fury*, 96.
[70] "British Commonwealth Carrier Operations in the Korean War."

[71] Commanding Officer and Commander Task Unit 95.1.1, Action Report 15 February through 26 February 1953, 9 March 1953; USS *Bataan* (CVL-29) 1952-1953 Third Far Eastern cruise book.
[72] USS *Bataan* (CVL-29) 1952-1953 Third Far Eastern cruise book.
[73] USS *Bataan* (CVL-29) 1952-1953 Third Far Eastern cruise book; William J. Sambito, *A History of Marine Fighter Attack Squadron 312*, 12-13.
[74] Commanding Officer and Commander Task Unit 95.1.1, Action Report 15 February through 26 February 1953; "Korean War 1950-1953."
[75] Commanding Officer and Commander Task Unit 95.1.1, Action Report 15 February through 26 February 1953; Sambito, *A History of Marine Fighter Attack Squadron 312*, 13.
[76] "MiG Alley" by John T. Correll; "Yevgeny Pepelyayev - top ace of the Korean War" (http://acepilots.com/korea/yevgeny.html: accessed 30 March 2020.
[77] "Yevgeny Pepelyayev - top ace of the Korean War."
[78] Dwight Messimer correspondence of 1 April 2020.
[79] Commanding Officer and Commander Task Unit 95.1.1, Action Report 15 February through 26 February 1953; Sambito, *A History of Marine Fighter Attack Squadron 312*, 13.
[80] Commanding Officer and Commander Task Unit 95.1.1, Action Report 15 February through 26 February 1953.
[81] "The Trainbusters Club" by Jerry Proc
(http://jproc.ca/haida/trainbus.html: accessed 4 April 2020).
[82] Ibid.
[83] Commanding Officer and Commander Task Unit 95.1.1, Action Report 15 February through 26 February 1953.
[84] Commanding Officer and Commander Task Unit 95.1.1, Action Report 6 March through 16 March 1953, 4 April 1953.
[85] Commanding Officer and Commander Task Unit 95.1.1, Action Report 6 March through 16 March 1953; "A Biography of Rear Admiral Shirley S. Miller, USN (Retired)" by Robert G. Miller
(https://www.navsource.org/archives/02/people/miller_shirley_s.pdf: accessed 28 March 2020).
[86] Commanding Officer and Commander Task Unit 95.1.1, Action Report 6 March through 16 March 1953.
[87] Ibid.
[88] *Bataan, DANFS*; USS *Bataan* (CVL-29) 1952-1953 Third Far Eastern cruise book.
[89] Naval Staff History B.R. 1736(54), *British Commonwealth Naval Operations, Korea, 1950-53*, 264.
[90] Ibid.
[91] *British Commonwealth Naval Operations, Korea, 1950-53*, 264; James F. Schnabel, Robert J. Watson, *The Joint Chiefs of Staff and National Policy, Volume III 1951-1953, The Korean War Part Two*, 225-226.
[92] *British Commonwealth Naval Operations, Korea, 1950-53*, 271-272.
[93] Ibid, 272-273.

[94] Ibid, 273.
[95] "The Battle of the Samichon River - the Hook" by Michael Kelly (https://www.awm.gov.au/articles/blog/battle-samichon-river: accessed 30 March 2020).
[96] Ibid.
[97] Herbert Fairlie Wood, *Strange Battleground: The Operations in Korea and their Effects on the Defence Policy of Canada*, 270-271.
[98] Ibid.

CHAPTER 4 NOTES:

[1] *Warrior* Summer 2010. (https://www.samfoundation.ca/Archived%20Newsletters/2010%20Summer.pdf: accessed 1 April 2020).
[2] J. D. Kealy, E. C. Russell, *A History of Canadian Naval Aviation, 1918-1962*, 2.
[3] Kearly, Russell, *A History of Canadian Naval Aviation, 1918-1962*, 1.
[4] Kealy, Russell, *A History of Canadian Naval Aviation, 1918-1962*, 2; "Jan Smuts" (https://www.britannica.com/biography/Jan-Smuts/Role-in-World-War-I: accessed 1 April 2020).
[5] Kealy, Russell, *A History of Canadian Naval Aviation, 1918-1962*, 5-6; David D. Bruhn, Rob Hoole, *Home Waters*, 270-271; "The RCN's First Eight Naval Pilots," *Warrior* Summer 2010, 5.
[6] Bruhn, Hoole, *Home Waters*, 271.
[7] Kearly, Russell, *A History of Canadian Naval Aviation, 1918-1962*, 6; "The RCN's First Eight Naval Pilots."
[8] Ut supra.
[9] "The RCN's First Eight Naval Pilots."
[10] Ibid.
[11] Kearly, Russell, *A History of Canadian Naval Aviation, 1918-1962*, 20.
[12] Ibid.
[13] Ibid, 22-23.
[14] Ibid, 23.
[15] Kearly, Russell, *A History of Canadian Naval Aviation, 1918-1962*, 23; "A History of HMS *Nabob*" (http://www.royalnavyresearcharchive.org.uk/ESCORT/NABOB.htm#.XooEe3JlCM8: accessed 5 April 2020).
[16] Kearly, Russell, *A History of Canadian Naval Aviation, 1918-1962*, 23; "Organisation of the Royal Navy 1939-1945" (http://www.naval-history.net/xGW-RNOrganisation1939-45.htm#24: accessed 3 April 2020).
[17] Kearly, Russell, *A History of Canadian Naval Aviation, 1918-1962*, 23.
[18] Kearly, Russell, *A History of Canadian Naval Aviation, 1918-1962*, 23; "World War II: Grumman F4F Wildcat" by Kennedy Hickman (https://www.thoughtco.com/grumman-f4f-wildcat-2361519); "Operation Offspring (ii)" (https://codenames.info/operation/offspring-ii/): both accessed 3 April 2020).

[19] Kearly, Russell, *A History of Canadian Naval Aviation, 1918-1962*, 23-24; "Operation Offspring (ii)"; "A History of HMS *Nabob*."
[20] Ut supra.
[21] Ut supra.
[22] Kearly, Russell, *A History of Canadian Naval Aviation, 1918-1962*, 26; "The Battleship Tirpitz" by José M. Rico
(https://www.kbismarck.com/tirpitz.html: accessed 3 April 2020).
[23] Ibid.
[24] *A Kearly, Russell, History of Canadian Naval Aviation, 1918-1962*, 26; S. W. Roskill, *The War at Sea 1939-1945. Volume III: The Offensive Part II*, 159.
[25] "The German battleship menace that was the Tirpitz"
(https://www.dailymail.co.uk/news/fb-6290343/What-Navys-Operation-Goodwood-Norway-Second-World-War.html: accessed 3 April 2020).
[26] "The near-sinking of HMS Nabob" by Sharon Adams
(https://legionmagazine.com/en/2019/08/the-near-sinking-of-hms-nabob/: accessed 3 April 2020).
[27] Kearly, Russell, *A History of Canadian Naval Aviation, 1918-1962*, 26; "A History of HMS Nabob."
[28] Kearly, Russell, *A History of Canadian Naval Aviation, 1918-1962*, 26; "HMS Nabob"
(http://www.forposterityssake.ca/Navy/HMS_NABOB_D77.htm: accessed 3 April 2020).
[29] Kearly, Russell, *A History of Canadian Naval Aviation, 1918-1962*, 26; "A History of HMS Nabob"; Eberhard Rössler, *Die Torpedos der deutschen U-Boote*, 79; Bodo Herzog, *Deutsche U-Boote, 1906-1966*, 319.
[30] Kearly, Russell, *A History of Canadian Naval Aviation, 1918-1962*, 26-27.
[31] Kearly, Russell, *A History of Canadian Naval Aviation, 1918-1962*, 27; "A History of HMS Nabob"; David Hobbs, *British Aircraft Carriers: Design, Development & Service Histories*.
[32] "A History of HMS Nabob."
[33] Kearly, Russell, *A History of Canadian Naval Aviation, 1918-1962*, 27-28.
[34] Kearly, Russell, *A History of Canadian Naval Aviation, 1918-1962*, 28-29; "A History of HMS *Puncher*"
(http://www.royalnavyresearcharchive.org.uk/ESCORT/PUNCHER.htm#.Xon-_nJlCM8: accessed 5 April 2020).
[35] Kearly, Russell, *A History of Canadian Naval Aviation, 1918-1962*, 29-30.
[36] Kearly, Russell, *A History of Canadian Naval Aviation, 1918-1962*, 30; Hobbs, *British Aircraft Carriers: Design, Development & Service Histories*.
[37] Kearly, Russell, *A History of Canadian Naval Aviation, 1918-1962*, 30.
[38] Kearly, Russell, *A History of Canadian Naval Aviation, 1918-1962*, 30-31; "A History of HMS *Puncher*"; Hobbs, *British Aircraft Carriers: Design, Development & Service Histories*.
[39] Kearly, Russell, *A History of Canadian Naval Aviation, 1918-1962*, 31.
[40] Kearly, Russell, *A History of Canadian Naval Aviation, 1918-1962*, 31; Hobbs, *British Aircraft Carriers: Design, Development & Service Histories*; "A History of HMS *Puncher*."

[41] Kearly, Russell, *A History of Canadian Naval Aviation, 1918-1962*, 31; "A History of HMS *Puncher.*"
[42] Ibid.
[43] Ibid.
[44] Ibid.
[45] "Commander Dickie Reynolds" (https://www.telegraph.co.uk/news/obituaries/1346476/Commander-Dickie-Reynolds.html: accessed 17 March 2018).
[46] "The British Pacific Fleet Task Force 57 Politics & Logistics: Sakishima Gunto, Okinawa Campaign, 1945" (http://www.armouredcarriers.com/task-force-57-british-pacific-fleet); "The Royal Navy's Pacific Strike Force" (https://www.usni.org/magazines/naval-history-magazine/2013/january/royal-navys-pacific-strike-force): both accessed 13 January 2020.
[47] "The British Pacific Fleet Task Force 57 Politics & Logistics: Sakishima Gunto, Okinawa Campaign, 1945";
[48] Mike Turner and Hector Donohue, *Australian Minesweepers at War*, 134-139; U.S. Naval Aviation in the Pacific, 41; "Operation "Meridian" – Palembang Oil Refineries, 1945" (https://www.navyhistory.org.au/operation-meridian-palembang-oil-refineries-1945/6/: accessed 24 January 2020).
[49] Turner, Donohue, *Australian Minesweepers at War, 134-139*; U.S. Naval Aviation in the Pacific, 41.
[50] Turner, Donohue, *Australian Minesweepers at War, 134-139*; "The British Pacific Fleet Task Force 57 Politics & Logistics: Sakishima Gunto, Okinawa Campaign, 1945" (http://www.armouredcarriers.com/task-force-57-british-pacific-fleet: accessed 13 January 2020).
[51] "The British Pacific Fleet Task Force 57 Politics & Logistics: Sakishima Gunto, Okinawa Campaign, 1945" (http://www.armouredcarriers.com/task-force-57-british-pacific-fleet: accessed 13 January 2020); Neil McCart, *The Illustrious & Implacable Classes of Aircraft Carrier 1940–1969*, 173.
[52] "Canada's last Victoria Cross winner – Lieutenant (N) Robert Hampton Gray, VC, DSC" (https://militarybruce.com/canadas-last-victoria-cross-winner-lieutenant-n-robert-hampton-gray-vc-dsc/: accessed 13 January 2020).
[53] Ibid.
[54] "Robert Hampton Gray VC, DSC" *The Crowsnest* Vol. 2 no. 12. Ottawa: Queen's Printer. October 1950. p. 16-7; "A Brilliant Flying Spirit" Lieutenant Hampton Gray, VC, DSC RCNVR by Stuart E. Soward (https://web.archive.org/web/20120415204124/http://www.navalandmilitarymuseum.org/resource_pages/heroes/gray.html: accessed 13 January 2020).
[55] "Brilliant Flying Spirit" Lieutenant Hampton Gray, VC, DSC RCNVR."
[56] Ibid.
[57] "Brilliant Flying Spirit" Lieutenant Hampton Gray, VC, DSC RCNVR"; "Canada's last Victoria Cross winner – Lieutenant (N) Robert Hampton Gray, VC, DSC."
[58] "Canada's last Victoria Cross winner – Lieutenant (N) Robert Hampton Gray, VC, DSC."

[59] "Our Victoria Cross Recipients" (https://www.fleetairarm.com/victoria-cross-medals.aspx: accessed 24 January 2020); David D. Bruhn, Rob Hoole, *Enemy Waters*, 141-145.
[60] "Sutton, Arthur William" (http://www.nauticapedia.ca/dbase/Query/Biolist3.php?&name=Sutton%2C%20Arthur%20William&id=21674&Page=40&input=1): accessed 24 January 2020).
[61] "Just One Cup of Fuel" by Dave O'Malley (http://www.vintagewings.ca/VintageNews/Stories/tabid/116/articleType/ArticleView/articleId/552/The-First-and-the-Last.aspx: accessed 16 January 2020).
[62] Ibid.
[63] Ibid.
[64] Ibid.
[65] "Cdr. William 'Bill' Atkinson" (https://navalandmilitarymuseum.org/archives/articles/high-achievers/cdr-william-bill-atkinson/; "Index of /documents/Royal Canadian Navy Citations" (https://www.blatherwick.net/documents/Royal%20Canadian%20Navy%20Citations/): both accessed 16 January 2020.
[66] "Cdr. William 'Bill' Atkinson."
[67] "HMS Formidable Roll of Honour" (http://www.maritimequest.com/warship_directory/great_britain/pages/aircraft_carriers/hms_formidable_67_roll_of_honour.htm: accessed 19 January 2020).

CHAPTER 5 NOTES:
[1] Kearly, Russell, *A History of Canadian Naval Aviation, 1918-1962*, 39; *Warrior Summer* 2010, 9; "825 Squadron."
[2] Kearly, Russell, A History of Canadian Naval Aviation, 1918-1962, 34, 36; Warrior Summer 2010, 9; "825 Squadron" (http://www.shearwateraviationmuseum.ns.ca/squadrons/825sqn.htm: accessed 5 April 2020).
[3] Kearly, Russell, *A History of Canadian Naval Aviation, 1918-1962*, 41; "HMCS Warrior – Histarmar" (http://www.histarmar.com.ar/Armada%20Argentina/Portaaviones/WarriorIndep/HMCS%20Warrior.htm: accessed 5 April 2020).
[4] Kearly, Russell, *A History of Canadian Naval Aviation, 1918-1962*, 42.
[5] Ibid, 42-43.
[6] Ibid, 45.
[7] "An Audience with the Pope" by Gerald Sullivan (http://www.forposterityssake.ca/RCN-Memories.htm#RCN-MEM-0053: accessed 5 April 2020).
[8] Kearly, Russell, *A History of Canadian Naval Aviation, 1918-1962*, 71.
[9] Kearly, Russell, *A History of Canadian Naval Aviation, 1918-1962*, 126; "HMCS *Magnificent*"

(http://www.forposterityssake.ca/Navy/HMCS_MAGNIFICENT_CVL21.htm: accessed 5 April 2020).

[10] Nicolas Tracy, Nicolas, *A Two-Edged Sword: The Navy as an Instrument of Canadian Foreign Policy*, 116.

[11] "There's a Moose in my Tub" by Gerald Sullivan (http://www.forposterityssake.ca/RCN-Memories.htm#RCN-MEM-0053: accessed 5 April 2020).

[12] "The Rat Patrol (Rats on the Maggie - 1951)" by Gerald Sullivan (http://www.forposterityssake.ca/RCN-Memories.htm#RCN-MEM-0053: accessed 5 April 2020).

[13] "There's a Moose in my Tub" by Gerald Sullivan.

[14] Ibid.

[15] "HMCS Magnificent" (http://www.forposterityssake.ca/Navy/HMCS_MAGNIFICENT_CVL21.htm: accessed 6 April 2020).

[16] Kearly, Russell, *A History of Canadian Naval Aviation, 1918-1962*, 81.

[17] Ibid, 82.

[18] Ibid.

[19] "The Coronation Spithead Fleet Review of June 15, 1953" by Alec Provan (https://www.nauticapedia.ca/Gallery/Spithead_Review.php: accessed 20 April 2020).

[20] "File:AD-4B on HMCS Magnificent (CVL 21) 1953.jpeg" (https://commons.wikimedia.org/wiki/File:AD-4B_on_HMCS_Magnificent_(CVL_21)_1953.jpeg: accessed 20 April 2020).

[21] "The increase in strength" (https://www.nato.int/archives/1st5years/chapters/9.htm: accessed 20 April 2020).

[22] Kearly, Russell, *A History of Canadian Naval Aviation, 1918-1962*, 94.

[23] "What was the Suez Crisis?" by Christopher Klein (https://www.history.com/news/what-was-the-suez-crisis: accessed 7 April 2020).

[24] Kearly, Russell, *A History of Canadian Naval Aviation, 1918-1962*, 94.

[25] Ibid.

[26] Kearly, Russell, *A History of Canadian Naval Aviation, 1918-1962*, 94-97; "HMCS Magnificent."

[27] Ut supra.

[28] Ut supra.

[29] "HMCS Bonaventure: Canada's Last Aircraft Carrier" by Kevin Patterson (http://www.sevenyearproject.com/canadas-rich-history-bonaventure.html: accessed 7 April 2020).

[30] Kearly, Russell, *A History of Canadian Naval Aviation, 1918-1962*, 99-101.

[31] Kearly, Russell, *A History of Canadian Naval Aviation, 1918-1962*, 102. "HMCS Bonaventure" (http://www.forposterityssake.ca/Navy/HMCS_BONAVENTURE_CVL22.htm: accessed 7 April 2020); "HMCS Bonaventure: Canada's Last Aircraft Carrier" by Kevin Patterson.

[32] "HMCS Bonaventure: Canada's Last Aircraft Carrier" by Kevin Patterson.
[33] Ibid.
[34] Ibid.
[35] "HMCS Bonaventure: Canada's Last Aircraft Carrier" by Kevin Patterson; "HMCS Bonaventure."
[36] *Warrior* Summer 2010, 38.
[37] Ibid.
[38] Ibid.
[39] *Vancouver Sun*, 12 February 1997.

CHAPTER 6 NOTES:

[1] Stewart B. Milstein L-7205, Operation Magic Carpet, Universal Ship Cancellation Society Data Sheet #31, April 2008.
[2] Ibid.
[3] W. A. Shurcliff, *Bombs at Bikini: The Official Report of Operation Crossroads*, 192-193.
[4] "Bikini A-Bomb Tests July 1946" (https://nsarchive.gwu.edu/briefing-book/environmental-diplomacy-nuclear-vault/2016-07-22/bikini-bomb-tests-july-1946: accessed 20 April 2020).
[5] Shurcliff, *Bombs at Bikini: The Official Report of Operation Crossroads*, 190.
[6] "USS *Independence* (CVL 22) and Operation Crossroads" (https://www.navyhistory.org/2016/08/uss-independence-cvl-22-and-operation-crossroads/: accessed 20 April 2020).
[7] Ibid.
[8] Ibid.
[9] USS *Cabot* (CVL-28) 1952 Mediterranean cruise book; *Cabot, DANFS*.
[10] *Cabot, DANFS*.
[11] *Bataan, DANFS*.
[12] *Monterey, DANFS*.
[13] *Langley, Belleau Wood, DANFS*.

CHAPTER 7 NOTES:

[1] Wingsy (https://politics.slashdot.org/comments.pl?sid=192598&threshold=1&commentsort=0&mode=thread&cid=15813107); "Ghosts of the East Coast: Doomsday Ships" by Karl C. Priest (http://www.coldwar.org/museum/doomsday_ships.asp): both accessed 17 April 2020.
[2] "Ghosts of the East Coast: Doomsday Ships."
[3] "Ghosts of the East Coast: Doomsday Ships"; "Inside the Government's Top-Secret Doomsday Hideouts" by Christopher Klein (https://www.history.com/news/inside-the-governments-top-secret-doomsday-hideouts: accessed 20 April 2020).
[4] "Inside the Government's Top-Secret Doomsday Hideouts."
[5] Ibid.

[6] USS *Wright* (CC-2) Welcome Aboard booklet - 1968-69.
[7] Ibid.
[8] Ibid.
[9] Ibid.
[10] "USS Wright (CC-2, previously CVL-49), 1963-1980" (https://www.ibiblio.org/hyperwar/OnlineLibrary/photos/sh-usn/usnsh-w/cc2.htm: accessed 19 April 2020).
[11] "Ghosts of the East Coast: Doomsday Ships."
[12] Ibid.
[13] Ibid.

CHAPTER 8 NOTES:
[1] USS *Arlington* (AGMR-2) 1967 cruise book.
[2] USS *Arlington* (AGMR-2) 1967 cruise book; *Saipan, DANFS*.
[3] *Saipan, DANFS*.
[4] Ut supra.
[5] USS *Saipan* (CVL-48) Far East and Around the World 1953-1954 cruise book.
[6] Ibid.
[7] Ibid.
[8] David D. Bruhn, *Wooden Ships and Iron Men: The U.S. Navy's Coastal and Inshore Minesweepers, and the Minecraft That Served in Vietnam, 1953-1976*, 113-114.
[9] USS *Saipan* (CVL-48) Far East and Around the World 1953-1954 cruise book.
[10] Ibid.
[11] Ibid.
[12] Ibid.
[13] Ibid.
[14] "USS Arlington.com" (http://www.ussarlington.com/: accessed 23 August 2019.
[15] *Arlington, DANFS*.
[16] "Detailed Report of TF 130 Participation in APOLLO 11 Mission" (https://www.history.navy.mil/content/dam/nhhc/research/archives/apollo-11/tf-130-apollo-11.pdf: accessed 23 August 2019).
[17] *Arlington, DANFS*.
[18] "Navy Recovery Ships" (https://history.nasa.gov/ships.html: accessed 24 August 2019).
[19] *Arlington, DANFS*; "Apollo 10 and NASA — Navy Collaboration in Search and Recovery Operations" (https://www.history.navy.mil/content/history/nhhc/browse-by-topic/exploration-and-innovation/navy-and-space-exploration/Apollo_10_NASA.html: accessed 24 August 2019).
[20] "Apollo 10 and NASA — Navy Collaboration in Search and Recovery Operations."
[21] Ibid.

[22] USS *Arlington* (AGMR-2) Middle Pacific 1969 cruise book; Bruhn, *Wooden Ships and Iron Men: The U.S. Navy's Ocean Minesweepers, 1953-1994*, 111.
[23] *Arlington, DANFS*.
[24] "President Nixon and President Thieu Meet at Midway Island, June 8, 1969" (https://www.nixonfoundation.org/2014/06/president-nixon-president-thieu-meet-midway-island-june-8-1969/: accessed 24 August 2019).
[25] USS *Arlington* (AGMR-2) Middle Pacific 1969 cruise book.
[26] "President Nixon and President Thieu Meet at Midway Island, June 8, 1969"; "Vietnam War Allied Troop Levels 1960-73" (http://www.americanwarlibrary.com/vietnam/vwatl.htm: accessed 24 August 2019).
[27] "What was Nixon's Vietnamization Policy?" (https://thevietnamwar.info/what-was-nixons-vietnamization-policy/: accessed 25 August 2019).
[28] "First U.S. troops withdrawn from South Vietnam" (https://www.history.com/this-day-in-history/first-u-s-troops-withdrawn-from-south-vietnam: accessed 25 August 2019).
[29] "H-033-4: 50th Anniversary of the First Moon Landing" (https://www.history.navy.mil/content/history/nhhc/about-us/leadership/director/directors-corner/h-grams/h-gram-033/h-033-4.html: accessed 23 August 2019).
[30] Ibid.
[31] "H-033-4: 50th Anniversary of the First Moon Landing"; *Arlington, DANFS*.
[32] Ut supra.
[33] "USS *Annapolis* - AGMR-1."

CHAPTER 9 NOTES:
[1] Hector Donohue, *From Empire Defence to the Long Haul, Post war defence policy and its impact on naval force structure planning, 1945-55*, 55-57.
[2] "VAT SMITH – Father of the Fleet Air Arm" (https://www.faaaa.asn.au/vat-smith-father-fleet-air-arm/: accessed 10 Aril 2020).
[3] Donohue, *From Empire Defence to the Long Haul*, 58-60.
[4] Ibid, 94.
[5] "HMAS *Sydney* (III)" (www.navy.gov.au › The Fleet › HMAS Sydney III: accessed 10 April 2020).
[6] "RAN Naval Aviation 1948-1957" by Kim Dubstan (https://www.faaaa.asn.au/heritage-ran-naval-aviation-1948-1957/: accessed 11 April 2020.)
[7] "HMAS Sydney (III)."
[8] Ibid.
[9] Ibid.
[10] Donohue, *From Empire Defence to the Long Haul*, 142-144.
[11] "HMAS Vengeance (I)" (www.navy.gov.au › The Fleet › HMAS Vengeance I: accessed 11 April 2020).

[12] "HMAS Sydney (III)" Part 2.
[13] "HMAS Melbourne (II)" (www.navy.gov.au › The Fleet › HMAS Melbourne II: accessed 11 April 2020).
[14] RIP CMDR Charles James Morris, RAN by Marcus Peake (https://web.archive.org/web/20160310082423/http://www.faaaa.asn.au/rip-cmdr-charles-james-morris-ran/: accessed 6 May 2020).
[15] "HMAS Melbourne (II)."
[16] Alastair Cooper, "1955-1972, The Era of Forward Defence" in David Stevens, ed., *The Royal Australian Navy: The Australian Centenary History of Defence, Vol. III*, 193.
[17] "HMAS Melbourne (II)" (https://www.faaaa.asn.au/photos/aircraft-carrier-hmas-melbourne/: accessed 14 April 2020).
[18] "China's aircraft carrier ambitions: seeking truth from rumours" by Ian Storey and You Ji, *Naval War College Review*, Winter 2004, 57.

CHAPTER 10 NOTES:

[1] Malcolm Brown, "Gledhill, Jeffrey Allan (1921–2011)," Obituaries Australia, National Centre of Biography, Australian National University (http://oa.anu.edu.au/obituary/gledhill-jeffrey-allan-16735/text28631: accessed 21 April 2020).
[2] "Pilotless Plane's Air Drama over Sydney" by Robert Kendall Piper, *Navy News*, 19 September 1980.
[3] "Recollections of a Firefly Pilot" by Norman Lee in T. R. Frame, J. V. P. Goldrick, P. D. Jones, Ed., *Reflections on the Royal Australian Navy*, 285-290.
[4] "Chockman the Brave" by Thomas Henry, *Slipstream*, April 1995.
[5] "805 Squadron" (https://www.navalofficer.com.au/805-2/: accessed 22 April 2020).

Index

Adams, Kenneth Frederick (Rear Adm., RCN), 114, 119
Agan, Alfred Hiram, 31, 33
Aldrin, Edwin, 164-165
Almond, Edward M., 22, 26
Amen, William T., 27-28
Anders, William, 158
Anderson, Gerald Arthur (Lt., RCNVR), 106-108
Andrewes, William G. (Adm. Sir. KBE, CB, DSO RN), 13-14, 21-29
Appleby, John L. (Lt. Comdr., RAN), 223
Armstrong, Neil, 164-165
Arrington, John Lindsay, 146
Asbridge, William Bell (Lt., RCNVR), 107-108
Atkinson, William Henry Isaac (Comdr., DSC RCN), 107
Australia/Australian
  Australian Army
    1st Australian Army, l, 218
    1st Australian Task Force (1ATF), xlvii
    Royal Australian Regiment
      1st Battalion (1RAR), xlvii, 182-183
      2nd Battalion (2RAR), 84-85
      3rd Battalion (3RAR), 55-59
      5th Battalion (5RAR), 6th Battalion (6RAR), xlvii
  Brisbane, 185
  Darwin, 191, 225
  Far East Strategic Reserve, xlv, xlviii, 185, 192
  Fremantle, 51, 176, 224-225
  Jervis Bay, 171, 178, 185, 187, 203
  Junee (NSW), 223
  Melbourne, 223-224, 226
  Monte Bello Islands, 176-177
  Mount Compass (south of Adelaide), 219
  Royal Australian Air Force
    No. 77 Squadron, xlviii, 45, 180
    No. 80 Squadron, xxi
    RAAF Base, Point Cook, 201
    RAAF Base Williamtown, 199-200
  Royal Australian Navy
    Naval Aviation
      Naval Air Stations, and Naval Shore/Training Establishments
        HMAS Albatross (RANAS Nowra), 171-172, 183, 199-202, 209, 221-223

254   Index

        HMAS Cerberus (Flinders Naval Depot), 201, 219
        HMAS *Kuttabui*, 202
        HMAS Leeuwin in Fremantle, Western Australia, 225-226
        HMAS Lonsdale in Melbourne, 226
        HMAS Nirimba (RANAS Schofields), 172
        HMAS Waterhen in Sydney, 226
     Fleet Air Arm
        723 Squadron, xxii, 171
        724 Squadron, 171, 200,
        725 Squadron, xlvii, 171
        800 Squadron, xxxvi
        805 Squadron, xx, xlvi, li, 40-50, 54, 171-178, 183, 189-191, 197-202, 211-225
        808 Squadron, xlvi, xlviii, li, 40, 51, 54, 173, 176, 202, 220-223
        816 Squadron, xx, xlviii, 171, 178, 183, 190-191, 202
        817 Squadron, xlvi, xlviii, 40-44, 54, 173-176, 183, 190-203, 220-221
        850 Squadron, 171, 178
        851 Squadron, 171
  Sydney, 102, 171-172, 178-192, 197-200, 218, 223-226
    Athol Bight, 183, 191
    Garden Island/Captain Cook Graving Dock, 178
Babbit, Arlene (Dick), 45
Becher, Otto Humphrey (Rear Adm., CBE, DSO, DSC & Bar RAN), 223
Bailey, Harold Edwin (Lt., DSC RAN), 52
Barbanes, William J., 68
Burrell, Henry Mackay (Vice Adm. Sir, KBE, CB RAN), xlviii, 180
Barrett, Joseph, 1, 8
Barrett, Robert E., 76
Beange, Guy Alexander (Comdr., DSC RAN), l-li, 52, 217-226
Bell, John F. (A/Sub Lt., RNVR), 108
Bidwell, Roger Edward Shelford (Rear Adm., CBE RCN), 95
Biggers, W. D., 148
Bluett, John Robert Tenison, (Lt., RN), l, 197-201
Borman, Frank, 158
Boulton, Angus George (Cdre., DSC RCN), 114
Bowles, Walter George (Lt. Comdr., DSC RAN), 52
Boyd, Denis William (Adm. Sir, KCB, CBE, DSC RN), 67
Bradley, Richard D., 76
Bratten Jr., Toria Joel, 146
Brehm, W. W., 148
Britain/British/UK
  Army
    27th Infantry Brigade, 55
    29th Commonwealth Brigade, 55
    Highland Light Infantry, 65
    King's Own Scottish Borderers, 56

Belfast, 109-111, 113, 120, 126-127
Barrow-in-Furness in Cumbria, 184
Devonport, 41, 171, 181
Falklands War, 193
Firth of Clyde, 91, 121, 124, 126
Glasgow, 100, 115-116, 124, 126, 185, 196
Greenock, 91, 120
Isle of Wright, 1-9
Liverpool, 90
Malta, 23-24, 65, 83, 120, 181
North Luffenham, 116
Plymouth, 120, 126, 181
Portsmouth, 96, 109, 120-121, 129, 177, 196, 218
Renfrew, 116
Rosyth, 95, 120
Royal Air Force
  RAF Birmingham, 196
  RAF Netheravon Airfield, 196
Royal Marines, No. 45 Commando, xliii
Royal Navy
  Aviation
    Fleet Air Arm
      No. 801 Squadron, 76-77, 103
      No. 802 Squadron, 54, 65, 67, 74
      No. 804 Squadron, 54
      No. 806 Squadron, 114
      No. 807 Squadron, 54, 83
      No. 810 Squadron, 54, 83
      No. 812 Squadron, 54
      No. 820 Squadron, No. 828 Squadron, No. 849 Squadron, No. 854 Squadron, No. 857 Squadron, No. 880 Squadron, No. 887 Squadron, No. 894 Squadron, No. 1770 Squadron, No. 1771 Squadron, No. 1833 Squadron, No. 1834 Squadron, No. 1836 Squadron, No. 1839 Squadron, No. 1844 Squadron, 103
      No. 825 Squadron, 54, 65, 67
      No. 827 Squadron, 54
      No. 837 Squadron, 218
      No. 846 Squadron, 91
      No. 848 Squadron, 103, 107-108
      No. 1830 Squadron, 103, 109
      No. 1831 Squadron, 218
      No. 1841 Squadron, 103, 108
      No. 1842 Squadron, 103, 107-108
    Naval Air Station
      Anthorn, HMS Nuthatch, in Cumbria, 219
      Lee-on-Solent, HMS Daedalus, 218

Machrihanish, HMS Landrail, near Campbeltown, 90
            Hatston, HMS Sparrowhawk, near Kirkwall, 168
            St Merryn, HMS Vulture, in Cornwall, 220
            Yeovilton, HMS Heron, in Somerset, 219
        Navy
            1st Cruiser Squadron, 91
            26th Destroyer Flotilla, 91
            British Pacific Fleet (11th Aircraft Carrier Squadron), xx-xxi, l, 102-108, 171-180, 218
            HMS Saker at Lewiston, Maine, USA, 218
            HMS Vernon, xxvii-xxviii
    Scapa Flow, 91-100
    Spithead, xli, xlix, 23, 111, 116, 121-122
    Tail-of-the-Bank, 90, 124
    The Clyde, 90-91, 100, 121, 126
Brown, George Firth Spencer (Comdr., DFC RAN), 52
Buchanan, Herbert James (Rear Adm., DSO, ADC RAN), 177
Burger, Alan D. (A/Lt., RNVR), 108
Burns, Eedson Louis Millard (Lt. Gen., CC, DSO, OBE, MC, CD), 125
Butterworth, Charles Edgar (Lt., DSC RCNVR), 106-107
Buxton, E. A., 148
Canada/Canadian
    Army
        25th Brigade, 55
        Princess Patricia's Light Infantry Regiment, 57, 86
        Queen's Own Rifles, 125
        Royal Canadian Artillery, 126
        Royal Highland Regiment, 126
    Baffin Island, 142
    Calgary, 125
    Esquimalt, 95, 111, 113, 124, 219
    Great Bear Lake, 108
    Halifax, 89, 109, 111, 114, 116, 118, 120-131
    Nova Scotia, 141
    Ottawa, 89, 111
    Royal Canadian Air Force
        1 Wing
            No. 439 Squadron, No. 410 Squadron, No. 441 Squadron, 115
        RCAF Station Uplands, 115
    Royal Canadian Navy
        Destroyer Division, Far East, 16
        Fleet Air Arm/Naval Air Squadrons
            No. 803 Squadron, No. 825 Squadron, 109-110, 114
            VF 870 Squadron, 129
            VS 880, 130
            Naval Air Station Shearwater (formerly Dartmouth Air Station), 114

Index   257

   Port Hawkesbury, Purbrook, Ontario, 89
  Vancouver, 90, 109, 124, 131
Carmichael, Peter (Comdr., OBE, DSC RN), 74-76
Cassels, James Halkett (Field Marshal Sir, GCB, KBE, DSO BA), 55
Cernan, Eugene A., 161
China/Chinese
  137th Division, 85
  Antung, 27
  Dalian, Guanzhou, 192
  The People's Liberation Army Navy (The PLA Navy or PLAN), 192
Chifley, Joseph Benedict, 169
Churchill, Winston, 167
Clarkson, Keith Elwood, 46
Cleeland, David, xxxix, 1-8, 81
Clifford, Eric George Anderson (Vice Adm. Sir, KCB, CBE RN), 83
Coleman, Joseph Lustrat, xxiii
Coleman, Ronald J., 50
Collins, Michael, 164-165
Colquhoun, Kenneth Stewart (Capt., DSO RN), 59, 63
Combs, Thomas Selby, 123
Connally, Richard L., 9
Cull, John T. (Lt. Col., RAF), 99
Dace, C. C., 148
Daigh, Harold D., 36-38
Daniels, Alan P., 76
Davis, Peter (Sub Lt.), 75-76
DeLong, Phillip Cunliffe, 36-38
DeWolf, Harry George (Vice Adm., CBE, DSO, DSC RCN), 111, 113-114
Douglas, Ken (Comdr., RAN), 189
Doyle, James H., 20-23
Dubber, Clifford Frank, 52
Duncan, Charles L., 73
Dutch, Brian Aubrey (Sub Lt., RAN), l, 211-215
Dyer, Kenneth Lloyd (Rear Adm., DSC RCN), 114
Elizabeth II, Queen, xlvii, xlix, 121-122, 176-180
Ellis, Brian (Sub Lt.), 75-76
Esmonde, Eugene (Lt. Comdr., VC, DSO RN), 105
Evans, Charles Leo Glandore (Vice Adm. Sir, KCB, CBE, DSO, DSC RN), 65
Ewen, Edward C., 21-22
Fabijan, Frank, 1, 8
Fahrion, Frank G., 136
Fell, Michael Frampton (Vice Adm. Sir, KCB, DSO, DSC & Bar RN), 52
Finlayson, William (Maj., AA), 58
Fitzpatrick, Francis John, 146
Fogden, Peter D. (Lt.), 76

Frame, Donald P., 35
Francis, Alfred Cecil (A/Lt., RNVR), 108
Fraser, Bruce Austin (Adm. of the Fleet, 1st Baron Fraser of North Cape, GCB, KBE RN), 102
Fraser-Harris, Alexander Beaufort Fraser (Cdre., DSC & Bar RCN), 114
Frewer, Frederick Charsley (Capt., RCN), 129
Gardner, William Daniel (A/Chief Airman, RAN), 52
Garland, Anthony M. (A/Lt. Comdr., DSC & Bar RNVR), 108
Gatacre, Galfrey George Ormond (Rear Adm., CBE, DSO, DSC & Bar RAN), 185
Genge, Edward Thomas (Lt., RN), 52
George, David Lloyd (1st Earl Lloyd-George of Dwyfor, OM, PC), 88
Giap, Vo Nguyen, 150
Gledhill, Jeffrey Allan (Capt., DSC RAN), xlix, 195-197
Glover, J., 148
Goldrick, Peter (Capt., RAN), 51
Gooding, Callis C., 45
Goodwin, Hugh H., 123
Gordon, Alexander Hughie (Capt., LVO, DFC RAN), 52
Gorton, John Grey (Sir., GCMG, AC, CH), 189
Grachev, Mikhail Fedorovich, 27-28
Gray, Robert Hampton (Lt., VC, DSC RCNVR), 106-108
Groos, Harold Victor William (Cdre., RCN), 126
Groves, John R. W. (Comdr., RN), 199
Haines, Carl (Sub Lt.), 75-76
Hancox, Phillip, 44-45
Harries, David Hugh (Rear Adm., CB, CBE RAN), 39, 42, 49, 52, 174-176, 221
Harrington, Wilfred Hastings (Vice Adm., CBE, DSO RAN), 219
Hartman, Charles Clifford, 25
Hauge, D. H., 35
Hazen, John Douglas (Sir., KCMG, PC), 88
Henderson, George R., 22
Henry, Thomas Frederick, l, 208-210
Hill, Malcolm A., 80
Hinchcliffe, Cecil I. (Comdr., RD RCN), 95
Horney, Harry Ray, 2, 64, 67, 70, 82
Houghton, Frank Llewellyn (Rear Adm., CBE RCN), 109
How, Richard Graham (Lt. Comdr., RN), 209
Hurricane HAZEL, 152
Hughes, Gordon Churchill (Sub Lt., DSM RAN), 51-52
Irwin, Charles W. (T/A/PO), 108
Jackson, Henry James (RCAF), 89
Japan
  Hiroshima, Maisura, Matsushima, Nagasaki, 104
  Itazuko, 69

Kobe, 66
  Kure, 9, 28-29, 46-49, 54, 61-66, 84, 175, 178
  Maisuru, 104
  Okinawa, 15, 19, 102-107, 150
  Onagawa Wan (Bay), 104-107
  Sakishima Islands, 102-103
  Sasebo, 23-29, 34-39, 43-47, 51-61, 65-70, 74, 81-84, 149-151, 175-178, 208, 222
  Tukushima, 107
  Yokohama, 150
Johnson, Louis A., 9
Johnson, Lyndon B., 146
Johnson, R. H., 36
Joy, C. Turner, 12-13, 25
Jupp, Donald G. (A/Sub Lt., DSC RNVR), 108
Keates, Walter J. B. (Sub Lt.), 77
Kemsley, C. A. (Capt., CA), 86
Kendall, Henry S., 135
Kennedy, John F., 129, 164
Kiggell, Launcelot John (Comdr., DSC RN), 52, 175
Kindell, Nolan M., 137
King, William Lyon Mackenzie (OM CMG PC), 112
Kissinger, Henry, 166
Knowles, Harold R., 35
Korea (North and South)
  Angag Peninsula, 49
  Annyong Reservoir, 3-4, 81
  Chacryong, 69
  Chaeryong, 44
  Changnin-do, 71-74
  Changyon, 48, 59-62
  Chinnampo, 3, 26, 44, 48, 60-69, 72, 74, 204
  Cho-do Island, 7, 48, 61, 70
  Chongchon River, 27, 77
  Chongju, 26
  Chonju, 25
  Choppeki Point, 64
  Clifford Islands, 21
  Haeju, 3-4, 16, 32, 44, 59-66, 71-76, 81-82, 203
  Hamhung, 17, 26, 36
  Han River, 2, 34-35, 44, 46, 51, 61, 72, 79
  Hanchon, 2-3, 48, 64
  Hojang-do, 37
  Hungnam, 17, 25-26, 47
  Hwangju, 35
  Imjin River, 57, 62

Inchon, 20-25, 33, 35, 49, 60, 74
Kojo, 42
Kaesong, 26
Kang-nung, 11
Kapyong River, 57
Kimpo, 8, 29, 44-46, 75
Koho-ri Peninsula, 59-60
Kowang San (Hill 35, "Little Gibraltar"), 56-57
Kunuri, 26
Mackau Islands, 21
Manchon, 74
Maryang San (Hill 317), 56-59
Mokpo, 21
Mu-do Island, 71
Ongjin, 48-50, 59-60, 70
Onjong-ni, 32
Osan, 11
Paengyong-do Island, 48-59
Pakchon, 25
Panmunjom, 51, 83-85
Pengyong-do, 70
Pohang, 17
Pohang-dong, 81
Ponghwa-ri, 61
Punchon, 61
Pusan, 17, 21, 35, 72
Pyongtaek, 32, 79, 84
Pyongyang, 3, 15-17, 25-26, 49, 51, 74, 80
Samchok, 11
Sariwon, 26, 35, 45
Seoul, 6, 8, 11, 20, 25, 32, 35, 57, 66, 69, 75, 84-85, 183
Sinchon, 60
Sogang-ni, 60
Sokto Island, 48
Songjin, 36
Sukchon, 68
Sunwido, 64
Suwon, 31-32
Taehwa-do Island, 44
Taedong River, 2-3, 15-16, 38
Taochon-do, 64
Wolmi Island, 22
Wongwon, 26
Wonju, 31
Wonsan, 17-18, 25-26, 33, 36, 42, 80
Yalu River, 26-28, 44, 72-80

Yesong River, 51
Yonan, 59, 64, 69, 203
Yongho-do, 50
Yuchon-in, 62
Korean Military
  South
    First Corps, 3rd Division, 6th Division, 8th Division, Capital Division, 25
  North
    4th Division, 11
Kraus Jr., James J., 69
Kum-Sok, No, 75
Logan, Brian E. W. (Capt., RN), 83
Lamb, William E., 28
Landymore, William, 71
Lay, Horatio Nelson (Capt., OBE RCN), 95
Lee, Norman Ernest (Cdre, RAN), 1, 201-202
Long, J., 148
Lovell, James, 158
MacArthur, Douglas, 12, 20, 26, 28
MacFarlane, George Richard (Comdr, RCN), 71
MacManan, Donald S., 137
MacMillan, Neil D. (Sub Lt., RAN), 44-45, 204
MacPherson, Cedric (Sub Lt.), 76
Mainguy, Edmond Rollo (Vice Adm., OBE RCN), 111
Maitland, Leslie Alan (A/Sub Lt., RNVR), 107-108
Mallace, Russ, 66-67, 74
Marshall, George C., 135
Martin, Harold M., 46, 51
Maunsell, Terence A. K. (Capt., RN), 63
Mayo, R. A., 148
McCain Jr., John S., 166
McDonald, Angus Lewis (PC QC), 90
McGregor, John T., 77
McGrigor, Rhoderick Robert (Adm. of the Fleet Sir., GCB RN), 91, 94, 101
McKinnon, A. L. (Chief Engine Room Artificer, RAN), 50
McLachlan, M. (Lt. RAN), 50
McNay, Peter Frank (Lt. Comdr., RN), 1, 186, 197-201
Milburn, Frank W., 34
Miles, George Ralph (Cdre., OBE RCN), 114
Miller, C. G., 148
Miller, Shirley Snow, 82
Miller Jr., William, 35
Morris, Charles James (Comdr., RAN), 185-187
Murray, Brian Stewart (Rear Adm. Sir, KCMG, AO RAN), 52
Nasser, Gamal Abdel, xliii, 125
Neal, Edgar T., 29

Nelles, Percy Walker (Adm., CB RCN), 90
Nevile-Jones, Richard (Lt.), 76
New Zealand
  HMNZS Cook (naval depot in Wellington), 219
  HMS *Philomel* (later HMNZS) in Auckland, 196, 218
  Royal New Zealand
    Artillery, 85
    Hopuhopu Military Camp at Ngaruawahia, 217
    Navy Volunteer Reserve, 217-218
    Waikato Mounted Rifles, l, 217
    Waiouru Training Camp, 217
Nixon, Richard M., 158-166
Norway
  Aalesund, Kilbotn, Vikeroy Island, Utsire Island, 100
  Bud, Haugesund, Hustadviken Lead, Kvitholm, 97
  Bodo, 121
  Gossen, Haarhamsfjord, Narvik, 91-92
  Kaa Fjord, 93
  Oslo, 156
  Skatestrommen, Vaagso Island, 98
  Stavanger, 99-100
  Tromso, 93
Nott, John William Frederic (Sir., KCB), 193
O'Brien, John Charles (Vice Adm., OC, CD RCN), 87
Operation
  COMMANDO, 57
  CROSSROADS, 136
  GOODWOOD, 92-93
  GRAPPLE, 111
  HURRICANE, 176
  MAGIC CARPET, xli, 134-135
  MARKET TIME, 158
  MERIDIAN, 102
  NEWMARKET, 100
  OFFSPRING, 91-92
  PREFIXM, 100
  RAPID STEP, 125
  SELENIUM, 97
  SHRED/GROUNDSHEET, 99
  STRANGLE, 174
Overton, Richard James, 61
Parker, Robert E., 28
Payne, D., 148
Patterson Jr., Russell G., 31-32
Pearson, Lester B., xliv, 125
Pepelyayev, Yevgeny G., 79-80

Prestley, Frank H., 35
Prince Henry (Duke of Gloucester), 177
Prince Philip (Duke of Edinburgh), xlvii, 122
Rawlinson, Gordon C. (T/A/PO Airman), 108
Rayner, Brian E., 76
Rayner, Herbert Sharples (Vice Adm., DSC & Bar RCN), 114
Ridgeway, Mathew, 31
Ripley, Ernest R., 76
Robbins Jr., Thomas H., 148
Rogers, William P., 165
Rohrsheim, Graham (Lt. Comdr., RAN), 189
Roland, Armand John (Sub Lt., RAN), 52
Romanick, Frank Maxim, 146
Roosevelt, Franklin D., xxxiii
Ross, James Finlay (Lt., RCNVR), 107-108
Rourke, William John (Rear Adm., AO RAN), 52
Ruble, Richard W., 21
Runyon, D. E., 148
Sandberg, Edward Donald (Lt., RAN), l, 211-213
Scott-Moncrieff, Alan Kenneth (Adm. Sir, KCB, CBE, DSO & Bar RN), 47, 50, 67
Seed, Peter William (Lt., RAN), 52
Shelton, Jeffrey J., (Maj., AA), 58
Sheppard, Donald John (Comdr., DSC RCN), 107
Sheppard, Robert Ross (Lt., RCNVR), 107-108
Ships and Craft
  Argentinian, *Independencia*, xxxviii
  Australian
    Anzac, 82, 180-181, 223
    Australia, 197
    Bataan, 14, 22, 36, 66, 70, 180-181, 197, 223
    Brisbane, 190-191
    Canberra, 169
    Junee, li, 223-224
    Kimberley, 66
    Melbourne, xv-xxii, xxxi, xxxix, xlv-li, 170-197, 208-226
    Murchison, 44, 207
    Queenborough, 202
    Shoalhaven, 14
    Sydney, xv-xxii, xxxvi-xli, xlv-li, 39-51, 53-54, 169-183, 185, 193, 197, 201-211, 217, 220-223, 226
    Tobruk, 47, 51, 206-207, 211
    Vampire, 202
    Vengeance, xxii, xxxvii-xxxix, xlv-li, 171, 179-181, 208, 211, 223, 226
    Voyager, 187
    Warramunga, 22, 50, 69-70, 219

Brazilian, *Minas Gerais*, xxxviii, 181
British
 Amethyst, 44, 70, 73
 Ajax, 77
 Alacrity, 14
 Ark Royal, 168
 Aylmer, 93, 95
 Belfast, 13-15, 34, 42-43, 47, 50, 53, 66, 70, 73, 206-207
 Bellona, 100
 Bickerton, 93-95
 Black Swan, 14
 Bligh, 93, 95
 Britannia, xlix
 Ceylon, 22, 70, 181
 Cockade, 78
 Colombo, 180, 223
 Colossus, xxxvii-xxxix
 Comus, 19, 42, 69
 Consort, 14-15, 22, 36, 69
 Constant, 64-67
 Cossack, 14-15, 42
 Courier, 99
 Devonshire, 91, 97
 Dido, 97, 99-100
 Eagle, xli
 Foam, 96
 Formidable, 93, 101-108
 Furious, 93, 197
 Glorious, 168
 Glory, xxxvi-xxxix, l, 12, 39, 53-65, 76-83, 174, 198, 201-203, 217-220
 Golden Fleece, 99
 Gothic, xlviii, 180-181
 Hare, 99
 Hart, 14
 Hercules, xxxix, 131
 Hood, 196
 Indomitable, xxi, xli, 103
 Implacable, xli, 103
 Indefatigable, xli, 91, 93, 101, 103
 Invincible, 193
 Illustrious, xli, 103, 105, 219
 Jamaica, 13-14
 Jewel, 99
 Keats, 93
 Kempthorne, 93, 95
 Kent, 91

Ladybird, 25
Magnificent, xxxix
Majestic, xxxix, xlviii
Myngs, 91
Nabob, xl, 87-95, 101
Nairana, 100
Norfolk, 97
Newcastle, 83
Newfoundland, 180, 223
Ocean, xxxvi, xxxix, xliii, 12, 53-54, 65-77, 83-84, 167, 178,
Perseus, xxxvii, xxxix, xli, 122
Pioneer, xxxvii, xxxix
Powerful, xxxix, xli, 110
Premier, 97, 99
Prince of Wales, 196
Puncher, xl, 87-101
Queen, 100
Savage, 100
Scourge, 91, 100
Searcher, 100
Serene, 99
Shropshire, 168
Strathmore, 201
Surprise, 24, 122
Terrible, xxxix, xlvi, 41, 171
Theseus, xxxvi-xliii, 12, 23-39, 54, 122
Tracker, 168
Triumph, xxxvi-xxxix, 9, 12-23, 54
Trumpeter, 91, 93
Unicorn, 60, 62
Vanguard, 120
Venerable, xxxvii-xxxix,
Vengeance, xxxvii-xxxix, xlviii, 171
Verulam, 91
Victorious, 103, 107, 196-197
Vigilant, 91, 95
Virago, Volage, 91
Warrior, xxxvi-xl
Wave, 99
Canadian
Algonquin, 91, 108
Athabaskan, 16, 21-22, 36, 46, 81
Beacon Hill, 95
Bonaventure, xxxix-xliv, 87-88, 110, 113, 126-131
Cayuga, 16, 22, 46, 64
Crescent, 111

  Crusader, 16-17, 78-82, 111, 124
  Haida, 16, 78, 81-82
  Huron, 16, 36
  Iroquois, xxx, 16, 66, 69-71
  La Hulloise, 122
  Labrador, 124
  Lucille M. Schnare, Pasadena, Uda A. Saunders, 89
  Magnificent, xxxix-xliv, 87-88, 110-126
  New Glasgow, 124
  Nootka, 16, 111
  Ontario, 108, 122
  Prince Robert, 108
  Quebec, 121-124
  Sioux, 16, 22, 46-47, 51, 91, 122
  Stadacona, 126
  Steller, 124
  Swansea, 122
  Triumph, 88-89
  Uganda, 108
  Warrior, xxxviii-xli, 87-88, 109-113, 124
 Dutch
  Evertsen, 22
  Piet Hein, 67
  Van Galen, 47
 French
  Bois Belleau, 30, 140
  Lafayette, 30, 140
 German
  Admiral Graf Spee, 77
  Bismark, 196
  Gneisenau, 105
  Prince Eugen, 105, 196
  R89, 92
  Scharnhorst, 105, 169
  Tirpitz, 77, 92-94, 104, 196
  U-156, 88-89
  U-354, 94
 Indian, *Vikrant*, xxxix, 131
 Japanese
  Amakusa, Etorofu, 104
  Kongo Maru No. 2, 106
  Nagato, Sakawa, 136
 Korean, *Kum Kang San*, 73
 Spanish, *Dedalo*, xxiii, xxviii, 30, 139
 United States
  Merchant Marine/Fishing Vessels

A. Piatt Andrew, Francis J. O'hara Jr., Sylvania, 89
Navy
  amphibious/auxiliaries/transports
    Annapolis, 153, 157, 166
    Arlington, 147, 153-166
    Chilton, Chipola, Chuckawan, 158
    Francis Marion, Guadalcanal, Hassayampa, Ozark, Rankin, Salinan, 159
    Guam, xxiv
    Hitchiti, Pakana, 137
    LSM-160, 137
    Northampton, xliii, 141-146, 153
    Ponchatoula, 185-186
    Princeton, 158-161
  combatants
    aircraft carriers
      Badoeng Strait, 29, 49, 51, 66
      Barioko, 60-61, 84
      Bataan, xxxiv, xxxvi, xxxix, xli-xlii, 1-6, 12, 14, 25, 29-38, 53-54, 63-74, 78-83, 133-135, 138-140
      Belleau Wood, xxxiv, xxxix, xlii, 30, 134, 138, 140
      Bennington, xxxii, 122
      Boxer, 32
      Bunker Hill, Franklin, Hancock, Intrepid, Lexington, Randolph, Ticonderoga, xxxii
      Cabot, xxiii, xxviii, xxxiv, xxxix, xli-xlii, 30, 133-139
      Cowpens, xxxiv, xxxix, 30, 134, 138, 140
      Enterprise, 191
      Essex, xxxii-xxxiv
      Hornet, xxxii, xlii, 158, 165-166
      Independence, xxxi, xxxiv, xxxix, xlii, 30, 134-137
      Kearsarge, 191
      Lake Champlain, 129
      Langley, xxxi, xxxiv, xxxix, xlii, 30, 134-140
      Leyte, 28
      Monterey, xxxiv, xxxix, xli-xlii, 30, 133-140
      Philippine Sea, 19, 27, 123
      Princeton, xxxiv, xxxix, xli, 30, 134
      Ranger, xxiii
      Rendova, 46, 66
      Saipan (CVL-48), later *Arlington* (AGMR-2), xxxiv-xxxv, xlii, 133, 140, 143, 147-166
      San Jacinto, xxxiv, xxxix, 30, 134-140
      Saratoga, 136-137
      Shamrock Bay, 96
      Sicily, 29, 66
      Wasp, xxxii, 121-122

Wright (CVL-49), later (CC-2), xxxiv-xxxv, xxxix, xlii-xliii, 121, 133, 140-146, 153
Yorktown, xxxii, 158
battleships
Iowa, 137
Missouri, 13, 66
New Jersey, 42-47, 83
Wisconsin, 121
cruisers
Manchester, 36
St. Paul, 33-35
destroyers
Arnold J. Isbell, 69
Carpenter, 158
Cochrane, 159
Collett, 46
English, 36
Frank E. Evans, 190
Goldsborough, 158
Hanna, 46, 78
Hank, 34
Hanson, 51, 78, 82
Higbee, 82
Hymann, 47
John R. Craig, 70
Lowry, 64
Marsh, 67
McCord, 78, 82
New, 158
Nicholas, 70, 159
Orleck, 80
Radford, 51
Rich, 158
Rupertus, 159
Sperry, 36
submarines,
Redfin, 123
Skate, 136
Simonds, James M., 76
Sinclair, Richard (Sub Lt., RAN), 48
Smith, Allan E., 25
Smith, Victor Alfred Trumper (Adm. Sir, AC, KBE, CB, DSC RAN), 168-169, 223
Smuts, Jan Christian (Field Marshall, PC, OM, CH, DTD, ED, KC, FRS), 88
Soviet Union, 139th Guards Fighter Aviation Regiment, 27-28
Stafford, Thomas P., 161

Stevens, Duncan Herbert (Capt., RAN), 187
Sthamer, Hans-Jurgen, 94
Storrs, Anthony Hubert Gleadow (Rear Adm., DSC & Bar RCN), 114
Stradwick, Walter Thomas (Sub Lt., RNVR), 108
Struble, Arthur D., 12-13, 31
Sturdee, Vernon Ashton Hobart (Lt. Gen. Sir, KBE, CB, DSO AA), 218
Sullivan, Gerald, 118
Sullivan, J., 148
Sullivan, Robert F., 1
Sutton, Arthur William (Lt., RCNVR), 105
Swart, Bouke K. (Sub Lt., RNNAS), 108
Sydney, Eugene Eljerfield Fernandes, 52
Tarshinov, Arkadii I., 28
Thieu, Nguyen Van, 161-163
Thornhill Jr., Henry Ehrman, 146
Thornton, Thomas, 8
Thrower, Anthony, 198-199
Townley, Athol Gordon, 189
Tunstall, Robert Joseph (Lt. Comdr., MBE RN), 52
Turner, Richmond K., 12, 25
Typhoon RUTH, 208, 221-222
United States
  Air Force
    2157th Air Rescue Squadron, xl, 6
    Air Resupply and Communications Service (ARCS), 6
      581st AR&CS Wing, 1, 6
        H-19 Helicopter Flight at Seoul City Airbase, xl, 1-8
  Army
    1st Cavalry Division, 17, 26
    8240th AU (formerly, Attrition Section Miscellaneous Division), Task Force LEOPARD, 72
    First Corps, 34
    Eighth Army, 26-31, 71-72
    Tenth Corps, 22, 26
    9th Infantry Division, 161
    24th Infantry Division, 11
    Task Force Smith, 11
  Marine Corps
    1st Marine Division, 22, 84
    Fighting Squadron/Attack Squadron
      VMA-324, 149-152
      VMF-212, 29, 31-32, 35
      VMF-312/VMA-312, 2, 35-38, 53-54, 64-83
      VMF-314, 30
  Navy/Naval
    Aviation

> Anti-Submarine Squadron VS-24, 158
> Fighter Squadron
>> VF-17A, 148
>> VF-31, 28
>> VF-52, 28
>> VF-54, 28
>> VF-111, 27
>> VMF-312, 38
>
> Helicopter Anti-submarine Squadron HS-4, 164
> Destroyer Division 72, 29
> Radiological Defense Laboratory, 137
> Underwater Demolition Team 11, 160

Space Program
> Apollo 8, 10, and 11, 154-158

Vanderpool, Jay D., 91
Walker, Walton, 12, 26, 31
Ward, Alfred Joseph, 33
Weber, Frederick C., 28
Webster, Ian, 211
West, Michael Montgomerie Alston Roberts (Gen. Sir., GCB, DSO & Two Bars, BA), 55
Westerman, Frank, 6
White, Robert Hastings, 146
Whitehead, Douglas R. (Sub Lt., RNVR), 108
Wilbur, James T., 72
Winstanley, Arthur, 52
Xing, Xu, 192
Young, John W., 161

About the Author

Commander David D. Bruhn, US Navy (Retired) served twenty-two years on active duty and two in the Naval Reserve, as both an enlisted man and as an officer, between 1977 and 2001.

After completion of basic training, he served as a sonar technician aboard USS *Miller* (FF-1091) and USS *Leftwich* (DD-984). He was commissioned in 1983 following graduation from California State University at Chico. His initial assignment was to USS *Excel* (MSO-439), serving as supply officer, damage control assistant, and chief engineer. He then served in USS *Thach* (FFG-43) as chief engineer and Destroyer Squadron Thirteen as material officer.

After graduation from the Naval Postgraduate School, Commander Bruhn was assigned to Secretary of the Navy and Chief of Naval Operations staffs as a budget analyst and resources planner before attending the Naval War College in 1996, following which he commanded the mine countermeasures ships USS *Gladiator* (MCM-11) and USS *Dextrous* (MCM-13) in the Persian Gulf.

Commander Bruhn's final assignment was executive assistant to a senior (SES 4) government service executive at the Ballistic Missile Defense Organization in Washington, D.C.

Following military service, he was a high school teacher and track coach for ten years, and is now a USA Track & Field official. He lives in northern California with his wife Nancy and has two grown sons, David and Michael.

Heritage Books by Cdr. David D. Bruhn, USN (Retired)

Battle Stars for the "Cactus Navy":
America's Fishing Vessels and Yachts in World War II

Enemy Waters:
Royal Navy, Royal Canadian Navy, Royal Norwegian Navy,
U.S. Navy, and Other Allied Mine Forces Battling the
Germans and Italians in World War II
Cdr. David D. Bruhn, USN (Retired) and Lt. Cdr. Rob Hoole, RN (Retired)

Eyes of the Fleet:
The U.S. Navy's Seaplane Tenders and Patrol Aircraft in World War II

Gators Offshore and Upriver:
The U.S. Navy's Amphibious Ships and Underwater Demolition Teams,
and Royal Australian Navy Clearance Divers in Vietnam

Home Waters:
Royal Navy, Royal Canadian Navy, and U.S. Navy
Mine Forces Battling U-Boats in World War I
Cdr. David D. Bruhn, USN (Retired) and Lt. Cdr. Rob Hoole, RN (Retired)

Ingram's Fourth Fleet:
U.S. and Royal Navy Operations Against German Runners,
Raiders, and Submarines in the South Atlantic in World War II

MacArthur and Halsey's "Pacific Island Hoppers":
The Forgotten Fleet of World War II

Nightraiders:
U.S. Navy, Royal Navy, Royal Australian Navy, and
Royal Netherlands Navy Mine Forces Battling the
Japanese in the Pacific in World War II
Cdr. David D. Bruhn, USN (Retired) and Lt. Cdr. Rob Hoole, RN (Retired)

On the Gunline:
U.S. Navy and Royal Australian Navy Warships off Vietnam, 1965–1973
Cdr. David D. Bruhn, USN (Retired) and
STGCS Richard S. Mathews, USN (Retired)

Salvation from the Sky: U.S. Navy, Royal Australian Air Force, and
Royal New Zealand Air Force Heroic Air-Sea Rescue in the Pacific in World War II
Cdr. David D. Bruhn, USN (Retired) and Stephen Ekholm

Support for the Fleet:
U.S. Navy and Royal Australian Navy Service
Force Ships That Served in Vietnam, 1965–1973

We Are Sinking, Send Help!:
The U.S. Navy's Tugs and Salvage Ships in the African,
European, and Mediterranean Theaters in World War II

Turn into the Wind
Volume I: US Navy and Royal Navy Light Fleet Aircraft Carriers
in World War II, and Contributions of the British Pacific Fleet

Turn into the Wind
Volume II: US Navy, Royal Navy, Royal Australian Navy, and Royal Canadian Navy
Light Fleet Aircraft Carriers in the Korean War and through End of Service, 1950–1982

Wooden Ships and Iron Men:
The U.S. Navy's Ocean Minesweepers, 1953–1994

Wooden Ships and Iron Men:
The U.S. Navy's Coastal and Motor Minesweepers, 1941–1953

Wooden Ships and Iron Men:
The U.S. Navy's Coastal and Inshore Minesweepers,
and the Minecraft that Served in Vietnam, 1953–1976

Printed in Great Britain
by Amazon